Queering Classrooms

Personal Narratives and Educational Practices to Support LGBTQ Youth in Schools

A Volume in Research in Queer Studies

Series Editors:
Paul Chamness Miller and Hidehiro Endo
Akita International University

Research in Queer Studies

Paul Chamness Miller and Hidehiro Endo, Series Editors

Queering Classrooms

Personal Narratives and Educational Practices to Support LGBTQ Youth in Schools

Edited by

Erin A. Mikulec
Illinois State University

and

Paul Chamness Miller
Akita International University, Japan

Information Age Publishing, Inc.
Charlotte, North Carolina • www.infoagepub.com

Library of Congress Cataloging-in-Publication Data

CIP data for this book can be found on the Library of Congress website:
http://www.loc.gov/index.html

Paperback: 978-1-68123-650-6
Hardcover: 978-1-68123-651-3
E-Book: 978-1-68123-652-0

Cover art comes from the original drawing, *Questions*, 2016 by Jordan DeWilde. Cover art is used with permission from the artist. The artist states, "This work represents the many questions gay students and gay teachers face in the field of education." He may be reached at jordandewilde@gmail.com

Printed in the United States of America

DEDICATION

This book is dedicated to every student I've known who has ever felt unsafe or unsupported in a school environment simply because of who they are. To those of you with whom I have worked over years who have struggled with your identity without the support of peers and teachers, you were my inspiration for this work. This book is for you.

—Erin A. Mikulec

This book is dedicated to all queer youth and teachers, and their allies, who fight to have a voice in this heteronormative world. Never give up!

—Paul Chamness Miller

CONTENTS

FOREWORD

Nelson M. Rodriguez
The College of New Jersey

I came out as a gay man during my undergraduate years at the University of Miami. Reflecting back on that time, I would characterize it as an overall positive experience. I didn't encounter much homophobia (that I noticed anyway) and the faculty and staff I interacted with, who knew or "suspected" I was gay, were always friendly and supportive. In addition, I met a number of other gay and lesbian students who became my support network and who always reminded me to laugh a lot. I also met my fabulous husband in college. In light of this positive set of experiences, stepping into and owning my gay identity within the context of being a student in higher education gave me hope that queerness, in any number of its forms, could actually thrive within institutions of higher learning. Something was lacking, however. What I didn't encounter as an undergraduate was much in the way of opportunities for the academic study of lesbian, gay, bisexual, transgender, and queer (LGBTQ) issues. Where was that knowledge? Was it in the closet, that is, buried in books on some upper floor of the library? And what about the queer professors—where were they? I often wonder how these absences also defined, however indirectly, my undergraduate coming out experience. Such a defining absence constituted my overall doctoral experience as well, especially as a student of education. Years later, it now makes so much sense to me why I have made an unapologetic commitment to queering my classes by way of engendering educational opportunities for my students to encounter, as well as to grapple with, "queer epistemologies."

Queering Classrooms: Personal Narratives and Educational Practices to Support LGBTQ Youth in Schools, pp. ix–x
Copyright © 2017 by Information Age Publishing
All rights of reproduction in any form reserved.

In *Queering Classrooms: Personal Narratives and Educational Practices to Support LGBTQ Youth in Schools*, Mikulec, Miller, and colleagues highlight the importance of carving out a space for LGBTQ studies within the field of education, especially within the context and concerns of teacher preparation. As many of us know, the academic knowledge on the subject of LGBTQ that preservice and practicing teachers encounter as part of their program of studies or professional training is, at best, spotty. This unevenness, and oftentimes blatant absence, is an important reminder that the enterprise of teacher preparation is situated at the intersection of knowledge and power; to be sure, teacher preparation represents a terrain of struggle, a site of ongoing contestation, over what knowledge should constitute the teacher preparation curriculum. If preservice and practicing teachers lack the opportunity to study LGBTQ issues in relation to questions of education, then it will be much more difficult for LGBTQ and heterosexual teachers to become advocates for LGBTQ youth in schools as well as to become agents of change more generally.

The editors of and contributors to this volume have organized an invaluable pedagogical opportunity for educators to study a broad range of LGBTQ topics in education with the goal of improving the lives of queer youth in school contexts. Utilizing a combination of personal narratives and LGBTQ scholarship within the field of education, we find in this volume a wealth of research and reflections on a number of issues that will be of use to current and future teachers, including overviews of the current landscape of LGBTQ youth in education, illuminating perspectives from practicing and preservice teachers, stories about how to utilize literature to support LGBTQ youth and to challenge heteronormativity in schools, and timely and useful insights on how practitioners and higher education scholars and educators continue to create supportive spaces for LGBTQ students across contexts of education. In all, *Queering Classrooms* challenges the politics of the constitutive discourse of teacher preparation by contributing to the radical hope and possibility of study.

CHAPTER 1

CHALLENGING THE STATUS QUO

Transforming and Queering Education

Erin A. Mikulec and Paul Chamness Miller

Over the last several years we have seen activists fight for lesbian, gay, bisexual, trans* and queer (LGBTQ) equity. Progress has been made in some areas of the world where, for example, same-sex marriage has been legalized, protections against forms of discrimination in employment and housing have been put in place, and even the inclusion of LGBTQ populations in hate crime laws. However, given the conservative nature of K–12 education and its blatant resistance to the inclusion of Others, this volume had as its aim to explore whether this educational milieu has improved over time. After all, as Carlson (2001) reminds us, "As queerness has become more open and 'out' in campus life, homophobia has had a more visible target to attack" (p. 297). So with an increased visibility of the queer community, we approached this volume by seeking authors who would share their own personal experiences and findings from original research to help illustrate the current trend in the K–12 setting.

According to The 2013 National School Climate Survey by the Gay, Lesbian & Straight Education Network (GLSEN), although school climate

Queering Classrooms: Personal Narratives and Educational Practices to Support LGBTQ Youth in Schools, pp. 1–7
Copyright © 2017 by Information Age Publishing

has improved for LGBTQ youth, many still experience a hostile environment and discriminatory practices (Kosciw, Greytak, Palmer, & Boesen, 2014). For instance, 69% of the nearly 8,000 LGBTQ students surveyed reported feeling unsafe at school because of their sexual orientation and gender expression, 64.5% reported hearing homophobic comments and remarks, 35% felt unsafe in either bathrooms or locker rooms, and 32.6% reported having been physically harassed because of their sexual orientation. Research also indicates that LGBTQ youth regularly experience verbal and physical abuse in schools, often feel unsafe or isolated, and are confronted with heteronormative systems and practices among peers and teachers. What is more, 49.5% of students reported that any intervention by school staff in response to verbal or physical harassment of LGBTQ students was ineffective (Kosciw et al., 2014).

Kosciw et al. (2014) also tracked their findings over time, and the statistics do suggest a cultural shift in terms of recognition of the issues faced by LGBTQ youth. However, according to Graybill and Proctor (2016), the current school climate can still be described as hostile, which can have a negative and damaging impact on attendance, academic performance, and educational outcomes (Greytak & Kosciw, 2014). The authors also state that support from teachers for LGBTQ youth is associated with more academic success in school and fewer issues with depression. Furthermore, as Kitchen and Bellini (2012) assert, a teacher's "duty of care" requires that teachers, regardless of their personal beliefs about homosexuality, provide a safe and supportive learning environment for all students that is free of harassment.

Unfortunately, there still exists a significant lack of support in schools, which novice teachers may experience upon beginning their careers. Preservice and novice teachers who identify as Allies may experience shock and disbelief that schools and fellow educators do not share in their support of LGBTQ youth. This may fly in the face of what they may have learned during their preparation or as a result of their own personal experiences with LGBTQ friends and family members. This kind of disconnect between theory and practice, so to speak, may leave Ally-educators feeling unsupported and isolated in their desire to engage in a meaningful way with LGBTQ youth in schools. To illustrate this point, several teachers, former students of one of the editors of this volume, were invited to contribute chapters to this book, but were denied permission by their school districts out of concern for what they may reveal about practices within their schools. How then, are novice teachers, even with instruction in LGBTQ issues in their preparation, to cope with doing what they feel is their professional responsibility to advocate and provide safe learning environments for all students, when institutional policies and practices inhibit this? Furthermore, how can teacher education help to prepare future teachers to work effectively with and advocate for LGBTQ youth?

Research indicates that teacher education with regard to LGBTQ youth is somewhat limited and that such issues, including recognizing homophobic bias and institutional heteronormativity, are often simply included as part of a unit on diversity or a multicultural education class (Gorski, Davis, & Reiter, 2013). Graybill and Proctor (2016) found that many educators feel underprepared and even uncomfortable in supporting LGBTQ youth due to underrepresentation during their preparation and subsequently in their professional development once they are hired. This lack of knowledge, skills, and available resources creates what Kitchen and Bellini (2012) describe as a "tension between confidence and uncertainty" (p. 220). Dismantling and reconstructing this tension requires that preservice teachers recognize and reconcile practices in which they have inadvertently participated during their own academic careers. For instance, even as students, preservice teachers likely observed a lack of intervention from teachers in the presence of homophobic remarks or institutional practices in schools that not only allowed anti-LGBTQ behaviors to persist, but also reified the message that they are acceptable (Greytak & Kosciw, 2014).

Regardless of the level of preparation a preservice teacher may have prior to licensure, as Hansen (2015) points out, there is no doubt that teachers, particularly secondary teachers, will work with LGBTQ youth in their classes and school communities, and therefore have a responsibility to be prepared to do so in a caring and supportive way. Without adequate preparation, we cannot expect novice teachers to recognize or respond to the issues surrounding LGBTQ youth in schools. However, such preparation must be meaningful and significant and carried out in a way that allows for preservice teachers to increase their own personal comfort level in working with LGBTQ youth (Jennings, 2015). This is not as easy as it may seem, given that undergraduate pre-service teachers, although adults, "may at times react with immaturity to serious problems posed by their peers" (Hansen, 2015, p. 52). However, teacher educators can encourage preservice teachers to interact and engage with LGBTQ youth through clinical field experiences, which are often an integral component in teacher preparation programs. Although it may not be possible to incorporate clinical experiences at schools like the Harvey Milk School of New York or the Alliance School of Milwaukee, clinical experience activities can be designed to help preservice teachers identify ways in which a school supports or hinders LGBTQ youth by observing the presence of and participating in a Gay-Straight Alliance (GSA) at the school, signage that identifies spaces as Safe Zones, and school policies on dress code related to gender expression. Clinical experiences can also include activities in which preservice teachers speak directly with their cooperating teacher about their perceptions of the school climate with regard to LGBTQ students or participate in GSA meetings or activities in which preservice teachers would then have the opportunity to engage with LGBTQ youth. Greytak and Kosciw (2014) found that having a personal connection to members of the LGBTQ community increased the likelihood that they would intervene on someone's behalf in a homophobic environment. Thus, increasing teachers' knowledge of the LGBTQ community may facilitate the development of practices that can enable them to work toward providing an inclusive and positive school environment. Greytak and Kosciw provide additional recommendations for ways in which teacher-education programs can provide opportunities for preservice teachers to become acquainted with LGBTQ students, "such as inviting LGBTQ youth speakers into their classes, engaging in service learning projects with organizations serving LGBTQ youth in the local community, or encouraging interaction with the college or university LGBTQ center or student group" (p. 420). Such experiences can have a powerful impact on preservice teachers that can increase their self-confidence in their abilities to intervene on the behalf of LGBTQ youth in their classrooms and schools. In addition, incorporating the issues of LGBTQ youth into teacher education is also no longer limited to introductory and general methods courses. More and more research is beginning to look at the needs of LGBTQ youth in terms of specific content areas, for instance music education (Bergonzi, 2009), physical education (Block, 2014), science (Lundin, 2014), and social studies (Maguth & Taylor, 2014).

LGBTQ-related issues in schools are not limited to students. Teachers who identify as LGBTQ may experience difficulties on their journey to become an educator as well, ranging from remaining in the closet throughout their preparation to feeling unsupported, once hired, by administration or their school community if they decide to come out (Kitchen & Bellini, 2012). Graybill and Proctor (2016) also found that teacher educators and preservice teachers who identify as LGBTQ have reported that not only is LGBTQ "content limited in the curriculum but the climate in many pre-service programs does not encourage discussion about LGBTQ issues" (p. 11). Furthermore, LGBTQ teachers also reported feeling isolated or unsupported within their schools and LGBTQ parents and guardians experienced discomfort and feelings of exclusion in their interactions with schools, limiting parental involvement in the education process (Gorski et al., 2013).

With this book, we hope to address the issues presented above in the current landscape of education and LGBTQ youth. The book is divided into four sections, each of which examines a different facet of addressing the issues of LGBTQ youth and how teacher education can work to facili-tate the preparation of teachers to address these concerns. While there is a research-based component to the book, we wanted to also emphasize personal narratives and the experiences of preservice teachers and prac-ticing teachers as well as teacher educators. In this way we can begin to understand the present climate in schools faced by teachers in an effort to inform the preparation of future teachers so that they may develop the knowledge and skills necessary to become advocates for LGBTQ youth.

The book begins with a section that describes the current landscape of LGBT youth in education. In this section, the authors reflect on how things have changed for LGBT youth as well as the challenges that still lie ahead. The second section brings perspectives from teachers in the field as well as preservice teachers during their preparation. These narratives share the experiences of undergraduate preservice teachers who had the opportunity to spend time in an LGBT-friendly high school as part of their clinical experiences, as well as a practicing teacher who shares his own journey in becoming a teacher. In the third section, we hear from teachers and librarians who share with us the ways in which they have used literature to support and advocate for LGBT youth and work to change the heteronormative practices within schools. The last section provides insights into how practitioners in both K–12 and higher educa-tion settings can and have created supportive spaces for LGBTQ students.

Finally, we recognize that working with the issues surrounding LGBT youth in schools is complex and includes not only students and teachers but others as well. Graybill and Proctor (2016) identify other school per-sonnel in addition to teachers that work with LGBTQ youth and are also in need of professional development such as school counselors, nurses, psychologist, and social workers. Although these support personnel are not the focus of this book, it points to the need to include the issues of LGBTQ youth in a number of university programs that prepare young professionals to work in schools. Therefore, while we must remember that there are a number of professionals who can have a positive impact on LGBT youth, we also believe that teacher educators have a special respon-sibility to prepare a corps of professional teachers ready to support and advocate for these students. As we know, teacher preparation programs have the ability to enable teachers to truly embrace the need for transfor-mation and tap into the power that they have to make transformation happen, because "only teachers have the power needed to raise critical issues about the functioning of schools" (Carlson, 1986, p. 34), including how LGBTQ youth and teachers are treated. It is in their preparation for becoming a teacher that preservice teachers learn to critically [reflect] on their own roles in the schooling process, [theorize] about what could be, and [work] to promote specific changes consistent with a broad vision of a just society ... to challenge the status quo in ways that are transformative rather than merely reformist. (Carlson, 1987, p. 307)

It is our goal for the readers of this volume to not only see how the educational system is still largely homophobic, as well as ill-prepared and unwilling to meet the needs of queer youth, but also to see that the system is not without hope. We hope that the pages within this volume illustrate some measures that teachers can take to begin to challenge the system, but perhaps more importantly to encourage the reader to begin to critically reflect on how this system continues to marginalize and silence queer teachers and youth. In so doing, our goal is to see more teachers and future teachers who will fight to give a voice to those who have for so long been and continue to be silenced.

REFERENCES

Bergonzi, L. (2009). Sexual orientation and music education: Continuing a tradition. *Music Educators Journal, 96*(2), 21–15.

Block, B. A. (2014). Supporting LGBTQ students in physical education: Changing the movement landscape. *Quest, 66*(1), 14–26.

Carlson, D. (1986). Teachers, class culture, and the politics of schooling. *Interchange, 17*(4), 17–36.

Carlson, D. (1987). Teachers as political actors: From reproductive theory to the crisis of schooling. *Harvard Educational Review, 57*(3), 283–307.

Carlson, D. (2001). Gay, queer, and cyborg: The performance of identity in a transglobal age. *Discourse: Studies in the Cultural Politics of Education, 22*(3), 297–309.

Graybill, E. C., & Proctor, S. L. (2016). Lesbian, gay, bisexual, and transgender youth: Limited representation in school support personnel journals. *Journal of School Psychology, 54*, 9–14.

Greytak, E. A., & Kosciw, J. G. (2014). Predictors of US teachers' intervention in anti-lesbian, gay, bisexual, and transgender bullying and harassment. *Teaching Education, 25*(4), 410–426.

Gorski, P. C., Davis, S. N., & Reiter, A. (2013). An examination of the (in)visbility of sexual orientation, heterosexism, homophobia, and teacher education coursework. *Journal of LGBTQ Youth, 10*(3), 224–248.

Hansen, L. E. (2015). Encouraging pre-service teachers to address issues of sexual orientation in their classrooms: Walking the walk & talking the talk. *Multicultural Education, 22*(2), 51–55.

Jennings, T. (2015). Teaching transgressive representations of LGBTQ people in educator preparations: Is conformity required for inclusion? *The Educational Forum, 79*(4), 451–458.

Kitchen, J., & Bellini, C. (2012). Making it better for lesbian, gay, bisexual and transgender students through teacher education: A collaborative self-study. *Studying Teacher Education, 8*(3), 209–225.

Kosciw, J. G., Greytak, E. A., Palmer, N. A., & Boesen, M. J. (2014). *The 2013 National School Climate Survey: The experiences of lesbian, gay, bisexual and transgender youth in our nation's schools.* New York, NY: GLSEN. Retrieved from http://www.glsen.org/nscs

Lundin, M. (2014). Inviting queer ideas into the science classroom: Studying sexuality education from a queer perspective. *Cultural Studies of Science Education, 9*, 377–391.

Maguth, B. M., & Taylor, N. (2014). Bringing LGBTQ topics in the social studies classroom. *The Social Studies, 105*, 23–28.

SECTION I

**LGBTQ YOUTH AND EDUCATION:
HOW FAR HAVE WE COME?**

CHAPTER 2

A PLACE WHERE THEY CAN BE THEMSELVES

Issues of LGBTQ Students [Revisited]

Michelle L. Knaier

In 2002, I was enrolled in an elementary/early secondary teacher education program in Central New York. As I reflect on that time, which I often do, I find myself grateful for my core group of professors who were adamant about promoting social justice and providing a democratic education for all students. These ideals were integrated within my teaching methods classes as well as in the development of my classroom management and teaching philosophies. Equality and equity were foundational themes for many theoretical discussions regarding K–12 classroom education. It was during this period when I wrote a paper titled, "A Place Where They Can Be Themselves: Issues of Gay, Lesbian, and Bisexual Students." Since that time, I've earned my master's degree in childhood education, obtained licenses to teach in both New York and California (K–12 multiple subject and biology), and served 5 years as a full-time science teacher in the public school system. Currently, I am pursuing a PhD in Curriculum & Instruction with a focus on curriculum studies, specifically multicultural and LGBTQ-inclusive education.

Now, 14 years after drafting that initial paper, I am revisiting and reflecting on what I wrote about lesbian, gay, bisexual, transgender, and

Queering Classrooms: Personal Narratives and Educational Practices to Support LGBTQ Youth in Schools, pp. 11–25
Copyright © 2017 by Information Age Publishing

queer (LGBTQ) youth and the issues this particular group faces in school settings. I approached this task with a varied perspective. As a queer, multicultural educator in the field of teacher education, I reviewed my words, thoughts, and arguments with much more life and teaching experience. I realized, with great despair, that the same issues and challenges faced by LGBTQ youth still exist so many years later. Though, to be clear, there has been improvement. When I compared the data from the Gay, Lesbian & Straight Education Network (GLSEN) *2001 National School Climate Survey*, the first of its kind, with the most recent *2013 National School Climate Survey*, most of the statistics highlighting the challenges faced by LGBTQ youth within the school climate have improved. This may be due to increased availability of LGBTQ-related school resources (Kosciw, Greytak, Palmer, & Boesen, 2014). Nevertheless, the school climate for LGBTQ students remains quite hostile (Kosciw et al., 2014), even if there has been a shift in societal acceptance of LGBTQ people.

The issues on which I focused in this now 14-year-old paper are just a sample of the hardships, inequities, and injustices that the LGBTQ student population still experiences. They include antigay name-calling, delayed social development, and lack of support for LGBTQ youth in the school setting. Although I argued in 2002 that K–12 teachers should implement LGBTQ-inclusive behavior and curricula, I did not argue for LGBTQ-inclusive teacher education as a solution to the underlying problem. It is now clear to me, based on my experiences and research, that such education is much needed. In this chapter, I first reproduce, in large part, the text of the paper I wrote in 2002 in order to highlight its current relevance. I then consider my former analysis in light of current data and observations, concluding that there is still much to be done to improve school life for LGBTQ youth, and that inclusive teacher education is an important element in achieving these tasks.

A PLACE WHERE THEY CAN BE THEMSELVES[1]

As a teacher, I hear antigay name-calling 9 out of 10 times I go into work, regardless of the school, district, or grade level. This happens on any given day, which suggests that this behavior occurs quite often. I hear gay bashing in elementary schools and in junior high and high schools. I even hear preservice teachers make antigay remarks. It is no wonder where young students learn homophobic behavior. Modeled by parents, teachers, and peers, this behavior greatly influences how young students perceive and treat LGBTQ people. According to GLSEN's 2001 (and 2013) *National School Climate Survey: Lesbian, Gay, Bisexual and Transgender Students and their Experiences in Schools*, 84.3% (64.5% in 2013) of lesbian, gay, bisexual or transgender students reported hearing homophobic remarks, such as "faggot" or "dyke." Further, 90.8% (71.4% in 2013) of the students frequently heard the expression "that's so gay" or "you're so gay" (Kosciw & Cullen, 2001; Kosciw et al., 2014). Unfortunately, teachers do not often challenge these remarks.

Both teachers and members of the general public send hidden messages to young people through the sort of disciplinary action they take against those who use antigay or racist epithets, the issues they introduce and discuss in school, and the types of gender-specific behaviors they accept and model. The 2001 GLSEN survey indicated that 81.8% (81.2% in 2013) of LGBT students reported that faculty or staff either never intervened or intervened only some of the time when homophobic remarks were made (Kosciw & Cullen, 2001; Kosciw et al., 2014). This statistic shows how gay, lesbian, and bisexual youth are often (and still) neglected, degraded, and unsupported in the school setting.

Every student has the right to learn in a safe and supportive environment regardless of race, ethnicity, creed, or sexual orientation. But often gays, lesbians, bisexuals, and transgender students are denied this right because teachers and administrators allow homophobic and transphobic behavior to be tolerated in classrooms and in schools. In what follows, I address challenges faced by these students, including antigay name-calling, delayed social development, and lack of support from teachers and peers. I also discuss the ways in which these challenges affect the lives of LGBTQ youth and suggest that educational reform may be key to solving these problems.

Challenges Faced by LGBTQ Students

The most common, not to mention degrading and disturbing, forms of harassment encountered by LGBTQ students are antigay name-calling and gay-bashing comments. Frankfurt (2000) reports that "antigay comments such as 'faggot,' 'dyke,' and 'homo,' [are] heard on an average of 25 times a day (that's every 14 minutes!)" (p. 64). And, according to Gordon (1994), "even first graders are now using such terms as 'faggot' to ridicule others" (p. 86).

The most disturbing aspect of these sorts of remarks is teacher silence. Bott (2000) claims, "an educator's silence supports discrimination" (p. 22). MacGillivray (2000) similarly suggests that "when students witness teachers punishing students for using the word *nigger* but not for using homophobic words such as *faggot*, that silence communicates the message that being GLBTQ [gay, lesbian, bisexual, transgender, questioning] is not OK" (p. 306, emphasis in original). McFarland and Dupuis (2001) concur, noting that "teachers may punish students for uttering racist remarks, but students who make homophobic comments are seldom challenged" (p. 172). And Bott (2000) adds, "Teachers and school librarians confront the issue [of gay bashing and antigay name-calling] only three percent of the time" (p. 22).

Teacher silence promotes homophobic behavior. Two suggested reasons for this silence are that teachers are so accustomed to hearing anti-gay remarks that they often let the name-calling slide (MacGillivray, 2000); and that teachers feel that homosexuality is a charged issue and therefore rarely confront children who use homophobic name-calling to humiliate and infuriate other children (Gordon, 1994). But the very reasons that teachers avoid speaking-up about homophobic behavior suggest why teachers should speak-up. These are the teachable moments teachers should take advantage of, even if it means putting their personal reputations on the line.

According to MacGillivray (2000), "Teachers are often unwilling to allow discussions on the topic of GLBTQ issues for fear of backlash from parents and administrators, of being labeled gay themselves, or of imposing values on their students" (p. 316). Woog (2000) asserts,

> If you're worried about having to defend yourself—don't. You can deflect the [accusation of being gay] by asking. "Why do you care? What does it matter to you what anybody else is? Why are you so interested in the topic?" You can do what a few teachers have done: Say, "Yes, I'm gay," and then "calmly" go on with the lesson. Of course, the class will be in an uproar. A few minutes later, you can say, "You know, I'm really not gay. But when I said I was—did that change your impression of me? What did you think? Wasn't I the same person I was before—and am now? Let's talk about this." Talk about your teachable moment! (p. 25)

Students should be taught that "the world is filled with many, diverse types of people—and that diversity is a source of excitement and celebration, not fear and hatred" (Woog, 2000, p. 23). Only through learning this will students become "good, decent, productive citizens of the world" (Woog, 2000, p. 23). Exposure to different lifestyles and cultures is a common area of study in school, and the gay culture should be included in these studies. Many students will not have the opportunity to travel or study at the college level and will not gain this exposure elsewhere.

Another issue that LGBTQ students must cope with is a delayed development of social relationships. MacGillivray (2000) points out that "heterosexuals are privileged because their identities as straight people as well as their opposite-sex relationships are affirmed and celebrated in every facet of the culture, from the popular media to the law" (p. 304). He goes on to add that heterosexuals take these privileges for granted and accept them as natural, without realizing that others are denied those same privileges. But in a society dominated by heterosexism—the belief that everyone is or should be heterosexual—LGBTQ youth *are* denied such privileges.

The assumption made by teachers and others that all students are straight underwrites which social relationships are modeled and encouraged. Therefore, when students enter the junior and senior high school years, where one usually learns about love and relationships, LGBTQ teens are often left out of the loop (Johnson, 1996). It is because these teens lack support and understanding that they do not socially develop until later in life.

Indeed, as adults, gays, lesbians, and bisexuals learn "all of the dating and falling in love skills that for most heterosexuals were part of the junior and high school experience" (Johnson, 1996, p. 41). While most junior high and high school students were exploring their sexuality, LGBTQ youth were preoccupied with hiding theirs. Elliot (2000) recalls what he used to concentrate on when he was in middle school:

> Feet slightly more than shoulder-width apart, legs and hips relaxed, arms firmed up ... I was ready to walk "straight" to my next class. I don't mean walking in a straight line to get from one classroom to the next; instead, I was focusing on walking in a manner that I perceived to be "heterosexual." (p. 40)

Today's youth should be focused on important issues, not worrying about walking like a heterosexual.

Yet another challenge faced by LGBTQ students—one that may have the greatest impact on them—is lack of support in the school setting. If LGBTQ students had the same support system that heterosexual, cisgender students have, they might not face any of the issues presented here. Schools can express a lack of support in many ways. For instance, the lack of LGBTQ representation in history and other curricula sends the message that people in the LGBTQ community have done nothing worthy of recognition—and this is certainly not true.

Representing LGBTQ issues in history and other curricula is important for LGBTQ students because they often lack role models. MacGillivray (2000) points out that "GLBTQ youth are one of the few groups of young people without parents who are like them as role models" (p. 308). He also notes that LGBTQ adolescents find themselves without other positive role models or peers with whom to make connections (p. 314). Given the lack of role models in LGBTQ youth's lives, "[by] including discussions of gender identity, sexual orientation, and discrimination against [LGBTQ] people in the curriculum, schools can help to destigmatize non-heterosexual identities and can deconstruct gender role stereotypes that limit all students" (p. 305).

As MacGillivray explains, "GLBTQ students should have the same opportunities as are accorded heterosexual students to discuss issues important to their identities as GLBTQ people, to learn about GLBTQ people in history, to learn about the GLBTQ community and their struggles for civil rights, and to go to school without fear of being harassed, tortured, or killed" (p. 315). Schneider and Owens (2000) add that "lesbians, gays, and bisexuals could also be discussed in history, anthropology, sociology, psychology, biology, and literature courses. The human rights struggle of sexual minorities could be a valid topic for contemporary issues courses" (p. 362). Furthermore, teachers can use the writings of Lewis Carroll and Emily Dickinson in literature classes (Chng & Wong, 1998). And books such as *Jack*, by A. M. Homes, and *The Arizona Kid*, by Ron Koertge, deal with homosexual issues and would be useful additions to the curriculum (Reese, 1998). These are just a few examples of how teachers can incorporate LGBTQ issues into their teaching and thus increase support of LGBTQ scientists, authors, and scholars—and recognize their accomplishments.

Schools also express a lack of support for LGBTQ students by inadequately educating students about homosexuality and bisexuality, including the awareness, protection, and guidance of and for LGBTQ students and their straight allies. Schneider and Owens (2000) argue that

> at the interpersonal level, educators need to communicate to students both formally and informally that they are open and supportive of their students. Moreover, they need to create a safe environment in which to learn and safe spaces where gay, lesbian, bisexual, and transgender students can go for help and support. (p. 362)

Bott (2000) further suggests that even if a school does not have an antiharassment policy, teachers should establish one in their own professional environment. This policy should state that "no form of harassment will be tolerated whether related to race, gender, age, sexual orientation, ethnicity, nationality, language, religion, physical appearance, [or] physical or mental capacity" (p. 22). Teachers can provide support for LGBTQ students by discussing such policies with students so they understand that using gay-bashing language is wrong and that it promotes discrimination based on sexual orientation.

Effects on the Lives of LGBTQ Students

Issues such as antigay name-calling, delayed development of social relationships, and lack of support from teachers and peers affect the lives of LGBTQ youth in a variety of ways. Some of these effects include physical and psychological abuse and isolation. For instance, hiding one's personal identity, dropping out of school, abusing drugs—and even suicide—are common practices of LGBTQ youth. McFarland and Dupuis (2001) point out that "one reason gay and lesbian students live silent and secretive lives is that to be visible, or to have come out as a teenager, means to place oneself at risk of verbal and physical abuse" (p. 172).

According to the GLSEN *2001 National School Climate Survey: Lesbian, Gay, Bisexual and Transgender Students and their Experiences in Schools*, 68.6% of LGBTQ students reported feeling unsafe at school because of their sexual orientation (55.5% in 2013). The survey also showed that 41.9% of LGBTQ students had been physically harassed (36.2% in 2013). Therefore, for fear of being picked on, harassed, or even physically attacked, many LGBTQ students chose to hide their true identities (Kosciw & Cullen, 2001; Kosciw et al., 2014).

Moreover, factors such as low self-esteem, social isolation, and depression have contributed to drug abuse and suicide attempts. Walling (1997) cites a 1989 study conducted by the US Department of Health and Human Services that found that gay and lesbian teens were three times more likely to attempt suicide than their heterosexual peers. Mental health distress, condemnation, and rejection cause many LGBTQ youth to use and abuse alcohol and other drugs (Grossman, 1997). Grossman (1997) also indicates that they are at risk for homelessness, HIV infection, and psychosocial developmental delays. LGBTQ youth often become homeless. They either run away because they cannot cope with their harsh, homophobic surroundings, or they are thrown away by a family who rejects them based on their sexual orientation or gender identity.

Educational Reform is Key

Despite the many challenges faced by LGBTQ youth, and the ways in which those challenges affect their lives, there is hope. Education is the key to curing homophobia and to omitting the acceptance of heterosexism as the norm in American society. Schools not only need to include LGBTQ-inclusive content, but also need to model the acceptance and honor the rights of all students, straight or gay. Our country is diverse, and the LGBTQ communities are a part of that diversity.

One way that educational institutions can support this diversity is to implement antidiscrimination policies. Since "many teachers fear retribution from parent groups, administrators, other teachers and students" for addressing controversial issues, they "need the protection of a clearly written policy as well as the support of their school district to effectively end antigay peer harassment in the schools" (MacGillivray, 2000, p. 320).

Teachers should come together and demand such protection from their administration.

Indeed, teachers cannot afford to not teach about LGBTQ identities, starting at the elementary school level. Straight children need to learn to accept their LGBTQ peers, and LGBTQ students need to learn to take pride in and accept themselves as they are at an early age. Bell, Weinberg, and Hammersmith (1981) explain that many gay, lesbian and bisexual adults report that they first became aware of their attraction to members of the same gender during late childhood. Chng and Wong (1998) note that "for those children who know at an early age that they are GLB, one of the most lonely and hostile environments is unfortunately, the place where they spend the majority of their time outside the home—their schools" (p. 72). This is because support and openness are not a part of young LGBTQ children's learning atmosphere. They also point out that "by the end of elementary grades, GLB children in American society have learned that heterosexuality is normative and homosexuality/bisexuality is shameful" (p. 73).

LGBTQ-inclusive teaching—and school support for such teaching—is key to overcoming these problems. As Chng and Wong (1998) explain, "the classroom is a natural forum for presenting accurate information to students, and materials about homosexuality and bisexuality should be included in the curriculum, when appropriate, to educate students about diversity of society" (p. 78). Schneider and Owens (2000) similarly note that "at elementary educational institutions, programs that discuss the fact that differences between people exist and that those differences have the potential to enhance our understanding of the world and one another could be implemented" (p. 362). Indeed, "in secondary educational institutions, more explicit discussion of identity development in general as well as specific identity developmental processes could provide students with relevant information that could help them explain and understand what they are experiencing regarding their sexuality" (p. 362).

LGBTQ students have a long way to go before society accepts them, without hesitation, for who they are. "Although homosexuality is more visible in today's American society than in previous decades, and society has become more tolerant of homosexuality and bisexuality, there has not been a corresponding decrease in cultural homophobia" (Grossman, 1997, p. 53). It is the duty of the educational system to provide all students with a safe and nurturing learning environment; to achieve this, homophobia must be addressed. Teachers and administrators need to work together to guide and support LGBTQ students. We need to provide an open and accepting atmosphere so that these students and their straight allies can succeed, not only academically, but also in developing and promoting their personal identities.

Whenever I hear a student, peer, or colleague voice an antigay slur, I confront them. Whether I express my intolerance of such language or inquire as to why the person chose to use a homophobic slur, I make it clear that gay-bashing is simply inappropriate. I try to make my classroom an open, safe place for all students, especially LGBTQ students. Furthermore, I will continue to research the effects of homophobia and how to decrease and eventually eliminate it within our schools. As a teacher and as a genderqueer, bisexual woman, I vow to educate students, peers, and colleagues on LGBTQ issues and why addressing these issues is imperative. Every student deserves to learn in an accepting and safe environment. And I strive to give my students just that—a place where they can be themselves.

FOURTEEN YEARS LATER ...

In the years since I wrote the paper appearing in the previous section, I have tried to use its lessons in my own work. I can proudly say that when I was a practicing teacher, my classrooms were always presented and nurtured as safe spaces for LGBTQ and allied youth. And now, as a researcher and instructor of undergraduate multicultural education, I continue to nurture such an atmosphere. But all in all, my actions were not enough.

Recent Advances and Remaining Challenges

The purpose of revisiting this paper from 2002 is to show current and future teachers that LGBTQ youth are still at risk, often invisible, and need support within classrooms. As noted above, in 1997, Grossman observed that "although homosexuality is more visible in today's American society than in previous decades, and society has become more tolerant of homosexuality and bisexuality, there has not been a corresponding decrease in cultural homophobia" (p. 53). This statement still holds true today, though much has changed in the American Gay Rights Movement since 2002.

Three rulings of the United States Supreme Court have advanced the LGBTQ civil rights movement since 2002: the 2003 decision in *Lawrence v. Texas*, holding that antisodomy laws in the United States are unconstitutional; the 2013 decision finding the 1996 Defense of Marriage Act (DOMA) unconstitutional; and the recent 2015 ruling in *Obergefell v. Hodges*, establishing that same-sex couples have the fundamental right to marry and that states cannot reserve "marriage" for heterosexual couples.

However, while these important rulings reflect progress, there is still much work to do.

For example, in many states discrimination based on sexual orientation and nonconforming gender expression continues. In other words, one can be legally fired from their job for being gay or transgender. Further, although the queer civil rights movement has advanced, I had hoped that much would have changed since 2002—I hoped, for example, that (a) LGBTQ youth and communities would be widely represented within curriculum and welcomed within school cultures; (b) antigay bullying and homophobic slurs would have been eradicated, or at least greatly diminished; and (c) teachers would be willing to actively discuss LGBTQ civil rights movements in classroom settings. However, I am disappointed that not much has vastly improved for LGBTQ youth in learning environments over the last 14 years—though I do understand that change is slow.

Thus, challenges remain. As educators, we should still be asking whether much has changed for LGBTQ youth. Are our teachers better prepared to educate and support this particular group of students? My own sense is that they are not. Accordingly, if there is a coda to my 2002 thoughts on the challenges faced by LGBTQ youth, it is this: educating *teachers* on how to be LGBTQ-inclusive might be one of the most powerful ways to address those challenges.

An Attempt to Address Inclusiveness in Teacher Education

Recent studies show that the benefits of LGBTQ-inclusiveness may not be merely theoretical. According to the GLSEN (2012) research brief, *Teaching Respect: LGBT-Inclusive Curriculum and School Climate*, LGBT students in schools with an inclusive curriculum are about half as likely as those in schools without inclusive curricula to experience high levels of victimization because of sexual orientation (16% vs. 32%) or gender expression (16% vs. 30%); are less likely to feel unsafe at school because of their sexual orientation (42% vs. 64%) or gender expression (28% vs. 41%); and are about half as likely to miss school because of feeling unsafe or uncomfortable (17% vs. 32%). These youth are more likely to feel comfortable talking to a teacher about LGBT-related issues (73% vs. 50%) and are more likely to have talked to a teacher about LGBT issues (80% vs. 64%). In addition, LGBT students are more likely to report that their classmates were accepting of LGBT people (61% vs. 37%); less likely to hear homophobic remarks (e.g., "that's so gay") and negative comments about someone's gender expression; and more likely to report that their peers usually intervene when hearing homophobic remarks (10% vs. 5%). These figures tellingly demonstrate the power and effectiveness of

LGBTQ-inclusive curricula. If school settings were more accepting of nonconforming students, such students might be able to seek out supportive faculty, staff, and peers to discuss private matters, just as their heterosexual, cisgendered peers are able to do.

But it is not fair to expect teachers to simply know how to construct, include, or integrate LGBTQ-inclusive behavior. They must be taught how to do so. This, however, is not always easy. As a queer instructor of Multiculturalism & Education, a core class offered within the College of Education at a Midwestern university, I personally attempted to address sexuality and gender-related topics within preservice teacher education. The majority of my students were white, heterosexual females enrolled in art, English, elementary, or science education programs; and the greatest tensions within the classroom occurred when content and discussions featured lesbian, gay, bisexual, transgender, queer, and other nonnormative or heteronormative behaviors and identities.

Due to the nature of this particular course, the readings and discussions related to a different topic or theme each week (e.g., critical thinking, social construction, equity/equality, identity, popular culture, ethnocentrism, stereotypes, families & sexuality, gender, personal agency, immigration, and privilege). Therefore, of the 16-week semester only 2 weeks were specifically dedicated to sexuality and gender issues within education and society. However, because of the way I identify (I am a bisexual, genderqueer female) I incorporated LGBTQ topics and gender norms and nonconformity from the first day of class when I asked students to share their preferred name and pronouns with the group. This exercise was often met with confusion as to its purpose and necessity but became clear as I modeled my introduction and explained my genderqueer identity. In particular, I do not think there should be a gender binary or gendered characteristics (e.g., males are brave and strong and females are pretty and sweet). Moreover, I believe that my openness about my queer identity served to comfort and create a safe space for my students. This is evident to me because several students either came out to me privately or came out publically to the class during the semester.

The course had standardized goals and expected student outcomes. But in addition to these, I stressed identity awareness and development. I encouraged my students to become aware of their personal identities as they developed their teacher identities, and to consider how this awareness and understanding of themselves would impact their future students. I also reflected on and developed my own identities as I exchanged ideas with and engaged my students. I tried to instill in my students that this is an ongoing process and should continue throughout their education and teaching careers (Jenlink, 2014). I also highlighted the importance of critical questioning, critical thinking, and critical reflection. Through sharing my identities and personal self-awareness, I modeled how to create a safe space and learning atmosphere for all students.

This course often offered the first opportunity for most of my students to openly discuss issues about race, socioeconomic status, and sexual orientation. I witnessed discomfort and distrust, evident in student silence, or openly expressed in written reflections. Usually, by the end of the final week of class, there were still a few students who had not contributed to classroom discussions; yet several students thanked me for allowing them the opportunity to share their thoughts on delicate topics. They confided that they could never have had these types of discussions with their parents, families, or peers, although many of them admitted that they were still "unprepared and/or unwilling to discuss queer issues as they relate to students and families, curriculum, and instruction" (Murray, 2015, p. 5).

Finally, even the religious identities of my students—most of them openly identified as belonging to Christian-based religions—did not seem to be an admitted barrier to their ability to accept others. I am hopeful for this generation of teachers. Many of them acknowledged tensions between their faiths and how they will provide an equitable education to LGBTQ-identified students they may encounter within their own classrooms. Nevertheless, many voiced that although they did not agree with LGBTQ lifestyles, no child ought to be discriminated against. This is a promising first step toward justice for LGBTQ students, since the majority of my college students, admittedly, had no idea that so many nonconforming identities (e.g., nonheterosexual, noncisgender) existed.

Creating and Teaching Inclusive Curricula

Because of the unawareness described above, and the lack of safe spaces where informative, constructive conversations can take place, we should be encouraging and developing LGBTQ-inclusive curricula within and across teacher education programs. One way to achieve this goal is by using frameworks such as the Queer Inclusion in Teacher Education framework (Murray, 2015) to develop teacher education curricula. In this way, teacher educators can provide an overview of LGBTQ history and evidence as to why such curriculum are needed; model LGBTQ-inclusive behaviors and language; provide examples of how K–12 teachers can make their curriculum LGBTQ inclusive; and offer a safe space to explore and (de)construct personal and professional identities through critical thinking, critical questioning, and critical reflection, with the purpose of knowing oneself in order to understand others (Banks, 2006; Gollnick & Chinn, 2004; Grant & Sleeter, 2011; Nieto & Bode, 2012).

Such curriculum and resulting teacher-student interactions would enable personal and teacher identity awareness and development. Identity awareness, development, and negotiation are vital factors within the LGBTQ community. While privileged, heterosexual, cisgender individuals never, or rarely, have to think about personal or professional identities, at least with regard to sexual orientation and gender, it is just not so for LGBTQ professionals (Jenlink, 2014; Kissen, 2002). LGBTQ-inclusive curricula would help nurture a safe space—and, hopefully, more dedicated time—for all teacher education students (e.g., lesbian, gay, bisexual, asexual, pansexual, straight, transgender, and cisgender) to engage in meaningful, constructive conversation and interaction geared toward promoting social justice and equitable education for LGBTQ youth.

Ultimately, through LGBTQ-inclusive teacher education, it is my hope that these practices will lead to LGBTQ-inclusive curricula implemented within K–12 classrooms. This implementation consequently should promote awareness of LGBTQ communities and identities, decrease the amount of bullying and violence toward LGBTQ youth, reduce the rate of suicide within the LGBTQ youth community, increase equal treatment toward and positive school experiences for LGBTQ youth, and diminish heteronormative behaviors and assumptions within the greater society. Ultimately, we need to provide *teachers* with the tools they need to create a place where students can be themselves.

NOTE

1. Small portions of this original paper appear in Knaier, M. L. (in press). Let's talk about LGBTQ-inclusiveness in K–12 curriculum. In J. Phillion, H. Sasser, & J. Rahatzad (Eds.), *Critical multiplicities in teacher education: Ethical considerations and alter-globalizations*. Charlotte, NC: Information Age. They are reprinted here with the permission of the publisher. Further, in what follows I largely stayed true to the original manuscript, but I edited and redacted some of the original language and content for the sake of publishing, professionalism, and inclusivity.

REFERENCES

Banks, J. A. (2006). *Race, culture, and education: The selected works of James A. Banks*. New York, NY: Routledge.

Bell, A. P., Weinberg, M. S., & Hammersmith, S. K. (1981). *Sexual preference: Its development in men and women*. Bloomington: Indiana University Press.

Bott, C. J. (2000). Fighting the silence: How to support your gay and straight students. *Voice of Youth Advocates, 23*(1), 22–26.

Chng, C. L., & Wong, F. Y. (1998). Gay, lesbian and bisexual (GLB) children: Implications for early childhood development professionals. *Early Child Development and Care, 147*, 71–82.

Elliot, B. (2000, Spring). Finding my stride: A gay student takes the bold step of being true to himself. *Teaching Tolerance, 17*, 40–41.

Frankfurt, K. (2000). A place for everyone. *Principal Leadership, 1*(2), 64–67.

Gay, Lesbian & Straight Education Network (GLSEN). (2012). *Teaching respect: LGBT-inclusive curriculum and school climate* (Research Brief). New York, NY: Author.

Gollnick, D. M., & Chinn, P. C. (2004). *Multicultural education in a pluralistic society* (6th ed.). Upper Saddle River, NJ: Pearson.

Gordon, L. (1994). What do we say when we hear 'faggot'? In B. Bigelow, L. Christensen, S. Karp, B. Miner, & B. Peterson (Eds.), *Rethinking our classrooms: Teaching for equity and justice* (pp. 86–87). Milwaukee, WI: Rethinking Schools.

Grant, C., & Sleeter, C. (2011). *Doing multicultural education for achievement and equity* (2nd ed.). New York, NY: Taylor & Francis.

Grossman, A. (1997). Growing up with a "spoiled identity": Lesbian, gay, and bisexual youth at risk. *Journal of Gay & Lesbian Social Services, 6*(3), 45–56.

Jenlink, P. M. (Ed.). (2014). *Teacher identity and the struggle for recognition: Meeting the challenges of a diverse society.* Lanham, MD: Rowman & Littlefield.

Johnson, D. (1996, Summer/Fall). The developmental experience of gay/lesbian youth. *Journal of College Admission, 152/153*, 38–41.

Kissen, R. M. (Ed.). (2002). *Getting ready for Benjamin: Preparing teachers for sexual diversity in the classroom.* Lanham, MD: Rowman & Littlefield.

Kosciw, J. G., & Cullen, M. K. (2001). *The GLSEN national school climate survey: The school-related experiences of our nation's lesbian, gay, bisexual and transgender youth.* New York, NY: GLSEN. Retrieved from http://files.eric.ed.gov/fulltext/ED464978.pdf

Kosciw, J. G., Greytak, E. A., Palmer, N. A., & Boesen, M. J. (2014). *The 2013 national school climate survey: The experiences of lesbian, gay, bisexual and transgender youth in our nation's schools.* New York, NY: GLSEN.

MacGillivray, I. (2000). Educational equity for gay, lesbian, bisexual, transgendered, and queer/questioning students: The demands of democracy and social justice for America's schools. *Education and Urban Society, 32*(3), 303–323.

McFarland, W., & Dupuis, M. (2001). The legal duty to protect gay and lesbian student from violence in school. *Professional School Counseling, 4*(3), 171–179.

Murray, O. J. (2015). *Queer inclusion in teacher education: Bridging theory, research, and practice.* New York, NY: Routledge.

Nieto, S., & Bode, P. (2012). *Affirming diversity: The sociopolitical context of multicultural education* (6th ed.). Boston, MA: Pearson.

Reese, J. (1998). Teaching tolerance through literature: Dealing with issues of homosexuality in English class. *International Schools Journal, 17*(2), 35–41.

Schneider, M., & Owens, R. (2000). Concern for lesbian, gay, and bisexual kids: The benefits for all children. *Education and Urban Society, 32*(3), 349–367.

Walling, D. R. (1997). Gay and lesbian issues. In D. R. Walling (Ed.), *Hot buttons: Unraveling 10 controversial issues in education* (pp. 147–166). Bloomington, IN: Phi Delta Kappa Educational Foundation.

Woog, D. (2000). Friends, families, and the importance of straight allies. *Voice of Youth Advocates, 23*(1), 23–26.

CHAPTER 3

SITUATING ALLY IDENTITIES IN RELATIONAL EPISTEMES

Learning With LGBTIQ People in Order to Make Supportive and Inclusive Decisions

Ryan Schey

When I began my first high school teaching position after graduating from a teacher preparation program, I strove to be an "ally" to lesbian, gay, bisexual, trans*, intersex, queer, and questioning (LGBTIQ[1]) youth, adults, and families in my new community. I participated in concrete actions such as establishing a Gay-Straight Alliance (GSA) with another entry-year teacher (see Schey & Uppstrom, 2010) and becoming a member of a teacher inquiry group, the *Pink TIGers*, focused on combating homophobia (see Blackburn, Clark, Kenney, & Smith, 2010 for a history of the early years of this group). In working as an activist, I uncritically assumed that I already knew what it meant to be an ally and that such a position could be unambiguous and uncomplicated. In other words, I thought that a person either was an ally or wasn't an ally. Since I was attitudinally supportive of social justice and was making intentional decisions in an effort to contribute to this goal, I thought I automatically was always an ally. After all, I was (and am) a straight cisgender man attempting to change a social system that marginalized(s) some people while giving others unearned privilege with respect to sexual identity and gender expression.

Year 1 of my teaching career eventually flowed into year 3 and then 5 and so on, each one introducing more complexity, ambiguity, and uncertainty into my LGBTIQ-focused (which at first was really LGB-focused) activism work. When I began my teaching career, I believed that doing social justice work would be challenging. However, I had thought that this difficulty would solely originate from the resistance of others in my school community. I didn't realize how complicated, nebulous, and contradictory my own role would be. What I had thought was clear-cut was anything but. During these years, there were moments that felt like successes. For example, one year on the National Day of Silence[2] I recall a "breaking the silence" meeting in our high school's courtyard after school where students screamed collectively to break their vow of silence, discussed their experiences from throughout the day, and participated in a small celebration of our GSA community. In moments like these, I felt I had built strong relationships with some LGBTIQ youth and was confident that my position in their lives was positive and affirming. At other times, I believe that I made mistakes that alienated and hurt some LGBTIQ youth due to, in part, my unexamined words and actions. For example, I still feel a deep pain and sense of regret around my words and actions in my relationship with one trans* youth, particularly with respect to the way in which I used humor in interacting with her regarding her name preferences. More generally, the complexities, tensions, and multiplicities of my experiences did not match up with the singular, fixed, and dichotomous definition of an ally that I had previously encountered and subsequently put into use. Due to my professional experiences and my involvement in a practitioner inquiry project conducted by the previously mentioned *Pink TIGers*, I have come to rethink what it means to become an ally to LGBTIQ youth, adults, and families in educational contexts.

In this chapter, I review current scholarship defining ally identities, propose a shift in our understanding of these identities, and then discuss a telling case of an interview with a lesbian-identifying student, Lana, which illustrates what this shift might look like for teachers and teacher educators. More specifically, I argue the need to shift away from understandings of ally identities that foreground a singular, fixed, and coherent ontology of people who are privileged due to their membership in macrolevel sexual and/or gender identity categories, especially with respect to the attitudes and intentions of these privileged people. Instead, I propose it is more efficacious for LGBTIQ-focused social justice work to employ understandings of ally identities that are situated in the epistemes of relationships among people who identify as LGBTIQ and straight or cisgender. My goal in rethinking what it means to become an ally is to help teachers and teacher educators to participate in decision making that results in interactions that a greater number of LGBTIQ people will more frequently experience as supportive, inclusive, affirming, and empathic. These localized interactions can in turn contribute to changes in educational structures that often marginalize, dehumanize, and/or delegitimize people as a result of their sexual identity and/or gender expression. In short, a shift from privileged ontologies to relational epistemes can help allies work to become more responsive, relevant, and meaningful for the people to whom allies claim to provide support through actions focused both on individuals and structures, which I discuss in greater detail in the conclusion.

CONCEPTUALIZING ALLY IDENTITIES ONTOLOGICALLY: CURRENT SCHOLARSHIP

Currently, common definitions of ally identities circulate both in scholarship and in materials produced by educational organizations primarily intended for practitioner use. Implicitly, both bodies of literature frequently utilize the ontology of privileged positionalities as an unexamined starting point for these definitions. Explicitly, they define the idea of an ally as a generalized social justice position involving an individual's membership in a macrolevel demographic identity group category that grants a degree of power and privilege—the very understanding I held when I first began teaching. In turn, this individual recognizes this privilege and then takes some sort of action intentionally designed to lessen oppression and increase justice. For example, Broido (2000) builds upon Washington and Evans (1991), defining "social justice allies [as] members of dominant social groups (e.g., men, Whites, heterosexuals) who are working to end the system of oppression that gives them greater privilege and power based on their social-group membership" (p. 3). The approach in this literature often focuses on the (potential) ally's attitudes and developmental process (e.g., Broido & Reason, 2005; DiStefano, Croteau, Anderson, Kampa-Kokesch, & Bullard, 2000; Edwards, 2006).

Some definitions move beyond generalized social justice stances toward specific considerations of LGBT[3] people. The Gay, Lesbian and Straight Education Network (GLSEN) provides a generalized social justice definition and then particularizes it: "An ally is any person who supports and stands up for the rights of LGBT people" (GLSEN, 2013, p. 5). Relatedly, some literature provides concrete action steps that illustrate how to apply the generalized social justice ally definition to LGBT-focused advocacy. To illustrate, Evans and Broido (2005) suggest "sponsoring speakers, movies, or plays on LGBT topics" (p. 51) while GLSEN's (2013) "Safe Space Kit" suggests "display[ing] Safe Space stickers or posters in your classroom or office" (p. 11). In these discussions, the ontological focus on privileged people's attitudes toward oppression and intentions behind their actions are central.

Without a doubt, these definitions have utility for LGBTIQ-focused activism work because they potentially foreground action and agency in relation to structural elements of power. If one overarching goal of teachers and teacher educators oriented toward social justice is to facilitate students' adoption of a stance of ally work as opposed to a stance of resistance, neutrality, or antiwork (see Clark, 2010a, 2010b), these definitions can be useful in highlighting that education is inherently political and ideological. Specifically, these ontologically focused definitions first emphasize action, suggesting that being an ally is not merely feeling sympathetic or believing in an abstract idea but additionally requires concrete localized action. Second, the emphasis on action characterizes people as agents and not merely as effects of power, thus foregrounding their potential to participate in social change. Third, these definitions recognize the role of power and social structures in producing oppression as opposed to focusing on characteristics of people who experience marginalization. In these ways, such definitions can be used to help individual pre- and in-service teachers become change agents who are aware of the need to consider how schools (re)produce oppression and inequality. In addition, much of the literature produced by educational organizations is accompanied by resources that teachers can immediately reproduce and use in their educational contexts.[4] In sum, they help contribute to individual action and agency in activism focused on changing educational contexts.

At the same time, by using the ontology of privileged individuals as a starting point, such definitions assume that the self exists *a priori* to social interactions. So, they employ "a positivist or structural theoretical framework, in which identity is singular and stable; that is, people either are or are not lesbian, gay, bisexual, or transgender (mostly not)" (Blackburn & Clark, 2011, p. 223). Furthermore, they assume that people who are not LGBTIQ either are or are not allies. As a result, ally identities become static and fixed as they are part of a larger taxonomy of identities made available to people through a series of binaries. The exception to this static rigidity is a possibility for a sort of redemption available to the (privileged straight cisgender) individual. This possibility frequently relies on a sort of consciousness raising or conversion narrative where the individual realizes his or her unearned privilege, accepts responsibility, and then makes atonement via efforts to change the system (e.g., McIntosh, 1998). However, through this narrative the social and discursive mechanisms that construct these identity categories are reified and naturalized.

In addition to naturalizing identity categories, current characterizations implicitly suggest that allies can always be identically defined because all people in marginalized positions always have identical needs. Otherwise, being an ally would mean more than an ontological combination of attitudes and intentions. By defining an ally with regard to social justice in general, such understandings homogenize across macrolevel categories of group identity (e.g., race or sexual identity) and erase possibilities for exploring the nuances of, for example, intersectionality and the multiplicity of lived experience. Next, they homogenize across experiences within LGBTIQ communities, implying that, for example, the needs of a lesbian couple with elementary school children in a Midwestern city are the same as the needs of a high school student in the rural South who experiences gender in a nondichotomous way. Finally, they homogenize across members of a particular identity category within the LGBTIQ acronym (e.g., bisexual or trans*), implying that all individuals who self-identify with a category will have similar and consistent needs and desires. Finally, it uncritically assumes that a singular action will be experienced as either wholly supportive or marginalizing, denying the possibilities of multiplicity and ambiguity.

In sum, in a well-intentioned effort to cultivate social justice, ontological definitions of ally identities elide the complex, fluid, and contingent nature of this work. They homogenize and naturalize both the identity categories and the experiences within such categories. In addition, they focus on the general dispositions of members of dominant groups who are potential allies because of how their macrolevel demographic identities position them in local interactions. In doing so, the people whose voices are already at the center remain in the center while those already at the margins stay at the margins. Conceptualizing ally work in this way teaches educators to work for social justice by primarily worrying about their own attitudes. It reifies ways of being that ignore the potential for people with experiences of marginalization to articulate unique insights regarding power, social structures, and social change (e.g., Dillard, 2000; Harding, 1993). While I do not deny the past utility and contributions of ontological conceptualizations of ally identities, I have come to question their limitations in realizing their stated goals.

CONCEPTUALIZING ALLY IDENTITIES EPISTEMOLOGICALLY: SHIFTING OUR TRAJECTORIES

In shifting how we understand ally identities, I draw upon poststructural and social constructionist theorists who understand meaning and identity as socially (re)produced in the micropolitics and power relations of everyday interactions (Butler, 1990/2007; Davies & Harré, 1990; Deleuze & Guattari, 1987, pp. 3–25; Erickson, 2008; Gee, 2008; Gergen, 2009; Jagose, 1996). In such a view, identity is not understood as an expression of an authentic and autonomous core self that is stable and coherent. Instead, it is contingent, heterogeneous, and fragmented. Therefore, becoming an ally is an ongoing process existing in the interactive space between people instead of within the interiority of a single person. It relies on epistemes (or ways of knowing) that are situated in trusting relationships between people who are positioned at the center and the margins in local interactions in relation to their macrolevel demographic identity categories. In detailing this shift, I draw upon Bucholtz and Hall's (2005) sociocultural linguistic approach to identities. Their heuristic utilizes five principles for understanding the interactive construction of identity: emergence, positionality, indexicality, relationality, and partiality. I discuss each of the principles next by explaining how it creates a shift for understanding ally identities. I then discuss what each might mean for straight and/or cisgender educators.

In doing so, I must include a caveat; my discussion is intended to be suggestive of future trajectories, functioning as a resource for readers to use in envisioning how such ideas can become meaningful and relevant in their educational context and practice. My discussion is not intended to be definitive or absolute, functioning as a set of static *a priori* action steps that anyone could unproblematically apply anywhere at any time. In this spirit, I offer five key sets of questions to serve as praxis epicenters for reflection and action. These are questions that, in retrospect, I wish I had been asking myself throughout my teaching career as I attempted to become an ally. With this in mind, I now shift to discuss Bucholtz and Hall's (2005) five principles and their significance for ally identities.

First, according to Bucholtz and Hall (2005), identities do not exist *a priori* to the social as decontextualized psychological phenomena that are the source of action, but instead they emerge through the use of interactive resources such as language. In this way, identities are a continual process; they are contingent and always shifting. So, ally identities do not exist based on preexisting ontological characteristics of privileged people; they are not defined through psychological phenomena such as feelings or intentions. Instead, ally identities emerge through interactions, specifically as people who are marginalized in relation to their sexual identity and/or gender expression experience interactions as supportive, inclusive, affirming, and/or empathic. In this way, ally identities are in constant formation and function strategically based on the dynamics in an educational context. They are situated rather than absolute and inevitable. While certain attitudes might predispose an individual to act supportively or unsupportively in a specific moment, such predispositions do not constitute acting as an ally. Instead, they are correlative. The concept of emergence can help straight and/or cisgender teachers and teacher educators to reconsider support as they come to understand that ally identities are not a one-time event but are instead ongoing efforts. So, in my own work, I find myself asking, How am I working in this moment to be experienced as supportive? While intentionality is not sufficient here, it is helpful as support is unlikely to happen by accident, especially in hetero/cisnormative (if not homo/transphobic) contexts.

Second, according to Bucholtz and Hall (2005), identities simultaneously encompass multiple tiers of interactional positions. Specifically, "(a) macro-level demographic categories; (b) local ethnographically specific cultural positions; and (c) temporary and interactionally specific stances and participant roles" (p. 592) all contribute to the moment-by-moment discursive work of identity formation. Reflecting upon these three tiers of identities highlights how people can be positioned intersubjectively as allies. It is vital to recognize that macrolevel demographic identity categories such as straight or gay are both produced by and productive of material effects in educational contexts (as current scholarship on ally identities already acknowledges). In other words, in relation to sexual identity and gender expression, some people experience privileging, naturalization, and valuation where others experience marginalization, dehumanization, and delegitimization. It is these categories that contribute to (re)production of inequitable relationships between privileged and marginalized people and make an ally identity available to privileged people. However, such effects do not operate monolithically or homogenously. Instead, they are constituted by the unique intersections of different facets of demographic identities alongside other tiers of identity categories such as locally significant or interactionally transitory positionalities. In this way, people emerge locally positioned as allies. In specific moments, such as a youth coming to a teacher for support, a person can be temporarily positioned as an ally and enact such an identity. Over time, reiterative acts can help solidify an ally or nonally (e.g., homophobe) identity as locally recognized.

For straight and/or cisgender teachers and teacher educators, it could be useful to recognize that an ally identity is not absolute in this view. Instead, for some LGBTIQ people in some instances, an individual such as a teacher will be positioned as an ally while at others that same teacher will not. Similarly, a single act can simultaneously have both supportive and marginalizing effects. As a result, I reflexively ask myself in my work, How are LGBTIQ youth, adults, and families experiencing me? What feedback and uptake come from others that can help me understand how I am (not) being positioned as an ally? What type of reputation and identity am I developing over time in my educational context?

Third, according to Bucholtz and Hall (2005), identities emerge in interaction via the use of linguistic, paralinguistic, and semiotic resources. More specifically, they argue that resources are available to people in different interactions and their use can point to (or index) the status of being a certain type of person. Although Bucholtz and Hall, among other scholars, have extensively explored the various types of discursive mechanisms that index identities, the existence of indexicality rather than its specific method of operation is most germane to my current discussion. When ally identities are located as indexically constituted in interactions, they are understood as existing within relationships as opposed to locating ally identities in attitudes or intentions (and thus understood as existing with internal psychological conditions). Because ally identities emerge through the intersection of macrolevel, locally significant, and transitory interactive positions, practitioners and researchers can come to investigate the empirical question of what languaging resources index, for example, ally or homophobe identities in a context. The principle of indexicality can thus encourage straight and/or cisgender teachers and teacher educators to adopt an inquiry approach to ally work. For me, instead of assuming a stance of knowing I can adopt one of openness and learning where I ask questions such as What can I do that will be relevant and meaningful in this context right now? What will others understand and experience as an ally action? What matters here and in what ways can I contribute to it?

Fourth, according to Bucholtz and Hall (2005), identities do not exist autonomously. Instead, they are situated within complex social relationships that involve intersecting relations such as "similarity/difference, genuineness/artifice, and authority/delegitimacy" (p. 598). Although Bucholtz and Hall's discussion emphasizes the tactical (de Certeau, 1984) nature of relating to different dimensions of identities, I extend their discussion to consider an explicitly voluntarist component of relationships: listening (e.g., Kinloch & San Pedro, 2014; Schultz, 2003). As Schultz (2003) argues, adopting a "listening stance" (p. 6) is significant in multiple ways: first, it "plac[es] the stories of individuals and groups who have been marginalized in the center of discussions" (p. 7); second, it attends to the "heartbeat or tenor of the group" (p. 8) and "requires proximity and intimacy" (p. 8); and third, by assuming "that everyone makes sense all of the time" (p. 9) it places people's fundamental humanity at the center of social action and transformation.

This idea can have great utility for straight and/or cisgender teachers and teacher educators as it prioritizes a relational epistemology. It foregrounds the question of how allies can go about knowing if they are actually being allies. Specifically, they can know they are allies by listening to LGBTIQ youth, adults, and families, by attempting to act on what they learn through this dialogue and then evaluating their actions based on the feedback and the results that are generated. This approach extends the previously mentioned inquiry approach. Such an understanding of ally work implies that it can and will never look the same across community contexts, across identities represented by the LGBTIQ acronym, across members self-identifying with an identity category, or even across an educator's different relationships. Instead, ally work will shift and change from moment to moment. It will be complex, fragmented, and even appear contradictory.

This approach means that allies will not show up to schools and impose preexisting notions of social-justice work onto the space but rather will work with LGBTIQ people to develop an activism trajectory that means something in that place at that time for those particular individuals. Such a stance embodies the suggestion that Blackburn (2014) makes: "Even the most well-intentioned straight allies must immerse themselves in the research and theory of LGBTQ scholars, authors, and artists to conduct insightful research focused on LGBTQ communities" (p. 53), an assertion that I extend to consider the work of well-intentioned straight cisgender people (e.g., me), who wish to participate in meaningful activism as teachers or teacher educators and not solely as researchers. So, in a continual effort to learn, I ask myself, How and where am I building space to listen? Where are new areas of learning and growth for me? How am I changing my decision-making to be more responsive to LGBTIQ youth, adults, and families?

Fifth, according to Bucholtz and Hall (2005), identity is partial, meaning that myriad factors beyond the self contribute to its situated and discontinuous construction. Such a view recognizes that identities are partially intentional and conscious, but they are partially an outcome of other aspects as well. For example, they are in part the results of certain habits and are "hence often less than fully conscious" (p. 606). They are in part negotiated with and contested by others, meaning that no single individual controls or decides identity. They are in part a result of broader social structures, that exist beyond the constraints of a given moment. Therefore, ally identities cannot be reduced to the attitudes and intentions of an individual teacher, but instead are a result of many social elements coalescing in a moment. Based on partiality, I work to reflect on what I take for granted: What do I assume about students, families, and other educators in relation to sexual identity and gender expression? How do my assumptions influence my actions and decisions? How can I reshape my future decisions based on my reflexivity? While it can be hard and even painful to honestly ask and answer these questions, it is an essential part of my ethical praxis.

In sum, working from Bucholtz and Hall's (2005) heuristic, I propose a new definition of how one can know when he, she, or they relationally emerges in an ally position:

> An individual is positioned as an ally when his, her, or their interactions are experienced as supportive, inclusive, affirming, and/or empathic by another individual who is marginalized, dehumanized, and/or delegitimized in relation to his, her or their sexual identity and/or gender expression.

This definition foregrounds the stories and experiences of LGBTIQ people in ally work through listening while dehomogenizing and denaturalizing such identities. It calls attention to structural operations of power but through the understandings of LGBTIQ people rather than preexisting and decontextualized analyses. In addition, it recognizes ally identities as a process of continual formation and thus as situated and fluid.

RYAN AND LANA'S CONVERSATION: AN ILLUSTRATION OF SITUATING ALLY IDENTITIES IN RELATIONAL EPISTEMES

I now turn to a brief discussion of excerpts from an interview I conducted with a lesbian student, Lana, to begin to explore empirically what shifting from an ontological to an epistemological understanding of ally identities might look like for teachers and teacher educators. Her interview comes from a larger research project conducted by the previously mentioned teacher-inquiry group, the *Pink TIGers*. This study centered on two questions: first, what do students, their families, teachers, administrators, other school personnel, and community members say about their experiences with advocacy for LGBTIQ and gender-creative people in schools? And, second, in the stories they tell, when, where, how, and under what conditions do they support LGBTIQ and gender-creative people in schools or not? The *Pink TIGers* conducted approximately 70 interviews and collaboratively analyzed this data. Lana's particular interview took place in my classroom during the summer after her graduation but before college. Over the 4 previous years, I had Lana as a student in multiple courses and she regularly visited me outside of class time. We often discussed life in general, and I was frequently a sounding board and caring counsel for her.

Lana's interview serves as a telling case illustrating the previous conceptual discussion of ally identities. As Mitchell (1984) explains, a telling case has the potential to be more analytically "fruitful" (p. 239) than a typical case because its qualities elucidate previously obscured relationships. The excerpts from Lana's interview are telling because they illustrate limitations of understanding ally identities through privileged ontologies while pointing to affordances of understanding ally identities through relational epistemes. Specifically, Lana pointed to support, inclusion, affirmation, and empathy when my interactions were consistent with a view of ally identities as situated within relational epistemes (a view that is therefore fluid, contingent, heterogeneous, and processual). She referenced misunderstanding, exclusion, denial, and antipathy when my interactions were consistent with a view of ally identities as located in the ontology of the attitudes and intentions of privileged people. At this juncture in the chapter, an argument grounded in an ontological understanding might outline a set of action steps for anyone to follow in any context at any point in time in order to do ally work. In contrast, I explore an example of myself as a teacher, researcher, and activist attempting interactively to become an ally in an effort to help readers imagine how they might attempt similar relational work in their educational contexts. Thus, this analysis is intended to be suggestive and illustrative rather than definitive and taxonomical.

As our conversation began, I shared with Lana my purpose for interviewing her and my goals for the project generally (i.e., to learn about her experiences of [non]support in schools and to understand ways to improve schools for LGBTIQ people). In response, she expressed anxiety about how people might interpret her words. She identified fear that she would need to speak definitively for all LGBTIQ people and that she needed to have the "right" things to say. Noticing this dynamic, I attempted to support and empower her voice:

(A) 1 Ryan: You seem anxious. Tell me about that.

2 Lana: I. Well. [laughs] I don't know. I think I kind of suck in that I'm more likely to offend other gay people than to be offended by anything that people say to me about it.

3 Ryan: Yeah.

4 Lana: So I don't want to be like, nasty, like ...

5 Ryan: No, you're going to be fine.

6 Lana: [laughs] Okay.

In the interview, when I noticed Lana's reticence to speak about LGBTIQ topics, I attempted to make space in the conversation for her to discuss her feelings, thus exploring their meaning and validating her point of view (A. 1). In the next turn, she responded with several starts, stops, and repairs (i.e., "I," "Well," "I don't know," and finally "I think ...") along with a nervous laugh. She was trying to find a way to help a straight adult who just didn't understand and didn't realize he didn't understand to begin to see her perspective. She eventually landed on the concept of "offense" as a way to frame her hesitance for me, a notion that invoked relational dynamics of harm, safety, protection, and personal interpretation. At its core, her comment attempted to assert the diversity and individuality of LGBTIQ experiences and protect each person's autonomy with respect to identification. She couched this idea in decorum by not wanting to "offend" (A. 2) or be "nasty" (A. 4). Foregrounded in her comments (A. 2) is a concern for how her words can impact other LGBTIQ people as opposed to merely a protection of herself. Unfortunately, instead of listening to her, I pushed her concerns aside and asserted my power as a straight adult with the institutional authority to define her experience (A. 5). She politely laughed and acquiesced (A. 6). I intended to enact the "good ally" identity through referring to my listening stance (A. 1) and interpersonal support (A. 5), but it was a failed attempt.

Ally definitions ontologically focusing on my attitudinal disposition and/or intentional choices are unable to explain my failure to be an ally to Lana in this moment. Thus, they have little utility for moving forward in social-justice work in this interactive context. They would commend my actions rather than reflexively explore their meanings, effects, and shortcomings. On the other hand, an understanding of ally identities based on relational epistemology highlights that Lana was not experiencing support, affirmation, or empathy in this interaction. It foregrounds her needs and, in turn, the importance of adjusting my approach if I am to be responsive to her needs in the moment and in conceptualizing a future advocacy trajectory. In the momentary interaction, I needed to shift to an approach focused on her in relation to me as opposed to her as spokesperson for all LGBTIQ people who would somehow help me develop a generalized set of decision rules for future actions. In the broader school context, I needed to consider how the high school could provide different and nuanced support for a range of LGBTIQ student needs.

Shortly afterwards, Lana attempted again to disrupt my tendency to equate and naturalize the desires of all LGBTIQ people. In doing so, she resisted my inclination to view ally work as autonomous or decontextualized. Specifically, she challenged this view as expressed in my homogenizing words when she asserted the varied and potentially contradictory preferences of LGBTIQ people. This excerpt comes immediately after I explained to Lana that I hope to learn from her ways to "be a better supporter and ally":

(B)   7   Lana: Are you talking about, like, things that are, like, ... like the politically correct term for things that, like, people are like, offended by, or, like, ...?

       8   Ryan: No, I ... well, and I think part of it, but that's a superficial type of thing.

       9   Lana: Yeah.

       10   Ryan: Because it's like, you know, if you use a certain word ...

       11   Lana: I don't think everyone would feel the same way about that.

       12   Ryan: Yeah.

       13   Lana: Some people think it's, like, a compliment.

As in (A), she again drew upon notions of decorum (i.e., "politically correct" and "offended" [B. 7]) in an effort to build my understanding regarding the diverse range of needs of LGBTIQ people. When I articulated that focusing on using "politically correct" terminology alone is "superficial" (B. 8), she affirmed that I was moving toward understanding her perspective ("yeah" [B. 9]).

In this moment, our conversation explores the question of terminology. Debates over the so-called correct terms can align with autonomous and positivist understandings of ally identities in that they emphasize selecting the correct or appropriate terminology and then applying it invariably across interactions. In doing so, such debates can elide considerations of how different words can function in different ways in different contexts for different LGBTIQ people, opening up the possibility for strategic and shifting language usage (e.g., Jagose, 1996; Sullivan, 2003). In other words, terminology can be fluid for individuals depending on which aspect of their identity they wish to foreground based on context and audience. In this spirit, Lana expressed (B. 11, 13) that different people had different feelings. Thus, the same language use in different interactions could index different relations and position people differently. In this second example (B), Lana again points to the shortcomings of an ontological understanding of ally identities: while someone might intend to use language in a supportive way, such an attempt might be experienced as unsupportive. As a result, that person could be positioned as a nonally or homophobe rather than an ally, an insight that becomes available once we shift to an epistemological understanding. Doing so foregrounds the need for educators to prioritize listening in relationships as a means of navigating the nuances of language use with specific people in the educational contexts rather than uncritically impose *a priori* assumptions about what words do or do not mean for people.

CONCLUSION

These excerpts from Lana's interview point to the complexity of the continual process of learning to interact supportively, inclusively, affirmatively, and empathically with the diversity of LGBTIQ youth, adults, and families who are part of a teaching context. In these small moments, Lana attempted to interrupt my tendency to homogenize and naturalize the diverse, and potentially contradictory experiences, needs, desires, and identities of LGBTIQ people. She attempted to disrupt *a priori* understandings of being an ally. In this way, Lana helps teachers and teacher educators understand the potential usefulness of foregrounding the perspectives of people who experience marginalization (as suggested by Harding, 1993). She reinforces what Bucholtz and Hall (2005) help us to understand via their identities in interaction heuristic: ally identities are always emergent, positional, indexical, relational, and partial. Becoming one is always a moment-by-moment interactive accomplishment. It is fluid and contingent, existing in the relational space between people. So, teachers and teacher educators can know they are allies in an interaction when they are experienced as allies instead of based on when they feel they are or intend to be. Straight cisgender people (like me) must continually engage in this admittedly hard world. While treating ally work as a set of decontextualized action steps that can be carried out in the same way by any person in any place at any time is possibly easier, more accessible, and more comforting than what I suggest, I believe that it is also less meaningful and effective.

In moving to a conception of ally identities as fluid and contingent, we open up the possibility of forgiveness and therefore invite more widespread participation in such work. Teachers and teacher educators, whether novices or experts with respect to making supportive and inclusive decisions, can understand that they can't and won't be perfect, so mistake-making becomes part of the process of becoming an ally. Relationships are messy and in this way involve missteps and repairs as people come to understand how to offer and receive support and care in ways that are reciprocally meaningful. Fixed and monolithic *a priori* notions of ally identities imply that teachers and teacher educators should have all of the answers before acting. In contrast, situating ally work in relational epistemes prioritizes inquiry, listening, and process. Such a view does not and should not be abused as a rationalization for repeatedly making the same callous mistakes or refusing to change. However, it does open up the space for trusting and caring conversations based on mutual vulnerability and forgiveness. Thus, this view can help undo some of the anxiety that educators can feel around the need to "get it right" or not attempt to do the work at all.

In closing, I suggest implications regarding three potential modes of support for ally identities situated in relational epistemes: individual relationships, structure-focused action, and pedagogies grounded in concrete social action. I discuss each next.

First, in working to provide support for LGBTIQ people, teachers and teacher educators can focus on individual relationships. By listening and learning relationally, they can understand the different variations of support and empathy desired by different people. In this way, the definition of ally work emerges from discussions in local contexts as opposed to being generated from outside and being imposed onto those specific relationships. So, teachers and teacher educators can work to strategically support the actions and needs of LGBTIQ people on a case-by-case basis, focusing on particularized actions. For example, in my relationship with Lana, this ally work took the form of being a sounding board for processing her day-to-day experiences. In doing so, I took actions that she articulated and understood as supportive and meaningful. However, as she points out about language use, not "everyone would feel the same way about that" (B. 11).

Second, in attempting to extend the work occurring in individual relationships, teachers and teacher educators must also focus on elements of the educational context. To only act and think in dyadic relationships masks the structural operation of power and potentially locates the "issue" in social-justice work in marginalized groups as opposed to the structures that construct inequality, exclusion, and hate via privileging and othering (see Martino, 2009). In this way, ally work that is grounded in relational epistemes must telescope outwards to disrupt and change structures that (re)produce homo-/transphobia and hetero-/cisnormativity. With respect to the details of Lana's interview, this work cannot simply position her desires and beliefs as speaking for all lesbians, all LGBTIQ people, or all people who experience marginalization. Instead, they indicate the need for ally work to change institutional practices via their corresponding patterns of individual manifestation that marginalize, interactive dynamics that dehumanize, and formal practices that delegitimize youth, adults, and families. The focus of such actions, for example, must be on opening up spaces for Lana's or other LGBTIQ students' identities to be understood on their own terms and not through *a priori* notions. In this way, ally work is not about elevating any one single person's voice as definitive, but instead about working with LGBTIQ people in order to determine locally significant trajectories of activism that value and humanize a diverse plurality of experiences and voices.

Third and finally, when ally identities are situated in relational epistemes, it challenges straight and/or cisgender teachers and teacher educators to learn to become allies through concrete social action (see also de

Castell & Jenson, 2007). While exploring one's attitudes and intentions can still be a useful part of teacher education oriented toward social change, it is not enough. By facilitating, for example, opportunities for preservice teachers to work to act as allies for youth and families in their field-based experiences and for LGBTIQ-identifying preservice educators in their university coursework, teacher educators can help these learners develop an intimate and experience-rich notion of praxis as they strive to become allies.

ACKNOWLEDGMENT

I would like to thank Kay Halasek for her support in drafting this chapter. She provided invaluable feedback on early drafts and organized the symposium where I first presented these ideas. Thank you to Mollie Blackburn, Michael Blancato, Caroline Clark, Kaitlin Clinnin, Scott DeWitt, Chad Iwertz, Ben McCorkle, and Tim San Pedro for their feedback during the symposium. I would also like to thank the young woman I call Lana and my fellow Pink TIGers (Mollie Blackburn, Megan Brown, Caroline Clark, Courtney Johnson, Jenell Penn, Jill Smith, Dorothy Sutton, Kim Swensen, and Lane Vanderhule) for enriching my work and my life.

NOTES

1. For the purposes of this chapter, I use the acronym *LGBTIQ*. Within the acronym, I use *T* to stand for *trans** in an attempt to represent the broad diversity of noncisgender people, their experiences, and their communities. I use *Q* to stand for *queer* to represent people who experience their sexual and gender identities fluidly and/or prefer for these identities to remain suspended. Additionally, I use *Q* to stand for *questioning* to represent people who question their identity status but do not identity with another element of the acronym.

2. From the Gay, Lesbian and Straight Education Network's (GLSEN's) webpage: "The National Day of Silence is a day of action in which students across the country vow to take a form of silence to call attention to the silencing effect of anti-LGBT bullying and harassment in schools" (for more information, see http://www.dayofsilence.org/).

3. Here and elsewhere when discussing the existent literature, I use variations in acronyms such as *LGBT* instead of *LGBTIQ*. I do so in an attempt to accurately reflect the discussions and perspectives in this work as opposed to imposing my terminology on it.

4. See, for example, GLSEN's "Educator Resources" website at http://glsen.org/educate/resources or the Human Rights Campaign "Establishing an Allies/Safe Zone Program" website at http://www.hrc.org/resources/entry/establishing-an-allies-safe-zone-program.

REFERENCES

Blackburn, M. V. (2014). Humanizing research with LGBTQ youth through dialogic communication, consciousness raising, and action. In P. Paris & M. T. Winn (Eds.), *Humanizing research: Decolonizing qualitative inquiry with youth and communities* (pp. 43–57). Thousand Oaks, CA: Sage.

Blackburn, M. V., & Clark, C. T. (2011). Analyzing talk in a long-term literature discussion group: Ways of operating within LGBT-inclusive and queer discourses. *Reading Research Quarterly, 46*(3), 222–248.

Blackburn, M. V., Clark, C. T., Kenney, L. M., & Smith, J. M. (2010). *Acting out!: Combating homophobia through teacher activism.* New York, NY: Teachers College Press.

Broido, E. M. (2000). The development of social justice allies during college: A phenomenological investigation. *Journal of College Student Development, 41*(1), 3–18.

Broido, E. M., & Reason, R. D. (2005). The development of social justice attitudes and actions: An overview of current understandings. *New Directions for Student Services, 2005*(110), 17–28.

Bucholtz, M., & Hall, K. (2005). Identity and interaction: A sociocultural linguistic approach. *Discourse Studies, 7*(4/5), 585–614.

Butler, J. (1990/2007). *Gender trouble: Feminism and the subversion of identity.* New York, NY: Routledge Classics.

Clark, C. T. (2010a). Inquiring into ally work in teacher education: The possibilities and limitations of textual practice. In M. V. Blackburn, C. T. Clark, L. M. Kenney, & J. M. Smith (Eds.), *Acting out!: Combating homophobia through teacher activism* (pp. 37–55). New York, NY: Teachers College Press.

Clark, C. T. (2010b). Preparing LGBTQ-allies and combating homophobia in a US teacher education program. *Teaching and Teacher Education, 26*(3), 704–713.

Davies, B., & Harré, R. (1990). Positioning: The discursive production of selves. *Journal of Theory of Social Behaviour, 20*(1), 43–63.

de Castell, S., & Jenson, J. (2007). No place like home: Sexuality, community, and identity among street-involved queer and questioning youth. In M. V. Blackburn & C. T. Clark (Eds.), *Literacy research for political action and social change* (pp. 131–152). New York, NY: Lang.

de Certeau, M. (1984). *The practice of everyday life* (S. F. Rendall, Trans.). Berkeley: University of California Press.

Deleuze, G., & Guattari, F. (1987). *A thousand plateaus: Capitalism and schizophrenia* (B. Massumi, Trans.). Minneapolis: University of Minnesota Press.

Dillard, C. (2000). The substance of things hoped for, the evidence of things not seen: Examining an endarkened feminist epistemology in educational research and leadership. *International Journal of Qualitative Studies in Education, 13*(6), 661-681.

DiStefano, T. M., Croteau, J. M., Anderson, M. Z., Kampa-Kokesch, S., & Bullard, M. A. (2000). Experiences of being heterosexual allies to lesbian, gay, and bisexual people: A qualitative exploration. *Journal of College Counseling, 3*(2), 131–141.

Edwards, K. E. (2006). Aspiring social justice ally identity development: A conceptual model. *NASPA Journal, 43*(4), 39–60.

Erickson, F. (2008). *Talk and social theory.* Cambridge, England: Polity Press.

Evans, N. J., & Broido, E. M. (2005). Encouraging the development of social justice attitudes and actions in heterosexual students. *New Directions for Student Services, 110,* 43–54.

Gay, Lesbian & Straight Educational Network (GLSEN). (2013). *The safe space kit: Guide to being an ally to LGBT students.* Washington, DC: Author. Retrieved from http://www.glsen.org/sites/default/files/SSK_2013_book.pdf [NOTE: This file has since been updated and is no longer valid. To view the current document, see https://www.glsen.org/sites/default/files/GLSEN%20Safe%20Space%20Kit%202016_0.pdf]

Gee, J. P. (2008). *Social linguistics and literacies: Ideology in discourses* (3rd ed.). London, England: Routledge.

Gergen, K. J. (2009). *An invitation to social construction* (2nd ed.). Thousand Oaks, CA: Sage.

Harding, S. (1993). Rethinking standpoint epistemology: What is "strong objectivity"? In L. Alcoff & E. Potter (Eds.), *Feminist epistemologies* (pp. 49–82). New York, NY: Routledge.

Jagose, A. (1996). *Queer theory: An introduction.* New York: New York University Press.

Kinloch, V., & San Pedro, T. (2014). The space between listening and storying: Foundations for projects in humanization. In P. Paris & M. T. Winn (Eds.), *Humanizing research: Decolonizing qualitative inquiry with youth and communities* (pp. 21–42). Thousand Oaks, CA: Sage.

Martino, W. (2009). Literacy issues and GLBTQ youth: Queer interventions in English education. In L. Christenbury, R. Bomer, & P. Smagorinsky (Eds.), *Handbook of adolescent literacy research* (pp. 386–399). New York, NY: Guilford Press.

McIntosh, P. (1998). White privilege: Unpacking the invisible knapsack. In P. S. Rothenberg (Ed.), *Race, class, and gender in the United States: An integrated study* (4th ed., pp. 165–169). New York, NY: Palgrave Macmillan.

Mitchell, J. C. (1984). 8.5.2 Typicality and the case study and 8.5.3 data collection for case studies. In R. Ellen (Ed.), *Ethnographic research: A guide to general conduct* (pp. 238–241). New York, NY: Academic Press.

Schey, R., & Uppstrom, A. (2010). Activist work as entry-year teachers: What we've learned. In M. V. Blackburn, C. T. Clark, L. M. Kenney, & J. M. Smith (Eds.), *Acting out!: Combating homophobia through teacher activism* (pp. 88–102). New York, NY: Teachers College Press.

Schultz, K. (2003). *Listening: A framework for teaching across differences.* New York, NY: Teachers College Press.

Sullivan, N. (2003). *A critical introduction to queer theory.* New York: New York University Press.

Washington, J., & Evans, N. J. (1991). Becoming an ally. In N. J. Evans & V. A. Wall (Eds.), *Beyond tolerance: Gays, lesbians, and bisexuals on campus* (pp. 195–204). Alexandria, VA: American Association for Counseling and Development.

CHAPTER 4

CONSTRUCTIONS OF CHILDREN AND CHILDHOOD

Implications for LGBTIQ Inclusion and Teacher Preparation Programs

Corrine M. Wickens

In today's society, 3% to 4%[1] of the population self-identify as gay, lesbian, or bisexual and 0.3% of adults in the United States self-identify as transgender (Gates, 2011). In a school of 500, this might mean that 15–20 young people may be gay, lesbian, or bisexual, or questioning their sexual identity, and one or two people may experience dissonance between their biological sex and their gender identity. While these percentages are based upon adults in the United States, LGBT individuals are coming out at increasingly younger and younger ages (Shilo & Savaya, 2011). Especially with the support of YouTube "coming out" videos, most notably the "It Gets Better" Project, LGBT young people are bravely declaring who they are in sometimes very public ways. In addition to the young people who may self-identify as LGBT, current studies estimate that 3 children per 1,000 are living in a same-sex headed household (Gates, 2013). But given the current limitations measuring same-sex households (Walther, 2007), this number is likely highly underestimated. Given the increased

Queering Classrooms: Personal Narratives and Educational Practices to Support LGBTQ Youth in Schools, pp. 45–62
Copyright © 2017 by Information Age Publishing

number of young people who are questioning their sexual or gender identity, who self-identify as lesbian, gay, bisexual, transgender, intersex, queer, or questioning (LGBTIQ), or are children in same-gender-headed households, it is contingent upon teacher education programs to effectively prepare teachers and administrators who will be serving these young people and their families.

However, the creation of LGBTIQ-inclusive classrooms has been stymied by ongoing ideological beliefs about LGBTIQ individuals, but most especially for the purposes of this chapter, ideologies around children and childhood. This is due to the protectionist discourses that are framed around children and childhood, but are infused in educational practices, selection of curricular materials for young people, and instruction and modeling within schools.

For the purposes of this chapter, I want to distinguish some language usage. Because ideologies discursively frame children and childhood in important and particular ways, when I refer to these ideologies, beliefs, and perspectives pertaining to young people, I use the language of "children and/or childhood." However, when I speak of young people themselves, not the ideologies, I indicate this through the labels of "youth" or "young people."

Thus, the purpose of this chapter is to address ideological and structural challenges to the creation of LGBTIQ-inclusive curricula and classrooms based on contemporary constructions of children and childhood. This chapter will explore how ideologies of children and childhood function as implicit and explicit regulators of heteronomativity and how calls for safety and protection in the name of children perpetuate heteronormative structures in schools, thereby limiting options for LGBTIQ-inclusion. This chapter will conclude with recommendations for teacher educators and teacher education programs to promote and model LGBTIQ-inclusiveness.

HETERONORMATIVITY AS INGRAINED IN SOCIETY AND EDUCATION

To understand ways in which ideologies of children and childhood impact LGBTIQ-inclusion, we must understand a central underlying assumption for this book and this chapter—the institutionalized processes of heteronormativity—as it manifests in society and in schooling systems through homophobia and heterosexism. Homophobia is commonly described as prejudice against individuals based on nonheterosexual orientation and is characterized as intense fear or hatred of those who desire individuals of the same gender (West, 2004). While homophobia emphasizes individual attitudes, behaviors, and beliefs, heterosexism underscores societal structures and power inequities. Herek (1998) defines heterosexism as "an ideological system that denies, denigrates, and stigmatizes any nonheterosexual form of behavior, identity, relationship, or community. It operates principally by rendering homosexuality invisible and, when this fails, by trivializing, repressing, or stigmatizing it" (p. 316). These two terms ground recent discourses on heteronormativity, which presumes and privileges heterosexuality and monitors "proper" and accepted gender identities through regulation of sexual arrangements. Within various educational contexts, heteronormativity informs and instructs educational practices through both official and unofficial discourses (Meyer, 2009; Pascoe, 2007).

EVOLVING CONSTRUCTIONS OF CHILDHOOD AND CHILDREN

One of the greatest challenges to creating LGBTIQ-inclusive classrooms revolves around contemporary ideologies of children. Although we can recognize that individual children can demonstrate a range of character traits—happy, playful, kind, generous, thoughtful, spiteful, mean, deceitful—as a society, we tend to conceptualize "childhood" and "children" in terms of innocence and asexuality (Stockton, 2009). As such, children require adults' protection from the evils of society, of which LGBTIQ identities and perspectives have been historically characterized. Over the last several centuries, there have been multiple ways of thinking about children and childhood, but I am going to discuss three of the most significant—children as "miniature adults," children as "incomplete beings," and children as "innocent."

Prior to the Industrial Era in the late 1800s and ensuing modernization, children were valued for their contributions of labor and household income. As a result, children were not segregated from the adult world. According to Plumb (1971), "Certainly there was no separate world of childhood. Children shared the same games with adults, the same toys, the same fairy stories. They lived their lives together, never apart" (p. 7). This conception of children as "miniature adults" was related to the economic function children provided the family: they were additional bodies to work on the farm and in cottage industries (Silin, 1995). Furthermore, living, working, and sleeping spaces were largely communal at this time, such that children were exposed to all the same experiences that adults were, including aspects of adult sexuality, where "not only was there no possibility of protecting children from any of the harsh realities of adult life, but the idea that it might be desirable to do so does not appear to have existed" (Jackson, 1990, p. 31). As miniature adults, there would have been no basis in protecting children from harsher aspects of life; and with communal living, there was no capacity to do so either.

Rather than simply being viewed as "miniature adults," children and childhood later came to be understood as persons in development and incomplete. Modernist psychological theories of childhood have significantly influenced this framing of children and childhood, emphasizing stages of development in which children are in a state of becoming (Erikson, 1968; Freud, 1938; Piaget, 1955). Indeed within this framework, adults' greatest concern about children is how the children are to be molded and shaped into the citizens that they will become (Stockton, 2009). As a result, "the child [had become] an object of respect, a special creature with a different nature and different needs, which require[d] separation and protection from the adult world" (Plumb, 1971, p. 9). Thus, childhood had come to be understood as a unique stage in life in which children needed to be encouraged and protected in secure, regulated environments.

Then in the Industrial Era, this notion of children as incomplete beings shifted into the now-prevailing discourse around children—that of children as innocent. This conception constitutes childhood as purer, more natural-like and yet untainted by adult learning and experience. A key aspect within the construction of children as innocent is that of children as asexual.[2] As Robinson (2013) has noted, "The hegemonic discourse of childhood is intimately linked with the concept of innocence, which is equated with purity, naivety, selflessness, irrationality, and a state of unknowingness, or being less worldly—all of which characterizes the child as vulnerable" (p. 42). Sexuality in the modernist era, however, has been constituted as an adult human characteristic, not part of humanity from birth. As such, sexuality has been positioned in opposition to a "natural" state of childhood innocence, and children within this framing considered void of sexual feelings and impulses.

Attending to these different conceptions of children and childhood, it is clear that while children are real people, the discourses around and about them are socially constructed, embedded in distinct sociohistorical contexts and generated not by children themselves but by adults. In fact, one of the central outcomes of the Industrial Era was to affirm and reify the notion of children and childhood as not adult. The child is innocent and pure, the adult knowledgeable and corrupted. The child is incomplete and in the process of becoming; the adult is fixed. The child is asexual, having not yet developed sexual impulses; the adult is sexual and engages in sex. These intertwining discourses constitute pivotal contemporary matrices of childhood. But it is also important to note that these discourses are established through an adult lens, perceiving life retrospectively and nostalgically, rather than being viewed from children themselves. Adults tend to hearken for "simpler days" of childhood and thus hold tight to the ideologies of childhood that accentuate the presumed innocence of childhood (Stockton, 2009).

These ideologies around children and childhood have become reified in contemporary discourses of children, exemplifying Foucault's (1972) "regimes of truth." To suggest that children are not inherently innocent and are by birth sexual beings could be constituted by many as near blasphemy. With regard to LGBTIQ inclusion and teacher preparation, these ideologies are infused into contemporary educational philosophies and pedagogies as stalwart, nearly unassailable practices. How we think about young people and what they are capable of is at the very heart of all education and thus the modeling and preparation in teacher education programs.

CONTROVERSIAL BOOKS, SAFE SPACES, AND LGBTIQ INCLUSION—OR NOT

How adults conceptualize children is likewise at the center of decision-making around what kinds of texts are included or not included in the curriculum. This section discusses competing agendas and perspectives related to LGBTIQ inclusion based upon different discursive frames around children and childhood. In the first three sections herein, I focus on issues around inclusion of controversial texts and censorship in public schools and libraries. In so doing, I demonstrate how different groups advocate for and use competing language around the "safety" of children through both LGBTIQ-inclusive policies or through anti-LGBTIQ-inclusive policies. Finally, I ground the rhetoric of the safety of children in ongoing, overlapping, and sometimes complementary (sometimes contradictory) ideologies of children.

Safety From Controversial Materials in Schools

What is appropriate for children and young people to read? What is appropriate (or inappropriate) to keep in school libraries for them to access? Teachers, librarians, and administrators often make daily decisions about what texts to include in their classrooms and in their libraries. Much of this decision-making is made based on considerations of age and developmental appropriateness. For some individuals, some texts more than others push the boundaries of what is considered acceptable or appropriate and thus are often considered controversial. In a recent study (Koss, Wickens, & Walther, 2011), my colleagues and I surveyed middle and high school teachers, librarians, and principals for their perceptions about the inclusion of "controversial" texts. For the purpose of that study, "controversial materials" was defined as "any topic that a parent or community member might challenge while specifically underscoring the most frequently cited reasons and categories for the ALA list of challenged and banned books" (p. 31; see also ALA, 2015a). The most frequently cited reasons for challenging a book include being sexually explicit, being unsuited for the age group, containing offensive language, violence, or references to homosexuality. In the last decade "other objections" have risen significantly to be the fourth most cited reason, most often citing the rationale "antifamily." As mentioned, antifamily indicates political and religious beliefs that define marriage solely between one man and one woman (Berger, 2002). Given this perspective, the phrase "antifamily" likewise indicates an opposition to marriage between same gender couples and LGBTIQ "lifestyles" generally.

Interestingly, teachers reported a high level of personal leeway in choosing curricular materials and still often chose not to include materials that would be considered controversial. One reason was fear of a parent phone call to administrators. But more significantly, a number of the teachers, librarians, and administrators saw themselves as community agents, standing in place of the parents in the school system. As such, they chose materials that would not go against local community norms. Moreover, these individuals framed their responsibility as school personnel "to protect children from dangerous and salacious material" (Koss et al., 2011, p. 37). In this way, they self-censored classroom and library materials in an effort to both adhere to local community norms as well as protect young people from potentially difficult or troubling topics.

Protection From LGBTIQ-Inclusion

These findings highlight important considerations as many politicians and conservative community activists have called for removal of books and materials largely dealing with LGBTIQ individuals in the name of "protecting children." For instance, in an effort to put forth a bill that would remove public funding for any library or school that included texts about gays or lesbians or by gay or lesbian authors, Alabama Representative Gerald Allen contended, "I don't look at it as censorship, I look at it as protecting the hearts and souls and minds of our children" (Holguin, 2005, para. 4). More recently, a community resident and parent, Ginny Maziarka from West Bend, Wisconsin, challenged 37 books in her local public library. She accused the young adult librarian and the library board of promoting "the overt indoctrination of the gay agenda" (Chosak,

2009). A few of the challenged books included *Baby Be Bop* by Francesca Lia Block (1995), *The Geography Club* by Brent Hartinger (2003), and Stephan Chbosky's (1999) *The Perks of Being a Wallflower* (Chosak, 2009).

While Maziarka first framed the book challenge around the promotion of a "gay agenda," she altered her language and discourse in the complaint to concern material she believed was sexually explicit or inappropriate for the age group (Chosak, 2009). This shift in language and rhetoric from explicit anti-LGBTIQ inclusion to more indirect phrasing and codes can likewise be seen in reasons given for other challenges in the "Top 10 Most Challenged Books of 2014" (ALA, 2015b). Of the 10 books, 6 of them include LGBTIQ characters, situations, or topics: *The Absolutely True Diary of a Part-Time Indian* (Alexie, 2007; ranked #1), *And Tango Makes Three* (Richardson & Parnell, 2005; ranked #3), *It's Perfectly Normal* (Harris, 1994; ranked # 5), *Saga* (Vaughan & Staples, 2013; ranked #6), *The Perks of Being a Wallflower* (Chbosky, 1999; ranked #8), and *Drama* (Telgemeier, 2012; ranked #10). Significantly, for nearly all of them, the primary reason given for challenging these books was that they were "anti-family" (ALA, 2015b). Not until very recently, these same books were cited for references to "homosexuality." Antifamily has come to represent political and religious beliefs that define marriage as only between one man and one woman and most often reifies traditional nuclear family structures (Berger, 2002). The rationale "antifamily" thus has simply shifted from "homosexuality" as a basis for censoring materials that normalizes LGBTIQ individuals and their civil rights.

Censorship and the Rise of Children's and Young Adult Literature

While overt censorship in public schools and public libraries is relatively limited, the fear of challenges, especially for public school personnel, often influences what texts and materials are purchased and what is taught. Much of the basis behind the challenges is the ideological belief that some topics are too difficult to be discussed with young people. In our contemporary era, such topics may range from issues of terrorism and 9/11 to cancer to gender identity and sexual orientation. These topics frequently become characterized as "adult" topics and knowledge, and texts and materials relating to such topics may be overtly banned, quietly removed, or never purchased in the first place.

Although "the assumption that children are too immature and impressionable for certain information, and that adults can and should keep such information away from them, has deep historical roots," overt censorship largely did not exist until the latter part of the 20th century (Bickmore, 1999, p. 17). Until the late 1960s, the primary organizations in charge of publishing and distributing children's literature were for the most part a homogenous group and simply did not purchase or promote books that they deemed inappropriate for young people. As such, they served as significant gatekeepers and regulators of children's literature, determining what was "good" for children to read (Simmons, 2000). As a result, literature for young adults was, as English educator Stephen Dunning remarked, "consistently wholesome and insistently didactic" (as cited in Simmons, 2000, p. 45).

All of this was to change in the late 1960s and 1970s. With the publication of S. E. Hinton's *The Outsiders* (1967), young adult literature authors began introducing contemporary issues and realism into their novels. Breaking multiple taboos, Hinton wrote about different school cliques; Paul Zindel wrote about teen sex in *The Pigman* (1968); Judy Blume about menstruation and masturbation in *Are You There, God, It's Me Margaret* (1970) and *Deenie* (1973), respectively; Robert Cormier about power in *The Chocolate War* (1974); and John Donovan about homosexuality in *I'll Get There. It Better Be Worth the Trip* (1969). With this new revolution in young adult literature, authors experienced greater freedom to write about death, suicide, divorce, sexuality—all the "unsavory" aspects of life, considered inappropriate for young people to know about, let alone read about, with pleasure (Blume, 1999).

Children's and young adult (YA) literature experts, especially librarians, balked at the sudden influx of complex, controversial issues arising in the literature. Is it really appropriate for youth to be reading of such things, they wondered?

> Yet when you say you want to write about a little boy whose mother committed suicide, people sometimes say: but should children know about these things? Is a child that age ready for that kind of experience? But no one asks a child in a real-life situation—are you ready for your mother to commit suicide, for your parents to get divorced? These things just happened, and the child, the adolescent, adjusts, copes because there is no alternative. (Klein, 1977, p. 82)

Almost forty years later, many adults maintain the same perspective: there are some topics just too sensitive, difficult, or inappropriate, too "adult," for young people. This perspective holds fast to the ideology of childhood as a state of innocence that must be preserved for as long as possible. As such, it is contingent upon adults to shelter and protect the community's young people from such topics. In this view, children are passive vessels with no ability to think about important issues for themselves and no personal agency. Likewise, missing is an evaluation of the presentation of the topic. In this case, the question shifts from "Is this topic too difficult for young people to discuss?" to "What is the most age-appropriate way to discuss this topic?" Thus, to understand issues of censorship in our public institutions that serve young people, we must deconstruct the ideologies of children that undergird them.

Paradox of "Safe"

At the heart of the dilemma of censorship is what it means to keep young people "safe" from texts and materials deemed too difficult or inappropriate for their age group. But this question of what it means for adults to keep young people "safe" is increasingly at odds regarding issues of LGBTIQ inclusion. "Safe" understandably means free of dangerous, threatening conditions, protected from potential harm, but what constitutes "safe" is highly disputed. As discussed, there is a strong push by some groups for schools and libraries to be void of materials that might contain troubling, challenging, or controversial content. Maziarka argued, "We expect our public library to protect children and empower parents to decide what their children can read" (as cited in Gaffney, 2014, p. 734). According to Maziarka, by including a wide range of YA fiction, most particularly LGBTIQ titles, librarians have taken the "once safe" public library and have made it "hazardous to youth readers." This issue of "safe" libraries has become a linchpin for such groups, asserting, "Your Library: No Longer a Safe Place" and "You no longer are a taxpaying supporter and/or patron of a family-safe library" (Maziarka, 2009). From this perspective then, "no longer safe" refers to libraries maintaining a wide and diverse collection of YA fiction that includes LGBTIQ titles, creating an environment in which children and young people can encounter books that are deemed "hazardous" to children's young minds and belief systems. Likewise, parents are not "free" to let their children wander the children's or young adult sections of the library unaccompanied, free from worry of what kinds of materials their child might pick up and begin reading.

While a number of groups refute the "safety" of public libraries for their children, keeping young people safe and free from harm has also been at the forefront of many LGBTIQ alliances and task forces at local, state, and national levels. Two structural supports critical to LGBTIQ youth and their feelings of safety are found in Gay-Straight Alliances (GSAs) and proactive antibullying initiatives with explicit protections for LGBTIQ youth. Currently, approximately 50% of middle, junior, and high schools support a GSA, often identified with "safe zone" (or its equivalent) placards. The Gay Lesbian Straight Education Network (GLSEN) reported the impact GSAs had for LGBTIQ youth in schools with a GSA, as compared to schools without a GSA. For instance, students with a GSA were less likely to feel unsafe because of their sexual orientation (46.0% vs. 64.4%) and experienced lower levels of victimization due to sexual orientation or gender identity (Kull, Kosciw, & Greytak, 2015).

With regard to antibullying initiatives, although youth who are gay or perceived to be gay based upon gender expression are disproportionately bullied, only about 10% of school districts include explicit protections based upon sexual orientation, gender identity, and/or gender expression (Kull et al., 2015). In schools with a comprehensive policy, students noted that the staff was more likely to intervene when hearing homophobic remarks, reinforcing a greater climate of safety. A recent bill before Congress would bolster these efforts through the Safe Schools Improvement Act of 2015 (SSIA). SSIA follows legislation already instituted by many states and school districts to define and enact laws or policies to protect the safety of LGBTIQ students in schools. The law would amend the Elementary and Secondary Education Act of 1965 (ESEA) to require each school and district that receives Safe and Drug-Free Schools and Communities Act funding to implement a comprehensive antibullying and antiharassment policy that enumerates categories of protection, including "a student's actual or perceived race, color, national origin, sex, disability, sexual orientation, gender identity or religion" (S. 311, 2015).

As demonstrated through the challenges to "unsafe" libraries and the calls for increasing safety through GSAs and comprehensive antibullying policies, the language for each of these political groups hinges on the issue of keeping youth safe. Notably, "safety" in near equal measure is used, on the one hand, as code for opposing LGBTIQ inclusion and as a mechanism of regulating social norms. On the other hand, "safety" serves as a critical tool for ensuring LGBTIQ inclusion through the creation of policies and practices that support students' physical and socioemotional well-being in schools.

Ideologies of Protection and Childhood

The issues of controversial materials, censorship, safe schools, and libraries demonstrate an ongoing tension between distinct but overlapping discourses of children and childhood that needs to be taken up in teacher-education programs. First, the slogan "Your library: No longer a safe place" underscores an ideology of children as innocent, needing protection from negative and corrupting influences (in this case, the gay agenda or antifamily propoganda). While currently less prevalent, this idea draws from discourses of gays as pedophiles, perverse individuals that need to be kept away from children. More significantly, such discourse recognizes the efforts at recognizing and normalizing LGBTIQ identities. The suggestion that LGBTIQ individuals are normal people with equal rights destabilizes the heteronormative structures and privileges that have been institutionalized in schools and in law. This idea connects to notions that marriage can only be between a man and a woman and that a family is defined as having a mother and a father, not two moms or two dads. Moreover, children are viewed as innocent in all matters deemed "sexual" and need to be sheltered from such "adult" knowledge and notions. Thus, any language or book that suggests otherwise is considered dangerous to this way of thinking and this framing of children and must be removed to keep children safe from these "harmful" influences.

Ironically, organizations and legislation advocating for GSAs in schools and comprehensive antibullying in part operate from a similar ideology of youth—that young people need to be protected from harm (as much as possible) and it is adults' responsibility to create environments that promote the emotional and physical well-being of young people. The difference here is that these advocates also operate from a perspective that adults need to let youth be who they are. Part of Jean-Jacques Rousseau's (1955) philosophy of the innocent child suggested that problems inherent in society lay with the world, not with the child, and children should be free to be whom they are. Thus, it is the responsibility of adults to care for and celebrate young people as they are, not whom adults think the youth should be or will be. But also from this humanist perspective, sexual orientation, gender expression, and gender identity are viewed as intrinsic to human nature; they are not learned, nor are they chosen. In this way, young people are accorded more agency than typical of the protectionist ideology of children and childhood.

In some ways, this framing of childhood creates an important bridge between conceptions of children as "innocent" and as "miniature adults." This framing leaves intact responsibilities of adults to create spaces that promote the socioemotional and physical well-being of young people. Unlike pre-Industrial Era days, contemporary conceptions of youth hold fast to the beliefs that young people should not be privy to everything adult and should be protected from abusive situations. In doing so, this conception of youth retains the contemporary sense that "kids should be kids" and also acknowledges young people's own personal agency and self-determination.

ROLES OF TEACHER-EDUCATION PROGRAMS AND COLLEGES OF EDUCATION

In this chapter, I have argued that a major limiting factor to LGBTIQ inclusion in K–12 schools is the ideologies around children and childhood that impact our thinking as teachers and teacher educators. I have demonstrated several different ways these overlapping, but oftentimes competing, ideologies are manifested in the practices and behaviors of public school and library personnel, as well as diverse community activist groups, such as in the language and rationale used by individuals and different interest groups to challenge books and materials in public schools and libraries, and in the advocacy work on behalf of LGBTIQ youth to create more GSAs and legislate the SSIA. In this final section, I specifically examine the role of teacher education programs with regard to LGBTIQ inclusion within the context of these ideologies of childhood and children.

First, in order to create LGBTIQ-inclusive classrooms and schools, teacher education programs need to provide opportunities for initial and advanced licensure teacher candidates to deconstruct the multiple ideologies of children, as well as the complex and often contradictory ways those ideologies permeate our language and our thinking. For example, the discourse of children as innocent suggests that children are inherently devoid of bias and prejudice toward others and that these attitudes are learned behaviors. But this ideology of innocence also often suggests that young people are passive recipients of adult constructions of meaning; that is, young people simply learn and mimic these constructions, be it on race, gender, age, ability, gender identity/expression, or sexual orientation. Indeed this framing of children contends that children do have the capacity to understand or process such topics and that children do not actively engage in negotiations around these topics. A significant body of research, however, has been conducted that demonstrates the dynamic processes young people, including very young children, use to understand and actively mediate discourses around race, gender, and sexuality (Blaise, 2005; Lewis, 2003; Renold, 2005; Thorne, 1993; Van Ausdale & Feagin, 2001). Thus, examination of ideologies of children and childhood in teacher education programs could help lead to more dynamic appreciation of the critical and agentive capacities of young people.

Second, teacher licensure candidates also particularly need opportunities to examine how these ideologies manifest themselves in the policies and practices within our public schools and libraries. For instance, one long-standing practice that is infused throughout education—developmentally appropriate instruction—presumes that young people should be taught in accordance to where they are developmentally at that time. Accordant with the developmental model, many educators argue that children (and young adults) are not developmentally "ready" to handle complex discussions of sexuality (or gender identity). As a result, such topics are relegated to the "adult world," the world of the knowledgeable and experienced (Cannella, 2001; Sawicki, 1991; Silin, 1995). Teacher education programs can help their teacher candidates analyze common educational practices for the underlying assumptions about young people. In the case of developmentally appropriate practice, teachers could distinguish between constructions of children that presume young people should not be exposed to or cannot handle discussing "difficult topics" and constructions of children that presume young people's innate capacity to construct their own meaning of such difficult topics, but in ways that they can understand.

Another more recent set of practices centers around issues of bullying. As noted previously, the majority of US school districts have antibullying policies, yet very few include specific protections based upon sexual orientation or gender identity/expression (Kull et al., 2015). With regard to ideologies of childhood, childhood innocence is typically conflated with sexual innocence. Sexuality in this perspective is framed as an adult attribute, not an intrinsic characteristic of one's innate humanity (Bruhm & Hurley, 2004). Likewise, any aspect of sexuality is frequently situated as sexual (i.e., having to do with "sex"), and this is considered by many as an inappropriate topic to discuss with young people, and public schools are viewed as inappropriate settings for such discussions. In order to enact comprehensive antibullying initiatives, educators must be able to discuss issues of sexual orientation as separate and distinct from "sex," and teacher education programs are critical venues for these discussions to begin to take place.

Third, teacher education programs are powerfully situated to help future educators unpack ongoing issues and rhetoric around censorship and self-censorship. The ALA (2015c) and the National Council of Teachers of English (2009) both have established guidelines and protocols instrumental for all teachers, administrators, and librarians to help avert censorship challenges proactively, as well as processes in the event of a censorship challenge. However, as Antell, Strothmann, and Downey (2013) note, "Some of the most insidious pressure comes not from external opponents and would-be censors, but from within" (para. 3) (i.e., self-censorship). They articulate multiple "traps" public librarians may fall into, which rationalize limited LGBTIQ library collections. Koss et al. (2011) also noted some other reasons that teachers, administrators, librarians/media specialists in public schools may engage in self-censorship. While attitudes in the United States toward LGBTIQ individuals has grown increasingly positive over recent years, school personnel may still hold the perspective that texts or topics that address LGBTIQ individuals are not appropriate for youth in their schools, based upon ongoing ideologies of children (Flores, 2014). As such, it is incumbent upon teacher-education programs to help school personnel unpack underlying assumptions of young people, as well as any other lingering bias, for the ways those assumptions can implicitly impact the selection of curricular materials.

Finally, in a study of homophobia and heterosexism in one college of education, it was clear that faculty and staff did not know how to discuss issues surrounding sexual orientation, gender identity, and/or expression (Wickens & Sandlin, 2010). Institutional barriers set issues of sexuality and gender identity apart from issues of race/ethnicity, nationality, culture, or language, which are commonly interrogated in these programs.

> One undergraduate, Barbara, commented that she felt the college had done a great job preparing her, as a future teacher, to discuss racial and ethnic differences among young children. She felt confident in her abilities to respond to students' questions about race and ethnicity such as, "Why is her skin dark? Why is her hair different, so curly?" However, Barbara felt much less prepared to address issues of sexual orientation and gender variation. She wondered, "What do you say when they say 'I have two daddies' or 'I have two mommies?'" (p. 14)

In order to effectively make a difference in the preparation of future educators, teacher education programs need to explicitly address sexual orientation and gender identity/expression in their programs. But to do that, they must also recognize the implicit connection between sexual orientation and gender identity with ongoing ideologies of children, especially the former.

Throughout this chapter, I have argued that childhood is socially and historically constructed and the meanings attributed to "childhood" change over time and context (Renold, 2005). Of modern constructions, the most pervasive and indeed hegemonic is the notion of childhood innocence (Robinson, 2013). A common phrase adults use is "Children are too young know about such things." "Such things" represents those topics deemed hard, dangerous, difficult, and thereby unspeakable and unnameable in the presence of children (Foucault, 1972). Thus, within this frame, it is the job of responsible adults to protect young people from such difficult topics as much as possible.

It is critical, therefore, that teacher education programs help current and future teachers critically analyze ideologies of children and childhood in the same light and importance as multiculturalism, racism, sexism, and other ongoing structural facets of human society and education. Given the paradoxical rhetoric around the word *safe*, it behooves teacher education programs to unpack the multiple and contradictory meanings with teacher candidates. It is also critical that teacher education programs underscore sexuality, sexual orientation, and gender identity as intrinsic aspects of human nature from birth. Relationships of sexuality, sexual orientation, and gender identity to curriculum and young people's participation in curriculum could then be more fully explored without the sense of trespassing social taboos. Thus, viewed from this perspective, integrating LGBTIQ identities into the curriculum becomes logical and presumptive. And in this endeavor, teacher-education programs must lead the way.

NOTES

1. The commonly accepted "10%" statistic for the lesbian, gay, and bisexual population is a misrepresentation of Kinsey's famous study of incarcerated males. The 3% to 4% represents an average percentage drawn from nine different studies that in different ways attempt to measure the numbers of individuals who self-identify as LGBT. Across these nine studies, percentages range from 1.2% to 5.6%. Different studies ask individuals to self-identify as LGBT or attempt to assess the constructs through questions around sexual attraction or sexual behavior.
2. Although children are generally considered asexual, there is a concurrent assumption of children's presumed heterosexuality (Robinson, 2013; Stockton, 2009). Tween girls holding hands, for instance, may be considered cute and innocent, a natural state that will give way to appropriate opposite-gender attractions and romance.

REFERENCES

Alexie, S. (2007). *The absolutely true diary of a part-time Indian*. New York, NY: Scholastic.

American Library Association (ALA). (2015a). *About banned and challenged books.* Retrieved from http://www.ala.org/bbooks/about

American Library Association (ALA). (2015b). *Frequently challenged books.* Retrieved from http://www.ala.org/bbooks/frequentlychallengedbooks

American Library Association (ALA). (2015c). *Essential preparation.* Retrieved from http://www.ala.org/bbooks/challengedmaterials/preparation

Antell, K., Strothmann, M., & Downey, J. (2013). Self-censorship in selection of LGBT-themed materials. *Reference & User Services Quarterly, 53*(2), 104–107. Retrieved from https://journals.ala.org/rusq/article/view/3458/3723

Berger, B. (2002). *The family in the modern age: More than a lifestyle choice.* New Brunswick, NJ: Transaction.

Bickmore, K. (1999). Why discuss sexuality in elementary school? In W. J. Letts IV & J. T. Sears (Eds.). *Queering elementary education: Advancing the dialogue about sexualities and schooling* (pp. 15–25). Lanham, MD: Rowman & Littlefield.

Blaise, M. (2005). *Playing it straight: Uncovering gender discourses in the early childhood classroom.* New York, NY: Routledge.

Block, F. L. (1995). *Baby be-bop*. New York, NY: HarperCollins.

Blume, J. (1970). *Are you there, God? It's me, Margaret.* Englewood Cliffs, NJ: Bradbury.

Blume, J. (1973). *Deenie.* New York, NY: Dell.

Blume, J. (1999). Place I never meant to be: A personal view. *American Libraries, 30*(6), 62-67.

Bruhm, S., & Hurley, N. (2004). *Curiouser: On the queerness of children.* Minneapolis: University of Minnesota Press.

Cannella, G. S. (2001). Natural born curriculum: Popular culture and the representation of childhood. In J. A. Jipson & R. T. Johnson (Eds.), *Resistance and representation: Rethinking childhood education* (pp. 15–22). New York, NY: Lang.

Chbosky, S. (1999). *The perks of being a wallflower.* New York, NY: Pocket Books.

Chosak, J. (2009, July 22). Parents ready to try banning books again in West Bend, WI: This time with a new library board. *NCAC.* Retrieved from http://ncac.org/blog/council-upholds-punishment-for-members-who-refused-to-ban-books-and-a-call-to-burn-books/http://ncac.org/blog/council-upholds-punishment-for-members-who-refused-to-ban-books-and-a-call-to-burn-books/

Cormier, R. (1974). *The chocolate war.* New York, NY: Dell.

Donovan, J. (1969). *I'll get there. It better be worth the trip: A novel.* New York, NY: Harper & Row.

Elementary and Secondary Education Act of 1965, Pub.L. 89-10, 79 Stat. 27, codified as amended at 20 U.S.C. 70.

Erikson, E. H. (1968). *Identity, youth, and crisis.* New York, NY: Norton.

Flores, A. R. (2014, November). National trends in public opinion on LGBT rights in the United States. *The Williams Institute.* Retrieved from http://williamsinstitute.law.ucla.edu/wp-content/uploads/POP-natl-trends-nov-2014.pdf

Foucault, M. (1972). *The archaeology of knowledge.* New York, NY: Pantheon Books.

Freud, S. (1938). *The basic writings of Sigmund Freud.* New York, NY: Pantheon Books.

Gaffney, L. M. (2014). No longer safe: West Bend, young adult literature, and conservative library activism. *Library Trends, 62*(4), 730–739.

Gates, G. J. (2011, April). How many people are lesbian, gay, bisexual and transgender? *The Williams Institute.* Retrieved from http://williamsinstitute.law.ucla.edu/wp-content/uploads/Gates-How-Many-People-LGBT-Apr-2011.pdf

Gates, G. J. (2013, February). LGBT parenting in the United States. *The Williams Institute.* Retrieved from http://williamsinstitute.law.ucla.edu/wp-content/uploads/LGBT-Parenting.pdf

Harris, R. H. (1994). *It's perfectly normal: A book about changing bodies, growing up, sex, and sexual health.* Cambridge, MA: Candlewick Press.

Hartinger, B. (2003). *The geography club.* New York, NY: Harper Tempest.

Herek, G. M. (1998). *Stigma and sexual orientation: Understanding prejudice against lesbians, gay men, and bisexuals.* Thousand Oaks, CA: Sage.

Hinton, S. E. (1967). *The outsiders.* New York, NY: Viking Press.

Holguin, J. (2005, April 26). *Alabama bill targets gay authors.* Retrieved from http://www.cbsnews.com/news/alabama-bill-targets-gay-authors/

Jackson. S. (1990). Demons and innocents: Western ideas on children's sexuality in historical perspective. In M. E. Perry (Ed.), *Handbook of sexology* (Vol. 7):

Childhood and adolescent sexology (pp. 23–49). Amsterdam, The Netherlands: Elsevier Science.

Klein, N. (1977). Growing up human: The case for sexuality in children's books. *Children's Literature in Education, 8*(2), 80–84.

Koss, M. D., Wickens, C. M., & Walther, C. S. (2011). Censorship and controversial materials in Chicagoland middle and high schools. *Illinois Reading Council Journal, 39*(1), 29–39.

Kull, R. M., Kosciw, J. G., & Greytak, E. A. (2015). *From statehouse to schoolhouse: Anti-bullying policy efforts in U.S. states and school districts.* New York, NY: Gay, Lesbian & Straight Education Network.

Lewis, A. (2003). *Race in the schoolyard: Negotiating the color line in classrooms and communities.* New Brunswick, NJ: Rutgers University Press.

Maziarka, G. (2009). *WISSUP = Wisconsin speaks up.* Retrieved from http://wissup.blogspot.com

Meyer, E. J. (2009). *Gender, bullying, and harassment: Strategies to end sexism and homophobia in schools.* New York, NY: Teachers College Press.

National Council of Teachers of English (NCTE). (2009, April). *The students' right to read.* Retrieved from http://www.ncte.org/positions/statements/righttoreadguideline

Pascoe, C. J. (2007). *Dude, you're a fag: Masculinity and sexuality in high school.* Berkeley: University of California Press.

Piaget, J. (1955). *The child's construction of reality.* London, England: Routledge.

Plumb, J. H. (1971). The great change in children. *Horizon, 13*(1), 4–12.

Renold, E. (2005). *Girls, boys, and junior sexualities: Exploring children's gender and sexual relations in the primary school.* London, England: Routledge Falmer.

Richardson, J., & Parnell, P. (2005). *And Tango makes three.* New York, NY: Simon & Schuster.

Robinson, K. (2013). *Innocence, knowledge and the construction of childhood.* New York, NY: Routledge.

Rousseau, J. J. (1955). *Emile.* New York, NY: Dutton.

Safe Schools Improvement Act of 2015. S. 311, 114th Cong. (2015).

Sawicki, J. (1991). *Disciplining Foucault: Feminism, power, and the body.* New York, NY: Routledge.

Shilo, G., & Savaya, R. (2011). Effects of family and friend support on LGB youth's mental health and sexual orientation milestones. *Family Relations, 60*(3), 318–330.

Silin, J. (1995). *Sex, death and the education of children: Our passion for ignorance in the age of AIDS.* New York, NY: Teachers College Press.

Simmons, J. S. (2000). Middle schoolers and the right to read. *ALAN Review, 27*(3), 45–49.

Stockton, K. B. (2009). *The queer child, or growing sideways in the twentieth century.* Durham, NC: Duke University Press.

Telgemeier, R. (2012). *Drama.* New York, NY: Graphix/Scholastic.

Thorne, B. (1993). *Gender play: Boys and girls in school.* Buckingham, England: Open University Press.

Van Ausdale, D., & Feagin, J. (2001). *The first R: How children learn race and racism.* Lanham, MD: Rowman & Littlefield.

Vaughan, B. K., & Staples, F. (2013). *Saga*. Berkeley, CA: Image Comics.

Walther, C. S. (2007). *Who counts? How the state (re)creates households* (Doctoral dissertation). Texas A&M University. Retrieved from http://repository.tamu.edu/bitstream/handle/1969.1/ETD-TAMU-1620/WALTHER-DISSERTATION.pdf?sequence=1&isAllowed=y

West, C. (2004). Homophobia and heterosexism. In J. Eadie (Ed.), *Sexuality: The essential glossary* (pp. 86–87). New York, NY: Oxford University Press.

Wickens, C., & Sandlin, J. A. (2010). Homophobia and heterosexism in a college of education: A culture of fear, a culture of silence. *International Journal of Qualitative Studies in Education, 23*(6), 651–670.

Zindel, P. (1968). *The pigman*. New York, NY: Bantam.

SECTION II

**REFLECTIONS ON PREPARATION:
VOICES FROM PRESERVICE
AND PRACTICING TEACHERS**

CHAPTER 5

HOPE FOR A BETTER TOMORROW

A Personal Narrative on the Need for Acceptance in Teacher Education Programs

Angela M. Jaime and Brody C. Tate

> The only thing they have to look forward to is hope. And you have to give
> them hope. Hope for a better world, hope for a better tomorrow, hope for a
> better place to come to if the pressures at home are too great. Hope that all
> will be all right. Without hope, not only gays, but the blacks, the seniors, the
> handicapped, the us'es, the us'es will give up. (Milk, 1978, para. 15)

Harvey Milk was the first openly gay elected public official in the United
States. His words above are from his famous "Hope" speech and are as
relevant today as they were in 1978. The difference between then and now
is that his courage has provided a foundation for the progress we see playing out today in the public eye, such as the right for all to marry in a mon-
umental decision by the United States Supreme Court on June 26, 2015.
Hope is the catalyst to progress and fuels our fire to address and change

*Queering Classrooms: Personal Narratives and Educational Practices
to Support LGBTQ Youth in Schools*, pp. 65–76
Copyright © 2017 by Information Age Publishing

the injustices of our society. Without hope we are lost and lose sight of what the future could be: positive and inclusive of all.

Hope, for the authors of this chapter, comes in the form of education and the need to improve the way we create inclusive and safe environments for students to explore, inquire, and question the world around them. There is a need to improve teacher education programs through updated curriculum and pedagogies, safe spaces created for open and honest dialogue, and support and collaboration established between teacher and student. The more they know, the better prepared they will be. Why shroud or dismiss the conversation of difference? It is the concrete and honest conversations that will prepare our students for the ever-changing world around them. If schools dismiss the conversation or avoid addressing the elephant in the room, students will have less informed conversations with each other as well as continue to develop hurtful and uneducated stereotypes they will use in their every day lives.

Educators are the main component in the machine of education, and they shape innovators and leaders throughout generations of students. Often the skillsets of students are left underdeveloped during undergraduate studies, and future educators are less prepared to enter the field after graduation, especially in the areas of multicultural education, diversity, and social justice education (Banks, 2013; Nieto & Bode, 2011). One area that continues to lack attention and visibility, even after much societal progression, is lesbian, gay, bisexual, queer, transgender, intersex, and asexual (LGBQTIA) education for preservice teachers. As Kitchen and Bellini (2012) put it, "While teachers and students are increasingly accepting, schools remain places in which LGBT-identified students experience considerable homophobia and bullying. Educators play a vital role in making schools safer for LGBT students" (p. 222). Both teachers and students impact the academic world and can develop safe or unsafe environments, and it is a teacher's responsibility to take action in preparing themselves for the LGBQTIA experiences that will occur in the school setting. Marsh (2002) and Schmidt, Chang, Carolan-Silva, Lockhart and Anagnostopoulos (2012) stressed the importance of educators' self-reflection on the subject of sexuality and affectional orientations before furthering students' understanding and implementation of inclusive practices (ALGBTIC, 2009).

While some researchers address and delve into LGBQTIA concepts and discussions, there is also a need to deepen and further the complexity of the conversations surrounding LGBQTIA issues and concerns (Gorski, Davis, & Reiter, 2013, p. 242). The more students know about the world they live in, the better informed they will be for their future.

The environment, both in and out of the classroom, influences students' development, discourse, and behaviors, which can impact social and mental well-being. For example, "The hetero-centric media expression of homo-sexuality reinforces prejudiced and inaccurate representations of gay people, which depersonalizes gay people as moral outsiders, a socially denied group deprived of equal rights and treatment" (Chung, 2007, p. 101). Even though society has become more LGBQTIA friendly, there is a large gap between educators and students in the dialogue that needs to occur on the topic of classroom inclusion. Chung suggested that common stereotypes need to be analyzed and challenged in the classroom in order to reach a deeper understanding of negative assumptions. Getting to the root of prejudice is key to students' understanding of stereotypes, generalizations, and racist labels. Teacher education programs provide opportunities to address different topics and "while we are politically committed to social justice, our pedagogy focuses on developing a relatively safe space for teacher candidates to examine and challenge their personal and professional identities" (Kitchen & Bellini, 2012, p. 223). We need safe spaces for our teacher candidates to explore, inquire and question their identities. A teacher who faces their own prejudice, is a better teacher for our kids.

PERSONAL NARRATIVE

In this chapter we sought to create a space where our voices take on a different form of inquiry and response. Through personal narrative, we tell some of our own stories and positive experiences either as a student or with our own students. The hope is that our words can provide affirmation for those successful in the classroom, encourage other educators to stretch themselves in their teaching, and for future teachers to take from our experiences helpful and encouraging stories toward their chosen career.

Brody

Growing up gay in Wyoming made me a lot of things: anxious, scared, angry, loved, humble, unique, and strong. Most importantly, my upbringing made me who I am today. My identity as a gay man changed in many ways with regard to educators who support my narrative, my identity, and those who pushed me forward to become a leader and a better person. I also recognize that as a white, gay male from rural Wyoming, I possess a lot of privilege other queer people do not. I have the privilege of my skin color, passing masculine behaviors, cisgender identity, along with other privileges I hold. I have lived in Wyoming, Utah, Texas, the United Kingdom, and Illinois.

I am the product of an Early Elementary Education teacher, mechanic, pilot, businessman, math guru, rancher, singer, and the outdoors. I was raised in a small, conservative, LDS (Church of Jesus Christ of Latter Day Saints), Wyoming town. I have known that I was a gay male from the time I was 4 years old. Growing up with a conservative family, I was told at a young age that boys were not meant to like other boys, play with dolls, like the color pink, dress too nicely, care about their grooming, and do nothing that would make them look "less like a man." I did not know that people in my childhood environment could have an impact on such a small, malleable child. I remember in kindergarten my peers told me that I could not play "house" as the mom, cook, maid, or any role that was for "girls," and the teacher agreed with them. In fifth grade, sex education was limited to hygiene changes; boys will start to smell and grow hair, and sex happens between males and females. Middle school is where passing notes equated to dating someone. At this stage in my life, I realized it was not socially acceptable to tell my friends I felt differently. I did not act like other boys did; I did not talk about girls the way other guys did in the locker room, or behave the way most guys did toward girls they liked. I became depressed and anxious; I was sick a lot, overweight, and in a really negative place during middle school. At this time in my life, a religious leader told me that if I choose to be gay, I should choose to no longer live in this world. Although I was not a true member of a church or a religious young man, I followed his advice and attempted suicide at the age of 14. For reasons beyond my knowledge, I stopped midattempt, called my aunt, and she saved my life by telling me I was loved, safe, and things would be okay. No child should ever be told they are broken, less than or not worthy of life itself. The thing is, I had very few people at the time that I felt I could reach out to. I stayed in the closet until I was 16 years old, when my Mom accidentally found out I was gay; I did not tell my Dad until I was 18 and it was over email. I was scared, lonely, a liar, an imposter, and most of all, I was afraid of being myself. I used school and learning as an outlet. I was in the top 10% of my class with a 3.98 high school GPA. In college, I became a campus leader and excelled in education. I lived for my college years and jumped into every opportunity. I started dating, had my first real kiss, and truly started to find the true me.

Looking back on my educational experiences in kindergarten through high school, I recall clear instances lacking development, proper educational practice, or severely outdated methodology used by my teachers. There were also the moments that saved me, reinstated my faith in education, and led me to pursue my master's degree in higher education. The people I owe most of my inspiration to are not celebrities; they do not make substantial salaries, and they most certainly do not receive the recognition they deserve. The people I am referring to are educators: teachers, mentors, supervisors, and professors. I look up to them. These educators encouraged my development in ways that others could not. These incredible people influenced me, not only intellectually, but emotionally as well. In high school, it was my science teacher, mentor and friend who guided me through the throngs of public education in a predominately Church of Jesus Christ of Latter Day Saints community in rural Wyoming. Wyoming is famously known for the hate crime and murder of Matthew Shepard. Being raised in an unhealthy environment for LGBQTIA youth, this teacher was my salvation, my rock, and my light at the end of a damp, dingy, tunnel. Her science courses and mentoring taught me life lessons that remain with me to this day. Her classroom was the intersection of knowledge, sanctuary, and self-exploration. The point is that I felt safe. She created an open-minded environment, stood up against all bullying, and made her classroom a place for exploration and learning. There was not a defining intervention, no giant poster that read "queers accepted here," nor some outstanding gesture that made the classroom safe. It was little things: her teaching methods, her openness to others that made me feel welcomed, and the use of inclusive language and rhetoric.

Upon graduation, I was given the opportunity to find myself in college, leave my hometown, and its lack of expectations behind. After exploring college life the first few semesters, I began to get involved. I heard about the suicides of bullied LGBQTIA youth across the nation and I felt like I had to take action in my Wyoming university town. In light of my interests in activism, I sought out the Shepard Symposium on Social Justice Committee. Dr. Angela Jaime invited me to a meeting to discuss my intentions of bringing a speaker to campus. During my first meeting, she helped me use my voice and encouraged me to use it. She said it was important to hear my narrative at a student/educator-focused symposium. That was one of the first moments that anyone had actually said the words to me "Your voice is important," and most importantly, I believed her. I was, from then on, part of the Shepard Committee. The following year I volunteered, became an intern for the Shepard Symposium with Dr. Jaime and have been a steering committee member for 5 years now. Dr. Jaime helped challenge me, pushed me to be better and to do my best, because she cared about my success and me. She wanted me to be the most amazing student and shape my intellect, refine my skills, and further my education to its limitless potential. She made me discover myself and be proud of who I am. Through her work, compassion, and sheer tenacity, she guided me to an amazing future. There are no words for what she has done for me and never enough praise for the educators that led me to where I am now.

I was once a timid, scared student and am now studying higher education and social justice to advocate for other students like me. Without these two incredibly influential educators supporting others and me for who we are, I can guarantee that I would not be the strong person I am today. My life would not have changed for the better; I would not have found myself and learned to trust, love, and have confidence in myself. My high school science teacher and Dr. Jaime are the sole reasons that I persevered through some of the most trying times in my life. Through their support, openness, belief in social justice and inclusion, they created an environment that allowed for interdisciplinary learning and integration of a healthy LGBQTIA community and space. My high school science teacher referencing her friends that are LGBQTIA or Dr. Jaime challenging me to think in new ways about myself and others changed the way I interacted with people, my vernacular, and the pursuits of my future opportunities. Allowing LGBQTIA learners to have a place and a voice is one of the most life-altering forms of education a person could use in the classroom. After all, rainbows can only appear once the sun comes out.

Angela

Education is the key. While this is a vague and an overused phrase, I am drawn back to its words so often in my career. For me, it's not the depositing of knowledge into our kids that is the priority, it is the opportunity to foster critical thinking, encourage exploration of interests, and expose students to other perspectives and ideals. This is the key I see as essential to the future success of our global society. Part of the journey toward using this key is creating safe environments for dialogue and inquiry, providing opportunities for self-reflection, incorporating current events and up-to-date curriculum, and actively being a change agent for our society.

I teach in a predominately white, middle class, rural state. I am an associate professor in the only teacher preparation program in the State of Wyoming. The courses I teach focus on multicultural, diversity and social justice education. I specialize in American Indian Education and have co-authored the statewide teaching endorsement called the *Teachers of American Indian Children Endorsement Program*. I am an adjunct and advisory faculty member in the American Indian Studies program as well. The work I engage in with students is largely controversial and highly charged at times. My job is to expose them to the global world around them and reflect on their own biases/prejudices. It is the intent of the courses I teach to encourage students to think outside the box they know and consider what teaching in a diverse and largely socially unjust society means to their classrooms and pedagogy. My courses are largely theoretical and self-reflective, both of which students struggle with because there is no clear solution or path to the answer. While the content of each of the courses I teach is challenging, it is the work in which I thrive. Albeit, while I thrive in this content area of education, it does come with its own frustrations and obstacles.

Over the course of my career I have struggled to find a groove in classroom discussion. As a graduate student I failed miserably in crafting a space for student-to-student and student-to-teacher dialogue. The presence of a power struggle between them and me seemed evident every semester. My lack of training to teach college-aged students, most not that much younger than me and sometimes older, played a key role in the students' frustration and mine. While in my doctoral program, like other students, I was focused on finishing and becoming a professor. In my quest for a career in higher education I failed to refine my craft as a facilitator in the classroom, rather than as a dictator. It also did not help that I was a woman of color and my students were mostly white. Over the past 11 years in my current position, I have worked diligently to focus on my facilitation and meeting my students where they are in their understanding and development rather than where I am. I also spend a great deal of time getting to know them early on in the semester. Each student arranges a time to meet with me during the first 5 weeks. I find that if a student and I are able to connect early on, then our semester together holds more trust and honesty. Sometimes there is a student who is most resistant to the curriculum and my style of teaching; I make it a goal to get to know them a bit better in our meeting and ask what they need from me to make the class more applicable to their future career.

I spend a great deal of time in the beginning of the semester talking with my students about the terminology they use in their personal lives and the classroom. We discuss the obligation we as educators have to create safe spaces for all students, not just the students in the middle or the "norm." I explain to them the importance of students' seeing themselves in the classroom, feeling as though it is their classroom. While artifacts in the room can seem like a superficial way to entice student learning, it is effective and can start the conversation between student and teacher. I encourage my students to think about the global community around them and to reflect the community their school is in, as well as the students in their classroom. Some of my past students have put up posters of various leaders from different cultures, ethnic groups and communities and others have posted the P-flag, the pink triangle and posters of famous speeches.

I have incorporated student moderators into the daily reading schedule. Students sign up to moderate and facilitate the discussion around a reading that interests them. This removes the focus from me as the professor and places it on them and an open learning environment. I meet with the student before their facilitation and help them with the questions they will ask their classmates. Some students bring in film clips or current events relative to the readings to jump-start the discussion. Having students facilitate the daily discussion puts less pressure on the students to participate. While I am still there in the room, I am a passive participant and only interject when I want to support student comments or if the discussion seems to be straying from the topic. Students take more ownership of the material when they have to lead the discussion.

More than any other aspect of my pedagogy and curriculum, I focus on self-reflection. After each class I reflect on the good and the not so good. I might do this by journaling or simply by taking a moment in my office. I teach my students to be reflective practitioners and I try to practice what I teach. Over the course of the last 2 years I have been learning what it means to be a mindful facilitator. This entails asking more questions of my students rather than giving them more answers and reflection. I lecture very little in my classroom. Instead, I ask the students to help one another find the answers and also find the answers within themselves. This is challenging when my classroom is composed of mostly white students and we are talking about white privilege; again, the student moderators play a key role in creating a safe place in our classroom.

One semester not so long ago, about 8 weeks into our semester, my diversity class and I were having a lively conversation around affectional orientation and gender. We had watched the movie, *Straightlaced: How Genders Got Us All Tied Up* (Chasnoff & Chen, 2009); the students were discussing what responsibilities teachers have when students raise issues in the classroom about LGBQTIA or gender identity. About 30 minutes into the discussion one of the students, Jeff, began to tell his story of coming out to his friends and family. He shared how hard it was to know he did not fit the mold his schools or community embraced and how hiding who he is made him feel sad and hurt every day. Jeff talked about his father's negative reaction to his being gay and his choice to leave his family and move away. His words were gentle and heartfelt while talking to his peers, pleading with them to be kind and accepting of all children, especially the ones like him. It was hard for me to not want to reach out to Jeff and hug him. His classmates were respectful of his story and expressed how grateful they were to him for sharing his story with them. Jeff told the class that he had never come out to a group of more than two or three before and certainly he had never come out to people who were not close friends or family. After class I hugged Jeff and thanked him for his words. Later that day he sent me an email with these words:

Hey Dr. Jaime,

I just wanted to E-mail you to thank you for creating such an open environment in our Diversity class. Today was the first time in my life that I was able to discuss my sexuality openly with a group of people, and feel like I wasn't going to be judged. It was something that was really difficult and scary for me to do, and I just wanted to say thank you. It was a great experience and I left the class feeling more empowered and confident about myself than I think I ever have. This class has opened my eyes to so many new things, and I thank you for allowing that to happen. I just wanted you to know how great today's class made me feel. Have a great Halloween.

Sincerely, Jeff

The email was an indication that this group of students felt safe in the classroom. This particular class consisted of several students who knew one another before my class through other courses or before college. Yet we engaged in several activities in the early part of the semester to foster community. Teaching for me has always been a struggle. Talking at students and dictating to them in the early years of my career did not serve the students or me well. Spending a great deal of time on building community and listening to my students, rather than dismissing them for lack of experiences, is working. This type of social reconstructionist teaching creates safe environments and allows students to open up and talk. Being mindful and present in my facilitating of the conversations has benefited my students and me; they feel heard and valued, and I feel as though I am getting to know them better.

In addition to my teaching responsibilities, I also serve on many committees and projects related to social justice. For the past 5 years I have chaired the Shepard Symposium on Social Justice (SSSJ). This event is a 4-day conference focused on activism, grassroots organizing, inclusion, and social justice from all disciplines. It has been a wonderful experience that has afforded me the opportunity to meet leaders in social justice education, work with amazing people on my own campus doing social justice work and to make a difference in the lives of students who have come to the Shepard Symposium.

In 1996 Omawale Akintunda and Margret Cooney from the College of Education at UW started the Symposium for the Eradication of Social Inequality. Their mission was to start the dialogue of faculty, staff, students, and the greater community on issues of social justice in the context of education. In 1998 Matthew Shepard was beaten and left for dead on the outskirts of Laramie; only days later would he pass away as a result of his injuries. The University of Wyoming, Laramie and the country were outraged that this young man had been killed for being himself, for being gay. Matthew Shepard is remembered as being not only a UW student, but for being a social activist. In 2002 the Symposium for the Eradication of Social Inequality changed its title to bare his name as a living reminder that life is precious and meaningful. It is in his name that we work every year to build a program and continue the dialogue around issues of inequality, social justice, diversity, and change. The anonymous donor for the Shepard Symposium was a hard worker for the Union Pacific Railroad and invested his money well. He was not a graduate of UW. He was a frugal man and sometimes lived in a small cabin on a piece of land west of Wheatland, Wyoming. He was a fan of film, Morris Dee, and the Southern Poverty Law Center. His first major gift to the University of Wyoming was an addition to the original Fine Arts Center, which allowed the Department of Theater and Dance to host an annual film festival and to teach acting for the camera. When Matthew was murdered, this donor was particularly disturbed by the brutality and senselessness of the loss. He established the generous gift to the University of Wyoming to endow the symposium in his memory. This donor has since passed, yet we remember and tell his story every year as a thank you to his courage and compassion.

It has been through the SSSJ that I have found a place to engage in meaningful work outside of the classroom. My interaction with individuals serving on the committee has been enriching. I have learned and been exposed to new theories, ideas, and personal stories. I have grown from these relationships and become a better person because of them. Our committee focuses a part of the program every year on LGBQTIA issues and concerns. Over the past couple of years we have become more involved in supporting and sponsoring GSA groups from Wyoming and the surrounding states. It is our intent to provide space for high school students to use their voices. We have been fortunate enough to have students come and present on panel discussions, movies they have made and projects they have completed in their home communities. This past year the SSSJ committee created GSA Day. We invited presentations and panels of students to voice their opinions, share the work they are doing in their schools, and be heard. It was a success and will continue to be a standing part of the program for years to come. Beyond the shine beaming from the students who participated and attended, their teachers, faculty advisors, and group mentors were present and active in the program. Their participation was an indication for me that the tides are changing— that teacher education might be changing to include more multicultural and diversity education and that social justice was present in their preparation for becoming an educator. The GSA Day and its success gave me hope for the future. We are all searching for signs and rays of hope in the work we are doing; for me, this was a day that hope was strong. I saw the possibility for a brighter and better accepting future for the world we live in through the GSA students who participated.

IMPLICATIONS FOR TEACHER EDUCATION AND CONCLUSION

So what does our narrative have to do with teacher education programs across the country and in a global society? Our purpose has been to expose our readers to the experiences we have had in and out of the classroom—the experiences we have had that have helped to shape our perspective and vision on education. It is through these stories we hope to engage a larger discussion of social justice education for preservice teachers and their students. Without the inclusion of hard conversations in teacher education programs we fail our students in not preparing them for the global society we live in every day. If we prepare future teachers to face their own biases and prejudices around difference then there might be more teachers like Brody's high school science teacher in the schools. We can encourage them to be open to the questions students will ask them, to have compassion without judgment toward students struggling with the societal inequities of school life, and encourage students to be inquisitive and questioning of the world around them.

Without the teachers and professors we have had or want to become, we would not have sought out the careers we have or are working toward having in the near future. We acknowledge the struggle of doing this work, yet accept the challenge to push our students and peers and teach from a social justice perspective. It is the students we see in the classrooms across the country whose lights are fading from a feeling of invisibility or rejection for who they are by their peers, teachers, administrators, and an overall school culture of acceptance toward LGBQTIA youth. It is our job as educators to embrace students, expose them to new ideas, foster their inquiries, advocate for them when injustices occur, and above all accept them. As cliché as it might sound, students are the future of our world and without the opportunities for them to grow and explore, we run the risk of losing out on a more inclusive and accepting society.

REFERENCES

Association of Lesbian, Gay, Bisexual, and Transgender Issues in Counseling (ALGBTIC). (2009). *Competencies for counseling with transgender clients*. Alexandria, VA: Author. Retrieved from https://www.counseling.org/docs/default-source/competencies/algbtic_competencies.pdf?sfvrsn=8

Banks, J. (2013). *Introduction to multicultural education* (5th ed). New York, NY: Pearson.

Chasnoff, D. (Prod. & Dir.) & Chen, S. (Prod.). (2009). *Straightlaced: How genders got us all tied up* [Motion picture]. San Francisco, CA: GroundSpark.

Chung, S. K. (2007). Media literacy art education: Deconstructing lesbian and gay stereotypes in the media. *International Journal of Art & Design Education*, *26*(1), 98–107.

Gorski, P. C., Davis, S. N., & Reiter, A. (2013). An examination of the (In)visibility of sexual orientation, heterosexism, homophobia, and other LGBTQ concerns in U.S. multicultural teacher education coursework. *Journal of LGBT Youth*, *10*(3), 224–248.

Kitchen, J., & Bellini, C. (2012). Making it better for lesbian, gay, bisexual, and transgender students through teacher education: A collaborative self-study. *Studying Teacher Education: Journal of Self-Study of Teacher Education Practices*, *8*(3), 209–225.

Marsh, M. (2002). Examining the discourses that shape our teacher identities. *Curriculum Inquiry*, *32*(4), 453–469.

Milk, H. (1978). *The hope speech*. Retrieved from http://www.danaroc.com/guests_harveymilk_122208.html

Nieto, S., & Bode, P. (2011). *Affirming diversity: The sociopolitical context of multicultural education* (6th ed.). New York, NY: Pearson.

Schmidt, S. J., Chang, S., Carolan-Silva, A., Lockhart, J., & Anagnostopoulos, D. (2012). Recognition, responsibility, and risk: Pre-service teachers' framing and reframing of lesbian, gay, and bisexual social justice issues. *Teaching & Teacher Education*, *28*(8), 1175–1184.

CHAPTER 6

ADVOCACY FROM ADVERSITY

Sculpting an LGBT Identity in Art Education

Jordan DeWilde

My journey to becoming an art educator began with a desire to teach and a passion for art. I repressed any questions I had about being gay in this profession until a number of experiences led me to find the answers. Bigotry and prejudice could have discouraged me if not for the support of my graduate program. With the freedom and encouragement to research issues I was interested in, I found the confidence to advocate for LGBT educators and students. I collaborated with professors and classmates to prepare preservice teachers to work with LGBT youth. I presented at conferences and to undergraduate courses of elementary education and art education majors. My research and experiences transformed me into a confident educator, prepared to make positive change.

SCARED BEGINNINGS

I found a seat in a crowded conference room while still in my first week at a new university. The lesbian, gay, bisexual, and transgender (LGBT) student group, Pride, was hosting a panel discussion in the Student Services

Queering Classrooms: Personal Narratives and Educational Practices
to Support LGBTQ Youth in Schools, pp. 77–92

Building. I was still new to campus, during my first year in the art education graduate and teacher certification program. I started going to Pride meetings to learn about issues affecting the LGBT community and to make new friends. I had been openly gay for almost 2 years, but I lacked any meaningful knowledge about LGBT issues or history and had very few friends who identified as gay. I listened as the Pride president introduced the career panel. Four individuals shared personal experiences of coming out in the workplace.

Two of the individuals were former public school teachers. They described horrifying stories of false accusations, harassment, and legal battles. One individual wrongfully lost her job and sued for defamation of character. Although she won her case, proving innocence, it did not make finding a new job in education any easier. The university I attended has a rich history of strong teacher education programs. When the panel was asked what advice they would give to the education majors in the room, they pleaded for students to seek a different career. I raised my hand and asked when these negative experiences that led to the end of their teaching career had taken place; two individuals responded they had left teaching in the early 1990s. The distance in time gave me some comfort, but the 90s were still too recent for me to believe I would be spared any discrimination as a gay educator. I was worried I had chosen a difficult path, but I knew my purpose was to teach, so I ignored their advice and continued on with my first semester.

Finding an Ally

I had only just begun the art education program as a graduate student, while also earning my teaching certificate. This nontraditional experience provided me with unique opportunities to choose research topics and share my perspective with other peers. During my first semester, I met one of the professors in the art education department. She was an outspoken LGBT advocate. Although I was never a student in any of her courses, she was one of the first people on campus I felt comfortable coming out to. I told her about the career panelists and what they had said about LGBT discrimination in education. She shared similar stories, but also explained the amount of progress that had been made. She encouraged me to research LGBT issues in art education as a possible thesis topic. I was immediately relieved to have found an ally in my department. I never even considered there might be research on LGBT issues specific to art education. I was extremely excited to discover answers to my own questions and possibly ease some of my concerns.

Disappointing Opposition

In the spring of 2010, I sat in a Curriculum and Instruction course as the professor lectured on issues of legality and ethics to a room full of future educators. The PowerPoint presentation went through slide after slide of what was not legal or not ethically appropriate for the classroom. A slide with the words "sexual orientation" immediately caught my attention. I assumed, and I suppose I had optimistically hoped, that this bulleted issue would be for the rights of gay and lesbian educators. To my great disappointment, the professor explained that under no circumstances should an educator disclose their sexual orientation to their students. She proceeded to give an example of a lesbian educator who lived an hour away from the community she taught in so that her students would not see her with her partner around town. The professor did note this may be an extreme caution, but the implication was that gay and lesbian educators were to hide this essential part of their identity. There was no time for questions or debate; this was simply stated and the professor moved on with the lecture.

I, however, was unable to focus on the remaining material. As a future educator, and gay man, I was certainly aware of the obstacles I may face from school administrators, parents, and students. I knew I risked wrongful termination. Although legally schools are prohibited from dismissing employees based on sexual orientation, at least in some states, little to no reason is required to terminate a nontenured teacher. Parents may believe the stigma that gay individuals prey upon children. Students may tease and create rumors based on the perceived sexual orientation of their teacher. I was prepared for many of these obstacles. However, I was somewhat shocked to be told my orientation was unethical for the classroom from one of my college professors. What was most alarming to me was that this presentation was given to a number of future educators. These students would soon become teachers who may be gay or lesbian themselves, but will also have gay and lesbian colleagues, students, and students of gay or lesbian parents. This implication of sexual orientation as unethical perpetuates stereotypes and social stigma that LGBT educators have struggled against for decades. As I pursued my passion to teach art, I strongly believed it was important that I had a good understanding of LGBT issues in education throughout history, along with current issues, and how I could use that understanding to create a safe and accepting environment for my future students.

Unfortunately this was not the last discouraging experience I had while attending my university. Prior to student teaching, education majors were required to do several hours of clinical experiences in a variety of classrooms. I was placed with a high school art teacher at a local school for a

6-week experience as part of a Curriculum and Instruction course. I was excited for the opportunity to learn from an art teacher and of course new students.

My excitement grew the first couple of days while I observed the students and discovered what curriculum unit I would later teach. On my third day of visiting, the teacher started to share his political and moral beliefs with me before class. These conversations turned my excitement to dread and discomfort for the remainder of my placement. The first indication of conflicting views came when the teacher described San Francisco, California, as a place for "sickos and weirdos," referring to the gay community. Throughout the 6 weeks, which happened to be during an election year, he often shared similar beliefs and questioned my own.

I tried my best to approach each day as a learning experience, because I knew I would not always have a safe environment to live and work in. The art education department provided me with so much support that I had forgotten how hate and ignorance could still be prevalent in the workplace. I finished the clinical experience without incident, and I believe the teacher felt we had gotten along quite well, but I was miserable each day. I stayed silent because ultimately he was responsible for my semester grade. I later expressed my discomfort in an exit survey. The experience was difficult, but it prepared me for potentially working with individuals with opposing views in the future.

Guided Exploration

The first opportunity to explore my concerns was later in a graduate course focused on researching different issues in art education. The professor facilitated a student-centered course and encouraged students to research issues of personal importance. Each week a new topic was discussed, and students were asked to present articles, opinions, and reflections. At first, I was apprehensive to suggest LGBT issues as a topic for the class to study. However after finding an ally in my LGBT-advocating professor, and a fellow classmate, I felt confident enough to express the importance of such research.

Gays and lesbians in education were not a recent development. In fact, LGBT individuals had been struggling for acceptance and equality in education since the 1700s with the first American schools. Traditionally, American schools were founded on religion and moral development. The very first community schools were taught by religious leaders and ministers. However, in 1701, a law was passed prohibiting ministers as teachers, so communities were forced to hire new teachers; but these educators were also expected to follow a strict moral code. These new teachers were predominantly women and were expected to remain unmarried and focus instead on their classrooms. The men in these schools were administrators. Their role was to supervise all aspects of education. This administrative role was considered manly, while the teaching profession was thought to be a nurturing, motherly profession. The few male teachers at this time were considered feminine and presumed to be homosexuals (Shannon, 2008).

By the 1920s, this womanly profession became criticized for feminizing young boys. The women who were expected to not marry were now seen as poor role models for young girls. Although it had been common for these women to be single before, communities began to speculate on the sexual orientation of single individuals. Older, single women educators were described as mannish and accused of corrupting children. During the time of World War II, schools began to hire married women as teachers. However, due to so many of the men leaving to fight overseas, women had begun to fill other job positions and left the teaching profession behind. At the end of the war, schools recruited male veterans to fill teaching positions (Shannon, 2008, p. 2).

During the 1950s, homosexuality became much more visible in urban areas. Throughout the nation, the general public was exposed to homosexuality through the publication of Alfred Kinsey's reports on sexual behavior. This increased awareness of homosexuals across the country led to schools hiring only individuals they found to be appropriate role models for students. This ideal role model was the married heterosexual. Also in the 1950s came Senator Joseph McCarthy's call for a homosexual witch-hunt. Schools began investigating the personal lives of any teachers thought to be homosexual. These teachers were removed and often arrested and imprisoned for being "immoral, emotionally unstable, and untrustworthy" (Shannon, 2008, p. 2). At this time, homosexuals were believed to be recruiting young people to their "alternative lifestyle," in addition to also sexually abusing children. As a result, many LGBT educators left the profession entirely. Those who remained were forced to retreat to the closet and keep a vital part of their identity a closely guarded secret.

The 1960s and 1970s brought about change for the LGBT community. In education gay and lesbian teachers brought their cases to court, challenging schools for their dismissal. In 1969 the California Supreme Court ruled "that being a homosexual was insufficient grounds in and of itself for dismissal" (Shannon, 2008, p. 3). Educators began to fight back rather than resign once their sexuality was disclosed. This progress toward equality faced a new opponent in 1977 when Florida Orange Juice spokeswoman Anita Bryant began the "Save Our Children" campaign. The campaign portrayed LGBT individuals "as being involved in a national conspiracy that was anti-God, anti-country, and anti-decency" (Shannon, 2008, p. 5). Members of the LGBT community were thought to be a threat to our nation's children, according to Bryant and her supporters. The "Save Our Children" campaign eventually encouraged state senators to introduce laws that targeted gay and lesbian teachers.

In 1978 the Briggs Initiative was introduced in California. This initiative, also known as Proposition 6, would allow the firing of any school employee found to be "advocating, soliciting, imposing, encouraging, or promoting private or public homosexual activity directed at, or likely to come to the attention of schoolchildren and/or other employees" (Shannon, 2008, p. 5). San Francisco supervisor Harvey Milk led a coalition of unions and organizations against the initiative and debated Briggs throughout the state. Teaching organizations such as the National Education Association, the American Federation of Teachers, and the California Teachers Association all opposed the Briggs Initiative. On November 7, 1978, California voters defeated the Briggs Initiative by a two-to-one margin. It is important to note that although this victory was made, many schools would still look for other reasons to fire known homosexuals to legitimize their dismissal.

CURRENT STRUGGLES

Many states still do not prohibit discrimination in employment based on sexual orientation. "In 2004, only 14 states had passed laws barring discrimination because of sexual orientation" (Blount, 2006). However, many city and local governments have ordinances to protect these citizens. The improved working conditions for LGBT educators is in large part due to the support of teachers' unions, educational organizations, and lobbying groups. Although LGBT activism in education has increased in recent years, many parents and schools still resist hiring openly gay and lesbian teachers and attempt to keep homosexuality out of the curriculum. According to Blount (2006),

> Many school officials still maintain informal practices of screening job candidates for possible sexuality or gender nonconformity. LGBT persons who are hired sometimes fear that their identities will be discovered, that they will be dismissed from their chosen profession, and that their lives will be made miserable through rumor, harassment, and social ostracism.

Obviously, there is still room for improvement. Schools need to recognize individuals of the LGBT community in order to create a safe learning environment for everyone. The persistence shown by LGBT educators "bespeaks their dedication to improving the lives of their students through education and the joy they find in teaching" (Shannon, 2008, p. 8).

According to a recent survey, "only 28% of people think a school board should fire educators based on their sexual orientation" (MacIntyre, 2007, p. 1). In 1987, the same survey revealed that 51% believed it was okay. The author attributes this decrease to the nation's willingness to have an open conversation about gay and lesbian issues in recent years. "When more and more people stand up to support their sons and daughters, their neighbors and friends, their home decorators and hairdressers, their teachers and health care providers, it makes a difference" (MacIntyre, 2007, p. 2).

According to information given at the Illinois Art Education Association (IAEA) 2009 conference, "80% of prospective teachers report negative attitudes toward gay and lesbian people" and "two-thirds of guidance counselors harbor negative feelings toward gay and lesbian people" (LBGT Stats, 2009, p. 1). These statistics are alarming because negative attitudes in the schools may result in a hostile environment for gay and lesbian educators. Additional information at the conference noted that gay and lesbian students often struggle with his or her own identity due to a lack of positive role models. "There are very few openly gay staff members or teachers in schools" and "the presence of openly gay and/or lesbian staff members is a crucial component of any school program seeking to reduce bigotry and provide support for gay and lesbian students" (LBGT Stats, 2009, p. 4). I look back at my own experience in school and wonder what a positive gay role model may have done for my own personal development. The conference presentation also expressed the importance of talking about gay and lesbian issues in the classroom because 27% of a typical class of thirty students will be directly affected by homosexuality in some way (LBGT Stats, 2009, p. 4).

Positive Representation

Not only is it important for LGBT educators to feel safe in their own schools, but their presence can also have a positive impact for the students. For LGBT students or students questioning their orientation, an educator closeted by his or her profession sends a message that being homosexual is something to be ashamed of, to hide, and such a message is wrong. I believe a better message to send would be that educators are not expected to conceal their orientation so that they could be positive professional role models for these students. This would be no different than a heterosexual teacher sharing a story about his or her family, displaying pictures on the desk, or having other general conversations that may include details of his or her personal life. To create a truly inclusive and safe environment for our students, the same should be expected for our educators.

Some educators assume there is no need to address issues regarding the LGBT community in their classroom. Some believe there are very few, if any, gay or lesbian students in their school. However, Goodman (1993) would argue that, "if you create an atmosphere in which every person feels safe to be himself/herself, you will discover that there are lesbian, gay, and bisexual students, parents, and staff in every school district" (p. 14).

School is often the first place children learn insults that describe the LGBT community. When these insults and slurs are used in the classroom, often the only repercussions students receive from teachers is a warning. Students who use the insults are told not to be mean, while the victims are comforted with the "sticks and stones" adage. Teachers rarely confront students' assumption that being gay or lesbian is an insult. Students fail to make a connection between the insults they use and the real-life homosexual individuals those insults hurt. Furthermore, "By failing to confront homophobic attitudes in students, schools become agents of injustice" (Goodman, 1993, p. 12). Bullying is an issue state legislature and educators have addressed in order to protect students at school. However, homophobia and LGBT discrimination have not shared the same attention. LGBT students are less likely than their straight peers to report victimization because they believe no action will be taken (Poland, 2010). The lack of resources and support for LGBT students is of great concern as these students are two to three times more likely to commit suicide than other youth.

There are a number of steps educators can take to create a safe environment for their students. First is to establish a strict antiharassment policy that includes sexual orientation and gender identity/expression. In addition to creating these "hate-free" zones, it is also important to educate students with information about the people affected by these insults. Teachers may also choose to support school clubs such as Gay-Straight Alliances and inform students of counseling services offered at the school, as well as community resources that pertain to LGBT youth issues. Although these implementations to the classroom directly affect students of the LGBT community, all students will benefit from building a safer classroom environment.

Often LGBT inclusion in curriculum is reserved for health or sex education courses, implying that homosexuality is about sex, not about history, literature, science, or any other field of study. However, as Prince (1994) notes,

If teachers honestly want to be supportive of gay students and to increase the ease at which these young people can live and develop as happy and productive individuals, they will achieve that goal only by the infusion of accurate and representative information into the curriculum. (p. 30)

Unfortunately, school curriculum often does not include LGBT role models who have made contributions to history, math, science, social services, and the arts. One of the most common ways to include LGBT issues in the curriculum is mentioning the sexual orientation of famous gay, lesbian, and bisexual persons during the natural course of teaching, because "true inclusion affects all subjects" (Prince, 1994, p. 30). With an art class, this would be the inclusion of artists such as Andy Warhol and Keith Haring. A foreign language class may offer a list of current issues debated in the United States to compare with other countries. One such issue could be gay rights. Similarly, a history class could address the LGBT community's struggle for equal rights while discussing civil rights. An English class could incorporate reading and writing on issues of sexism, feminism, and other gender issues found in literature dating back to the 18th century. There are several creative ways that connect LGBT community issues to course content. By providing students with an opportunity to learn more about the LGBT community, teachers may encourage a better understanding of sexual and gender diversity. This also allows teachers to present students who identify as gay or lesbian with information they may relate to.

CREATIVE EXPRESSION

My first opportunity to connect to curriculum as a gay student and future educators came in a research methods for teaching high school art education course in the spring of 2008. The assignment was to create a sculpture focused on our own identity. Through creating my own sculpture and observing the presentations of my peers, I learned that creating opportunities for students to express themselves is a great way to reach students from all backgrounds, including those who may identify as LGBT.

I created a sculpture to symbolize my experience coming out years before. Around the time I came out and the months preceding, I wrote several poems and lyrics about relationships and internal struggles I was facing. The sculpture took the form of several handwritten colorful sheets of paper crumpled and assembled into a sphere that hung above a clear plastic trashcan. Around the trashcan I drew symbols to describe my experience. One such symbol was an open padlock to symbolize the freedom I would eventually feel after living an openly gay life. I also included a flashlight to symbolize the attention I felt was given to this one specific aspect of my identity. Finally, there was a camera to symbolize finding a way to focus life through my own lens.

The assignment also required us to write an accompanying poem or prose that we would read as part of our presentation to the class. Although many of my classmates had become my close friends, this was the first time I addressed my sexuality to some of my peers, and certainly the first time I had ever done so in an academic presentation. Months before I would have never dreamed of having the courage to do so, but the opportunity and environment constructed by my professors allowed me to speak about my experience with pride. The assignment was a great moment for me personally, but it also showed me how I might present similar opportunities to my own students.

ENCOURAGED RESEARCH

I continued through the art education program, always looking for opportunities to research and grow as both a gay student and a future educator. I started to transition my focus less on gay educators and more on how I could best help LGBT students in my future classroom. In September 2010, the news frequently reported unfortunate suicides of LGBT youth. Although statistics had previously reported LGBT youth as more likely to commit suicide than straight peers, the frequency and media coverage spurred a new sense of urgency. Bullying prevention became the proposed solution and certainly is a valuable effort in preventing discrimination leading to such tragedies. However, in addition to policy and management, schools may wish to consider implementing positive LGBT representation or issues into the curriculum.

Opposition to a gay-friendly curriculum is inevitable, but is necessary to create truly inclusive classrooms across all grade levels. Many may find such themes inappropriate for elementary students, but in reality children may be struggling with orientation and/or gender identity in these very early grade levels. Students may also come from LGBT families and should also feel safe, included, and represented in their schools.

VISUAL CULTURE

As a graduate student, I was required to take a seminar course titled Visual Culture. At the end of the course each student had to choose a topic and present to the class before writing a lengthy research paper. My professor encouraged all of us to spend time with a research topic we were interested in. I took this opportunity to explore how visual culture, television, comic strips, toys, and such may affect the gender socialization of children and the drawings they create.

Items of visual culture have worked to create specific boundaries for what is considered masculine or feminine. From anatomical prints dating back to the 18th century to the Bratz dolls and superheroes of today, visual culture has certainly played a role in gender socialization. Particularly with the Bratz dolls and superheroes of popular youth culture, children are surrounded by images and products demonstrating "appropriate" appearance and behaviors for men and women. This exposure has helped mold children's identity, but also affects how they view others and the world around them.

Duncum (1997) demonstrates this theory with his research of unsolicited drawings of Western children (p. 107). Duncum found several consistent differences in the drawings of young boys and girls with many different research studies throughout history. He has found that the general themes in childrens' artwork has changed very little over time. The differences found in these drawings can be attributed to gender socialization.

He also notes that of all the surveys that have examined children's unsolicited drawings, their interest was found in ordinary life, fantasy, peaceful scenes, and strong physical action. All of these surveys found "strikingly different gender preferences" (Duncum, 1997, p. 108). Boys typically drew means of transportation and weaponry, while girls drew flowers and houses. Boys seemed to be more interested in machinery and battle than girls, who favored growing things. Boys were also noted as depicting sports scenes in their drawings. One of the most favored subjects of children of both genders was the human figure. Boys drew superheroes, as well as funny or weird made-up characters. Girls, on the other hand, drew an older female with fashionable clothing. Just as the Bratz dolls are viewed as an idealized female to young girls, the same perception is found in their drawings.

Duncum (1997) explains that by applying gender schema theory, "it is possible to understand these preferences as guided by an internal mechanism to conform to gender-based standards and stereotypes" (p. 109). With exposure to gender norms in society, exemplified in visual culture, the child develops an understanding of what is and is not appropriate for his or her specific gender. This leads to a censoring affect when creating artwork in order to fit in with their classmates, because "usually without being consciously aware, children select their subjects in accord with what they conceive to be appropriate subjects for their gender, and consequently they find these rewarding" (p. 109).

In some cases, the same subject matter is created by both boys and girls. He uses drawings of horses as an example. For girls, the drawing of a horse may convey ideas of nurturing and family, but for boys the horse is a symbol of transportation, power, and strong physical action. In other words, "Boys and girls may draw what appears to be the same subject matter for a very different reason or purpose due to their gender socialization" (Duncum, 1997, p. 111).

Duncum (1997) concludes by linking these tendencies in children's drawings to the influence of popular media. Just as bedtime stories, fables, and myths of the past found their way into children's artwork, now so have themes from movies and television. Visual culture is not only shaping the child's identity but is also shaping the visual imagery they themselves create.

One way in which society has constructed these gender roles is by implementing visual culture. Callen (1997) referenced the work of Bernard Albinus' early anatomical studies as depicting the male body as the universal norm (p. 606). This was the body against which all women were to be measured. This body implied that men were superior and women were perceived as the "Other," whose only purpose was for reproduction. Our understanding of ourselves and our own experiences is often found by observing others through visual imagery. We are born a specific biological sex, but we learn our appropriate gender roles from socially and culturally constructed norms in visual culture. As children, we are surrounded by visuals that catch our interest. Those interests are constructed by society and reinforced in our toys, comic books, television programs, and films. These examples of popular culture demonstrate the appropriate behaviors and attitudes for young boys and girls. Visual culture helps develop our identities but also develops our understanding of our world and how we interact with others in society. We censor our own actions in accordance to these norms as we judge those of our peers. We play a role in the creation of images in mass culture directly by making artwork or producing other imagery, and indirectly by our consumption of goods such as dolls and comic books. Although it is society that creates the specific gender roles for men and women, visual culture is the evidence of that socialization.

I continued researching LGBT issues in visual culture and art education by studying inclusive children's books. I knew I was interested in teaching art at the elementary or middle school level, and I was looking for age-appropriate lessons or resources for my students. Although students may not yet identify as LGBT at a young age, they may have relatives or friends who do, and I believe all students could benefit from a more inclusive curriculum.

LGBT-INCLUSIVE CURRICULUM

One suggestion for achieving an inclusive curriculum is to feature books with characters and stories that reject the heteronormative social structures. Children's books in particular for elementary classrooms could make an impact on all students, not just those of the LGBT community. Many of these books send positive messages such as "be yourself," messages all children can benefit from. The characters and story may not even specifically read as a book about gay issues, but to a student sensitive to issues of identity or different family structures, these books can be a huge source of comfort.

Many schools have adopted multicultural books into class curriculum for similar reasons of representing the entire student body rather than a cultural majority. Rajput (2009) describes books as both mirrors and windows. He believes books to be like mirrors because the reader is able to see themselves in the text or illustrations. However, he also states books may be like windows because readers are allowed to see into the lives of others. Rajput was given the difficult task of speaking to preservice teachers on the topic of children's books that address racism and sexism. In 1980, the Council on Interracial Books for Children produced a list of 10 criteria when analyzing a book that is inclusive. At the top of this list is to check the illustrations.

Rajput (2009) acknowledges the importance of finding children's books to represent all students, including those who are members of underrepresented groups. He notes that minorities are more than groups based on race or ethnicity, but may also include groups like the LGBT community. *I'll Get There. It Better Be Worth the Trip* (Donovan, 1969) was the first young-adult book with gay content to ever be published. However, the book's characters only perpetuated stereotypes of homosexuals. Gay characters were depicted as either doomed to a life of despair or as predators. Rajput (2009) condemns the use of such literature and instead encourages the use of gay-friendly children's books in the classroom. He includes question to help determine inclusiveness such as, "How would children of same sex parents react? Or children who are questioning their sexuality?" (p. 66). He advocates for the use of truly inclusive literature to help promote tolerance, respect, and social justice.

Illustrators Maya Gonzalez, Linda de Haan, Stern Nijland, Lynette Schmidt, and Carol Thompson have all created visual representations of gay-themed stories in children's books. Formalistically, the illustrators are very different. However the content and overall message of their stories is all the same; love may be found in a great variety of situations and combinations of people. Just as Rajput (2009) analyzed classic children's books for racism and sexisim, educators should consider implementing more inclusive illustrated works.

Demand for gay- and lesbian-themed children's books increases as the definition of the American family evolves to include the LGBT community. Books that depict racially homogenous LGBT characters serve as an alternative to the heteronormative perspective. However, there are children's books available that feature racially diverse LGBT characters as well. Including children's books in the classroom that address issues of homosexuality exclusively are great steps for promoting tolerance and understanding. Still a further step would be to include well-developed stories featuring gay and lesbian characters without creating an "other" out of the LGBT community. Educators should consider searching for truly inclusive resources to create a positive learning environment where all students feel represented and appreciated.

Advocacy Opportunities

As my knowledge of LGBT issues in art education grew, I was given more opportunities to share information with peers. For 3 consecutive years I was asked to present information about LGBT students, bullying, and the value of inclusive curriculum to an undergraduate course titled Art for Diverse Populations. I spoke to preservice teachers about issues they may face teaching students who are questioning their sexual orientation or identify as LGBT. Art is often a subject area where students express themselves creatively and sometimes more openly than they might in other classes.

Once again the art education department at my university was not only providing me with a safe environment to explore my interests, but they were also encouraging me to share my findings with peers. I was able to have productive conversations with students who may not support the LGBT community politically or morally but could understand the importance of supporting gay students through policy and curriculum.

Building on these small presentations, I wrote a proposal to present at the Midwest Bisexual Lesbian Gay Transgender and Allies College Conference on the topic of LGBT issues in education. I spoke a great deal about the need for teachers to support gay students, but I also provided information about the history of LGBT educators. I wanted to provide some comfort to education majors like me who may have been scared to enter the teaching profession. I gave reasons for being an openly gay educator, such as in order to be a positive role model for all students. I acknowledged the improvements in legislation to protect the rights of LGBT educators, and I stressed the need for inclusive curriculum.

Transition to the Classroom

I carried my grand ideals into student teaching and learned a balance of optimism and the real world of teaching. Although I strongly believe an openly gay educator with a LGBT-inclusive curriculum can be of great benefit to all students, I learned how much of the world is still not quite ready. Teachers must consider job security, the workplace environment, and community standards before implementing their own philosophy in the classroom.

During student teaching, I experienced occasional homophobic comments from my cooperating teachers. One teacher made inappropriate comments about a gay couple she saw trying on clothes at the local mall. My other cooperating teacher was hesitant for me to teach about openly gay artist Keith Haring, because he "was not a good role model." These comments were minor insults but still had an impact on my working relationship with these teachers. I learned how to subtly include opportunities for LGBT inclusion and collaborate with colleagues who may not be as supportive.

Homosexuality in education cannot be kept in the closet. Education is about the sharing of ideas and learning by making meaningful connections to course material. That learning is hindered when both educators and students are expected to deny an essential part of their identity. This denial causes a withdrawal from the learning experience. By creating an environment that is safe and accepting for everyone, students are able to make those connections as unique individuals. School may be the only safe space a student struggling with these issues can turn to. That is why it is so important to address the LGBT community. By providing students with positive role models and accurate information, educators are given a great opportunity to make a difference in the lives of their students. This opportunity is what every educator hopes for, and is possible by creating a safe environment for all students.

CONCLUSION

As a graduate student earning my teaching certification, I had a unique opportunity to follow my own interests and share with others. After reflecting on all of my experiences, I know the opportunities were what gave me such a strong education. I am now a 3rd-year elementary art teacher, and I try to provide my own students with a variety of opportunities. I work in a small, rural, and conservative town, so I remember the lessons I learned about collaboration while earning my certification. I know I was very fortunate to be encouraged by the art education department. The great support I received gave me tremendous confidence as I began teaching, and I believe all of the experiences, both positive and negative, helped prepare me as a gay man, an advocate and educator.

REFERENCES

Blount, J. M. (2006). Lesbian/gay/bisexual/transgender issues in education. In F. English (Ed.), *Encyclopedia of educational leadership and administration*. Thousand Oaks, CA: Sage.

Callen, A. (2002). Ideal masculinities: An anatomy of power. In N. Mirzoeff (Ed.), *The visual culture reader* (pp. 603–615). New York, NY: Routledge.

Donovan, J. (1969). *I'll get there. It better be worth the trip: A novel*. New York, NY: Harper & Row.

Duncum, P. (1997). Subjects and themes in children's unsolicited drawing and gender socialization. In A. M. Kindler (Ed.), *Child development in art* (pp. 107–114). Reston, VA: National Art Education Association.

Goodman, J. M. (1993). Lesbian, gay, and bisexual issues in education: A personal view. In D. Walling (Ed.), *Open lives, safe schools* (pp. 9–16). Bloomington, IN: Phi Delta Kappa Educational Foundation.

LGBT Stats. (2009). *Proceedings of the IAEA state conference* (pp. 1–5). Lisle: Illinois Art Education Association.

MacIntyre, M. (2007). Support for gay educators on the rise. *NEA Today, 26*, 1–2.

Poland, S. (2010). LGBT students need support at school. *District Administration, 46*(1), 44.

Prince, T. (1994). The power of openness and inclusion in countering homophobia in schools. In D. Walling (Ed.), *Open lives, safe schools* (pp. 29–34). Bloomington, IN: Phi Delta Kappa Educational Foundation.

Rajput, T. (2009). Questioning your collection. *Knowledge Quest, 38*(1), 62–69.

Shannon, V. (2008). Teachers. In *GLBTQ: An encyclopedia of gay, lesbian, bisexual, transgender, and queer culture*. Retrieved from www.glbtq.com/social-sciences/teachers.html

CHAPTER 7

PREPARING TO ENTER THE FIELD

Reflections From Preservice Teachers on Learning to Work With LGBTQ Youth

Nora Dunne, Kevin Goffard, and Jacqueline Svetich

A VISIT TO "THE SCHOOL,"[1] BY NORA DUNNE

Teaching is such a difficult profession, for so many reasons. We are responsible for providing content knowledge to students who probably are not really interested in learning our content. Besides that, we spend our days dealing with teenagers who are trying to figure out who they are and what they want to do with their lives in the future. LGBT students, along with all students, are often struggling with their identity during high school. LGBT youth often feel like they are different and that they do not fit in. As teachers, we are the ones who are there to support these kids for the majority of the day. We have the responsibility to be there for students and support them as they go through this process. Teachers give students support when they do not have any other adults to encourage them to become better people and find success. I think that this makes

Queering Classrooms: Personal Narratives and Educational Practices to Support LGBTQ Youth in Schools, pp. 93–107
Copyright © 2017 by Information Age Publishing

teaching such a rewarding job, but it also places a great responsibility on us as teachers.

When I entered the teacher education program, I did not have a great deal of knowledge about working with LGBT youth. From watching the news and reading articles in newspapers and online I knew that there were definitely issues with how society treats people who are different in general. I had read some articles about the struggles that LGBT youth in particular face. I knew about bullying and harassing students and about the problem with suicide among LGBT youth. However, I personally had not had experience with the struggles these students were facing. I also had not seen severe bullying in my own high school or in the schools where my clinical and field experiences took place. I knew there were problems and these things were happening, but I did not have firsthand experience. To me, it felt like severe bullying was happening in a different world.

We discussed working with LGBT students in several of my classes. We talked about how diversity plays a role in the classroom and how to encourage students to appreciate differences. However, I did not see a great deal of diversity in my teacher education classes or in the classes I observed. While we discussed diversity, we were not truly exposed to it. Visiting The School changed this. This school is a charter school that is part of the regular public school system, with a focus on being a safe community for all learners, regardless of sexual or (a)gender identity, race, ethnicity, body size, income, or any other excuse one may have for bullying another student. It is also a school where the bully can learn through restorative justice how to live in a society without bullying and how to restore broken relationships because of his or her actions.

The first time I went to The School, it was definitely a culture shock. The atmosphere was very different than that of a typical school. Students called their teachers by their first names and had a significant role in the daily working of their school community. Many students engaged in a restorative justice class, which allowed them to participate and help solve problems within their school. Many of these students had struggled with school in the past, and I saw how much pride the students took in their school's atmosphere. I think it was very beneficial to be put into an environment that was so different than what I had ever seen. I learned so much from this school, and I know that these experiences made me a better educator and will benefit my future students. As an educator, I will make sure that the atmosphere in my class allows students to participate and take ownership of their community. One way I hope to do this is by spending time at the beginning of the year forming classroom rules as a class. This will allow students to help decide on the rules that they feel are important and will make them feel like they play an important role in the classroom. Visiting this school illustrated for me how important it is to allow students to take ownership of the classroom.

I visited The School twice. Both times were very eye-opening experiences. Listening to some of the stories that the students told me broke my heart. There were students who had been both physically and emotionally harassed for not fitting in. These students were wonderful, bright, caring people, but some people could not see this in them. It was so upsetting to me, because these kids were amazing people. They welcomed us with open arms, despite the way they had been treated in the past. I had heard stories on the news about bullying, but I really have not witnessed severe bullying firsthand. I could not believe some of the things these students had experienced from others. It especially surprised me because all of the students I talked to were such friendly and caring people. I would have never thought that kids could be capable of such horrible actions, and I was so surprised that these great kids had been treated so poorly in the past. Equally surprising to me was how welcoming these kids were to us, despite how they had been treated in the past. Visiting this school has really reinforced the idea that school needs to be a safe place for these students.

I was also heartbroken to hear about the education some students had been receiving. Some of the kids that I talked to had endured horrible experiences with teachers and education in general. They had felt like teachers did not care about them. Some kids told me at previous schools they would sit in a room with a computer and do busywork all day. They did not feel challenged and they hated school. This was hard for me to hear because I feel like as teachers, it is our job to care about and challenge students. First off, I always want my students to think that I care about them and their problems. I also want to challenge my students academically. Students are capable of so much, but they need to be challenged. I was also disappointed to hear that students had not felt cared for at other schools, but there was definitely enough love to go around at The School! You could tell just by watching how much the teachers cared about their students. The students would hug their teachers and talk to them. By watching the students and teachers interact, you could just tell there was a great amount of respect and trust between them.

Some students at this school have had very difficult lives. Talking to these kids helped me realize that I will have students who have gone through things that I cannot even imagine going through. My goal as a teacher is for students to feel like they can trust me and come to me when they have problems. I want my students to feel that they can trust me and that I care about them, as I have seen the students at this school come to trust their teachers. The teachers at this school have really tried to make a safe place for students. They really work hard to make sure that students feel safe and accepted, especially if they did not feel accepted at other schools.

This is really what I would like to bring into my future classroom. I know that some kids do not feel safe at home. They do not trust their parents or guardians, and they feel like they need to keep their guard up at all times. Often, these students will feel unsafe at school as well. I believe these students are the ones whose trust I need to gain the most. I hope that I am able to help these students break down the walls that they put up. I could tell that the teachers at the school were able to gain the trust of their students. The students would hug their teachers and would talk to them, telling them about what was happening in their lives. I could tell that the teachers had gained the trust of their students, which helped the teachers create a better learning environment for the students.

One thing that I have really thought a lot about is a question that I heard while at the school. One of the teachers asked, "Should we have a lot of schools like The School, or should we have a little The School like this in every school?" Although I think The School has helped so many kids and stops kids from falling through the cracks and dropping out, this should not really be the goal. It makes me so sad to think that there are so many kids who have been teased, bullied, and ostracized enough to need to leave their school.

I think that our goal as teachers should be to make every school have a little bit of The School. I believe that if teacher education programs bring future teachers to The School, schools similar to this program, or start programs to work with diverse students, we will be able create many schools that have a part of The School in them. Every future teacher takes something from visiting The School, and we will bring this experience into our future classrooms. We can bring these experiences to our classroom and share the experiences with other teachers. By doing this, we can make all of the schools that we teach at a little bit like The School rather than creating a lot of schools like it.

Both times I went to The School, I participated in a "restorative justice" class. In this class, students work together to help solve problems within the school. Both times I observed, this class ended in a discussion. My professor always asked the students what they got from our being there, and what they wanted to tell us as future teachers. Many of them said they liked sharing their stories and they liked knowing there were future teachers who really cared about students. Again, this made me realize that there are so many students who do not have people, whether it is a teacher or parent, who care for them and want them to succeed. I want to make sure my students know that I will always be there for them.

I really think that LGBT youth are not any different from any other students. All students just want to feel loved and accepted for who they are. Being different is scary in high school, and I'm sure LGBT youth are sometimes afraid to share who they really are. This is so much more difficult when they do not have a place where they feel safe. I want to ensure that my classroom and my future school are places where students will feel safe. Students at The School know that they will be accepted for who they are. Some students may not have a safe place at home; this makes it even more important to make schools a safe place for them.

The restorative justice class helped these students create a safe environment for themselves and their classmates. The students in these classes engage in peace circles that help students solve problems with each other. These students are trying to prevent problems from becoming worse, because many students at The School had behavioral problems, and one more strike against them could end their educational career. This tactic shows just how much the teachers at The School want their students to succeed. They are trying to do everything possible to prevent their students from taking actions that would cause problems for their futures. If suspended or expelled from this school, these students will have nowhere to turn. The teachers use restorative justice as a way to keep help students work through problems and keep them in school.

I really liked sitting in on the restorative justice classes. I think that this is something all schools should implement in some way, and I thought it was a great opportunity for all of the kids at The School. The members of the class receive experience in peacemaking and problem solving. The students who are brought in receive a chance to work through their problems with other students and receive an outside perspective that is not a teacher. It gives these students a chance to work through their problems and the solutions before they take action themselves and receive a punishment that could destroy their opportunity at the school. This also helps the students form a community. This community is another reason students feel safe at The School.

It really amazed me how this class led students to work together and form a community. The students at The School were very diverse, and this classroom was no exception. There were kids whom you would never expect to see working together in this class. There were students who were of different races, socioeconomic background, sexual orientation, and gender identity, and they all appreciated each other and their different opinions. They respected each other and the ideas that each of their classmates had. They all were supportive and encouraged each other, and they all helped solve the issues that came about in the school. I think that this really reflects on the teachers at the school. They have been able to get all types of students to work together across whatever may make them different from each other. The kids in this class truly formed a community and were able to support each other and help each other solve problems. As an outsider, I was so surprised to see how well these students interacted. They all truly cared about each other and were supportive of their goals, thoughts, and problems. The students in this restorative justice class really illustrated to me what a tight-knit community this school really is.

I think that community is really important in making a school feel safe for LGBT students. Students will know they have somewhere safe to go and feel safe with their peers. I think that part of the success of The School is that the students feel safe interacting with each other. The students form a "peace circle" (modeled after many indigenous communities' method for resolving conflict) if they have a problem, and they know that they can trust their peers. So many of the students at The School have been bullied previously, so I think it is important to them to know that they can trust and go to their peers. It is also important for students to have adults that they can trust, but it is also important for them to have classmates whom they can trust and who treat them well. In the end, all students want to feel accepted by their peers. The teachers at this school have helped create a community and build trust within the community. Friendship is such an important part of high school, and the teachers at the school helped create a place where the students can develop friendships and support systems.

I think that going to this school has been very important in my preparation to become a teacher. It has helped prepare me to work with LGBT students, but it has also helped me think about how to meet the needs of all students. This school was much different than any school I had ever previously been to. I think that it was a good experience for my classmates and me. It gave me a taste of something completely new and gave me some experience in classrooms that are not as typical as other classes I have observed. This new point of view has been important in my development as an educator.

This experience is something that I will be able to take into my classroom that others may not have. I have now had experience working with students whom many schools had obviously given up on or rejected. Granted, two visits is not a lot of experience, but many future teachers are not put into these different types of environments at all. I will be able to bring these experiences into my future classroom and help make all of my students, including LGBT students, feel like I care for them and want to help them succeed. I hope to make my classroom an environment where students feel safe and feel like they are able to express themselves and their opinions openly. I want all of my students to be able to say what they believe without a fear of being ridiculed or hurt. Going to this school has helped me really think about what type of environment I want my future classroom to be like for my students.

I think one of the most important parts of preparing to be a teacher is putting yourself into as many different situations as you possibly can. As a teacher, you never know who your students are going to be or what to expect in your classroom. You can never be fully prepared for what is going to happen. From what I have learned in my teacher education classes, the best way to prepare yourself is to put yourself into as many different situations as you can. I think that going to this school was so beneficial in my preparation to become a teacher, because it helped put me in many different situations that I would not have been in if I had not gone to this school, which helped me look at students in a different way. I think that these experiences have helped me grow as a teacher and have helped make me a better educator. I will be able to use this experience in my classroom in the future, and I also hope to be able to share these experiences with my colleagues.

SEEING THROUGH A DIFFERENT LENS, BY JACQUELINE SVETICH

Before college I didn't even know what the acronym LGBT meant. I always considered myself a nice person, so regardless of how my peers saw themselves, I was typically friends with everyone. Once my professional education started at the university, the terms *diversity*, *differentiation*, and *multiple learning styles* were drilled into my head as important methods that needed to be implemented in my classroom. I began to hear the term *LGBT youth* and I started to reflect on how I saw this in my high school; they were labeled the "weird" kids, the kids who didn't have friends, and the kids that were bullied. Then I thought about how they acted in class and remembered that they were reserved, stuck to themselves, rarely participated in class, and struggled. Throughout my education I have had multiple discussions about how important positive environments are and why it's imperative that students feel accepted and involved within a classroom. A lot of our discussions turned to bullying and how 90% of the time the students who were being bullied were LGBT youth. As time went on I got the opportunity to look more in-depth at how environment and inclusion of diverse students really impact a classroom through clinical experiences, anecdotes, and assignments. But it wasn't until I went to The School that the importance of those terms truly clicked for me.

This school was like nothing I had ever seen before. The more I learned about The School, the more I fell in love with it. I fell in love with the culture and acceptance that was present at this school. The founder and head teacher of The School had a mission and outlook that I found brilliant as well as heartfelt. She changed the stereotypes of "those kids" and the "us and them" and gave them the respect, recognition, and attention they deserved. The School was a place where everyone was not only accepted for who they were but their personas were celebrated. As I walked around the school I got to meet other teachers who shared that same mission and outlook, and it was evident that the staff at The School work hard at creating a safe environment where students are treated fairly regardless of background.

I was lucky enough to visit the school twice: once when I was a sophomore and again when I was a senior. Both times I had different experiences. The first time I went I was more of an observer and getting to know what the typical day of a student was. When we first arrived, we walked in and multiple students immediately greeted us. They were completely open and the students introduced themselves to us, saying, "Hello everyone! My name is and I am bisexual." You could tell how much they love their school; immediately the students wanted to take us on a tour, get to know us, and talk about their educational experiences. I learned what classes they liked the most, what teachers they liked the most, and why they liked this school over other schools. When I asked these questions I got consistent responses: "We don't have to hide who we are;" "I'm accepted for who I am;" and "I have a great relationship with my teachers, they listen to me, they hear me." I also got to experience and participate in a flash mob, which was my personal favorite. The teachers and students went downtown and we performed popular line dances called the Turbo Shuffle and the Wobble. This was really a cool experience because the teacher taught them how to do the Turbo Shuffle and the students showed us before we headed downtown for our flash mob. It was an awesome way for the kids to connect with each other and teachers but also with us. They instantly made us part of their community, and it was a blast!

Once the flash mob was over, we came back to school and I shadowed more students. This school is not traditional and it was a brand new experience for me. Students were given freedoms that I was not used to, and they had a say in their school community. Everyone had an open line of communication. There was a level of mutual respect between the teachers and students. It was very informal; teachers were called by their first names, and the students were extremely independent. As I sat through classes I was amazed at how engaged and involved everyone was. Students were working collaboratively together, asking great questions, and staying on task. The difference I saw between this class and other classes that I had been in was that there was a trans* female and open same-sex relationships within in the class. There was no change to the flow, no distractions, and no insecurities. Each student, regardless of how he or she identified, was confident and was given the chance to work toward bettering their education in a safe classroom environment. This made me reflect back on how LGBT youth in my high school acted, and I wondered why there was such a difference in the dynamics of the students, which brought it all back to the importance of that sense of community.

By far the best experience that I took away was during my second visit, specifically my time spent with the students participating in restorative justice. This school is one of few schools that uses this practice to get students to communicate openly with teachers and peers. It is a way in which students are able to express themselves about problems, issues, topics, or discussions within and out of the school. Students are invited to share their feelings using talking pieces (typically a stick or piece of wood, where only the person holding can talk) without fear of judgment; it is built entirely on trust and honesty. This program, in my opinion, is what makes this school such a tight and close community. Not only do the students use this method in their school, but they also travel to conferences and other schools to teach educators and professionals how they can incorporate restorative justice into their establishments to help create that same close and safe environment.

When restorative justice was first introduced to me, I was extremely skeptical: I couldn't understand how they got diverse students to open up and talk about their feelings. I felt that most students would laugh at the idea or refuse to participate. I couldn't be more wrong. I got to work with a beginner group and an advanced group. It was an eye opening experience in not only my professional world but in my personal world. As we went along I found myself amazed at what these students were going through outside of school. They have real problems—grown-up problems that I couldn't even begin to understand—on top of just going to school. They were dealing with severe depression, anxiety, pregnancy, abuse, learning disabilities, and behavioral problems. I was fortunate growing up and going through school; I didn't have identity issues and I felt comfortable in my own skin. I had a supportive family and great friends, so it was hard for me to imagine what it was like for others who were going through life-changing events. Perspective really shifted for me. Listening to them talk and open up about what was happening in their lives made me realize that school may not have been their first priority, but that doesn't mean that they should just be cast aside and ignored. There needs to be that communication that restorative justice offers. They should be loved and supported as the individuals that they are, especially when it comes to the classroom. I would be furious if I saw any of my students being bullied or bulling. I've learned that it is important in setting the tone of the class that bullying is not acceptable under any circumstance.

Visiting and participating in The School was by far the best way that I could have worked with LGBT youth. Hearing their perspectives of their school and teachers and witnessing how they interact with their peers has helped me understand the importance of relationships and acceptance of each student. As a new teacher I found that getting to know who my students are has helped me best meet their individual needs. That being said, I recognize that not all students are willing to open up and talk about their feelings or tell me what is going on in their lives. However, now I know that it's still just as important for me to build relationships and build that trust where students can feel comfortable to talk to me. Students have lives outside of school and external factors, whether that be bullying or other extenuating circumstances, and that can affect their performance in school. It is an important and huge part of my job to be flexible, understanding, and respectful of students' identities and any other issues that are occurring in their lives. LGBT youth are like any other student who needs the support of their teachers to feel accepted and welcomed into the classroom. School may be the only place where they can escape their problems, so it is vital that teachers be there for them to create, sustain, and enforce a safe and nurturing environment.

NEW UNDERSTANDINGS ABOUT LGBT YOUTH, BY KEVIN GOFFARD

One of the qualities of a successful educator, in my opinion, is being able to work effectively with a multitude of students of all abilities and backgrounds. One of the biggest and possibly fastest rising groups in terms of civil rights today is the advancement of rights for the LGBT community; and with that, the LGBT community is becoming more prevalent and integral in our schools as well Coming from a high school that served a community that was of a higher socioeconomic status, the complex issues regarding the inclusion, education, and livelihood of the youth who were LGBT was not an issue that was really brought to my attention a lot. My school had a Gay-Straight Alliance, but beyond that basic program, that was the extent that we heard about anything regarding LGBT youth. It's sad that looking back we did not have a more active involvement with these youth, but then again it was still in the process of gaining momentum in our nation as well. Now there is a much bigger awareness of LGBT youth in my old high school, but one that I wouldn't consider to be drastically different than when I was there. So coming to the university from my high school and then going into the teacher education program, the thought of all of the challenges that the LGBT students faced in schools was minimal. While I knew there were some struggles they faced, including bullying, the extent of those challenges was something that I had no idea about and thought that it wouldn't have been much more different anywhere else than it was in my school. Throughout my teacher preparation career, my understanding has evolved when it comes to issues regarding LGBT youth.

Something that I love about the liberal arts education process is that your view of the world becomes so much bigger, so much more open, and you are able to learn or even be exposed to things that you wouldn't have been exposed to before. This is what happened when I came into the theatre teacher education program. I was able to have the opportunity to be exposed to some of the underlying issues that surrounded this complex issue of LGBT youth, especially in our schools and society. There was exposure to the "It Gets Better" video series, in which the LGBT community could talk about their experiences. Through a lot of those images, it was heart-wrenching to hear about some of the stories that these kids had to endure just because they weren't cisgender heterosexual. One in particular was about a boy, about 14 years old, and we heard his story. But sadly, ultimately he decided to take his own life because of the pressures of the bullying and negative treatment he got just for being gay. There were countless other stories that presented similar experiences: some who had attempted suicide, some who were contemplating suicide, some who were beat up, and some who were threatened. These stories presented a much bigger problem and one that is very prevalent in our schools today.

One of the hardest things is to go into a school and see some of these events being played out day after day. While observing, it is easy to hear the words gay, homo, fag, lesbo, and such being thrown around like they don't mean anything. However they do. Regardless of whether or not it is being directed at someone who is LGBT or not, just the mere saying of the word is enough to do damage. Although the LGBT community uses this word as a form of identity, where it crosses the line, and what I have seen in schools, is when it is used in a negative way to represent something that may not even be connected with their sexual identity. The saying, "That's so gay" is one that is popular, and while the pure purpose of this expression may not be to demean LGBT people, it does. Although the word "gay" is not a bad word, I feel that the meaning we put behind the word does a lot more damage than the actual word itself. These new uses of words helps reinforce stereotypes and sets up an expressway for bullying.

It has been now a couple years that I have worked alongside populations that are exclusively or a majority LGBT, and the issue of bullying is always brought up. Now, bullying can happen to any student, and the type of bullying can change from one situation to the next. However, from my experience of becoming a teacher and reading articles on case studies and fieldwork, the LGBT community experiences significant bullying because it can be physical, mental, sexual, emotional, virtual, or a combination of them all. It can take place anywhere, both in and out of school, on the streets, at home, at work, while also being done by members of both the LGBT and the non-LGBT community. As a preservice teacher, it was mind-boggling that a student of any gender could be bullied not just in school, but anywhere, and it could be done by anyone. I have heard stories of bullying and abuse by classmates, family (including parents), co-workers, strangers, as well as fellow members of the LGBT community. Something that complicates it even more is that in some areas, the LGBT community is not unified. For these youth, the aspect of bullying is so complex and can have such a number of factors going on. As stated above, non-LGBT kids can and do experience this same type of bullying; however, my experience has shown that LGBT students seem to be more likely to experience this in their lives.

So how did my viewpoint change? I believe a couple factors went into it, and it sure wasn't an overnight experience. This deepening understanding was the result of coursework both in the College of Education and my Theatre Education classes, both of which involved clinical field experiences. To be brutally honest, you can read all the articles you wish. You can watch all the videos that you can watch. You can hypothesize all you want. However, nothing, and I repeat, nothing, comes close and is more impactful than hearing someone talk about their experiences face to face—being in their environment, being there, not behind a screen or a sheet of paper, but there in the present moment. This attitude of being there in the moment came about really from my experience at many clinical sites, including one of the most impactful ones: The School. I had the opportunity to travel to this school during my Issues in Secondary Education class. This school is specifically designed for students who were struggling in regular public schools. A lot of these students belong to the LGBT community, many of whom are out and as a result were bullied in many ways. By taking advantage of this opportunity, I was able to spend a day with the students at this school. Certainly, one day is pretty brief, but in that short amount of time I learned an amazing amount, which helped to further my understanding of the issues surrounding LGBT youth in schools. One of the most impactful experiences was sitting one-on-one with these amazing students. However, hearing their stories was hard to experience, because after all these are kids. Kids just like I was, and yet they were ones who were bullied; some were abused, and some had experiences happen to them that I couldn't even imagine happening to me. We heard their stories about their oppression from other students, community members, and even their own family members, just because of their sexuality. We heard stories of how they were bullied so hard and so much that they tried to commit suicide and had marks from cutting themselves. We heard how they ultimately stopped succeeding in school due to not feeling safe or comfortable in an environment where they should.

Hearing these students' stories had to be some of the hardest things I have had to do during my time here as a teacher candidate. This is a reality and a problem in today's schools. Despite the negativity though, the students also gave me a sense of hope and inspiration. Because they came to The School, they felt safe and welcome, as well as having a sense of trust from their teachers and peers so that they could be who they are without the fear of being rejected or turned away. By doing this, they then began to make great strides in their schoolwork.

Something that I enjoyed most about this experience, I think, is that this new understanding has helped open my eyes and has taught me a lot of valuable lessons that I can bring with me when I go to student teach, and ultimately teach on my own. What's even better is that the things that I have learned can be applied to all students. That's the beauty in what you can learn. So what did I learn? Here are a few examples:

1. I learned to provide a learning environment that is supportive of all students that allows for those students to grow in a positive direction. No matter what, students need to feel safe. They need to feel that they are welcomed and supported. They need a place in which they can succeed. This includes building a trust relationship with the students. The more they trust you, the more you can help them succeed.

2. Not everyone is what he or she appears to be—a simple lesson, but one that I feel is often times overlooked. Everyone has a backstory and everyone's experience is different. By learning to look at that backstory, we can begin to maybe see why they do the things that they do, or why they act a certain way. Some of a teacher's biggest questions about a student's personality or actions can be answered by just looking at the students' journey and what they have been through. This is a definite lesson that I am grateful for learning.

3. Knowing that while there may not appear to be an issue at a school does not mean that it does not exist. Looking back, my high school has made great efforts, but I can begin to see some of these things that LGBT students go through being played out, and before this experience, I was oblivious to it. So while the problems may not be obvious to everyone, the problems still exists, and it is up to teachers to try to address those in their classrooms as well as in their schools.

If given the opportunity to give advice to preservice teachers, one of the first things I would say is this: You have to be aware of the background of the issue that you are going to face. The systemic issues that are in place, not just in education but also in society, are dramatically complex, with no single or easy solution. However, that should not discourage us, both preservice and practicing educators, from trying to combat the problems in our own classroom. We may not be able to change the world; however, it is possible to change our classrooms, the hallways in our schools, and perhaps even the communities we live and work in. And the preservice teachers of today have a greater opportunity to create and start change right at the beginning of their careers. We have grown up with these issues being at the forefront of our society. We have grown up in a time when at least some people are more open and aware of the LGBTQ community. As a result, if trends continue, we will begin to see an even bigger increase in the presence of these issues in the schools we work at, which in return will require us as teachers to take action and combat these issues. In addition to growing up with these issues, we have also seen firsthand the issues that currently exist when talking about LGBTQ youth in our school system. Unfortunately, as is too often the case, the LGBTQ students are given unfair treatment due to the systematic elements that are currently in place in the schools and society. Therefore, being so close to these issues for a lot of our lives will, in some respects, give us good background knowledge of these issues, which in return, will provide us with the best possible way to respond.

My second piece of advice is that it is critical that you develop genuine rapport with your students, especially when addressing LGBTQ concerns. If you cannot change anything outside the walls of your classroom, at the very least, you have the power to create a classroom climate that is safe and welcoming. I would argue that one of the biggest issues that plague these students is the lack of resources or availability of these resources that these schools have for LGBTQ youth, especially in areas that might be poorer, more religious or conservative. What's more, many students cannot count home as a safe environment, as the home may be a place of neglect, abuse, or even abandonment. Students may not be able to turn to friends, as they may have lost friends or are afraid of rejection by their peers. You, as a teacher, the person who sees them 5 days a week, can be that person whom they can trust to go talk to, to get advice, and be supported in who they are and what they are doing. However, unless the students trust that you are there for them and on their side, this relationship cannot be formed. While seemingly small, the effect that this trust can have on the students can be profound, and it might be the difference between a student dropping out or staying in school. Whether your students are LGBT or not, if you can get students to trust you, you will have a much better chance of reaching out to them and helping them get better academic success and create a more welcoming culture and place for students to be.

One thing that I have learned is that it is crucial to know that some-times doing this won't be easy. Controversial issues such as this one can be difficult to navigate, and as a response, you might think that it is better to just give up. However, it is imperative that you do not. You are sometimes the last resource, the last hope that many of these students have. You may have to act alone or do 100 things before you start to see the results, but you cannot become discouraged. Through this, it is imperative that you continue to believe in what you are doing and what you are fighting for. You have to trust that change can occur and believe that one day these students, and the LGBTQ community as a whole, will be able to go through life, school, and work being equal and without discrimination. As I have witnessed and have experienced, if you can keep this optimistic hope, even during the dark moments, as well as a trustful connection with your students in an inclusive environment, you will be a better teacher as a result and have much more success with connecting to and helping the LGBTQ youth in your classroom.

These are just some of the many lessons I have learned and will take with me as I enter into my career as a teacher. While in no way am I saying that I am an expert with LGBT youth, I do feel I have learned a lot and know a lot more than students who have not been given this opportunity, which leads me to the question of why this is important. Like myself, many students whom I have talked with throughout my time at the uni-versity have had little to no knowledge of the issues facing LGBT youth. This just goes to show the lack of awareness that our society has when it comes to these students in our schools. The issues surrounding the LGBT community as a whole are becoming part of a bigger dialogue. But we cannot make the mistake of thinking that although progress has been made there is not much more to do. We are still battling equal rights for people of different races, for women, for at-risk youth, for the people who are underrepresented in our schools and society. Yes, we have made strides to address those issues; however, to say that they are gone is simply not true. We pride ourselves on the notion that everyone has the right to a chance of success in the United States, but how can they be successful if we don't give them the chance to be successful? They deserve the same rights everyone else has because they are human beings. We know our strengths and the areas we need to improve on. So let's get to work and start to make a difference for the better.

NOTE

1. The name of the school has been renamed to protect this particular learn-ing community.

SECTION III

**USING LITERATURE TO ADDRESS ISSUES
OF LGBTQ YOUTH IN SCHOOLS:
FROM THE CLASSROOM TO THE LIBRARY**

CHAPTER 8

READING THEM IN

Using LGBT Child and Young Adult Literature in Preservice Teacher Education

Paul Venzo

A young woman is standing in line at a university café. An older woman is next to her in the queue and strikes up a conversation. They talk briefly about their courses and about the lunch menu, and—of all things—motorbikes; the younger woman is carrying a helmet under her arm. The older woman asks, "So when did you come out?" The younger woman replies, "Um ... Just then?"

This is—fairly obviously—not my coming out story. However, this is a true account of the experience of a friend of mine who has kindly agreed for me to print it here. This is because both of us are queer-identifying teachers who have worked with young people in the tertiary sector over many years, and we know well the powerful effect on identity and identity formation that is wrought by the university education system. For us, going to university was bound up in questions about our politics, our aspirations, and our sexuality. Even in the queue at the café, it seems there was a lot to be discovered.

Tertiary education has an important role to play in shaping how we think, talk, and feel about ourselves and about others, particularly when it

*Queering Classrooms: Personal Narratives and Educational Practices
to Support LGBTQ Youth in Schools,* pp. 111–126
Copyright © 2017 by Information Age Publishing

comes to aspects of subjectivity and identity. For one group in particular this will be crucial, because of the impact this might eventually have on the lives of young people—preservice teachers.

Contemporary research on preservice teacher training on sexuality education is a growing field, with notable contributions from Simkinson (2009), Carmen, Mitchell, Schlichthorst, and Smith (2011), Marshall (2011) and Ollis, Harrison, and Maharaj (2013). More specific, lesbian/gay/bisexual/transgender (LGBT) studies about preservice teacher sexuality education are the focus of work done by Robinson and Furfolja (2001) and Mudrey and Medina-Adams (2006). Research has also been conducted from the point of view of students as recipients of sexuality education (Gowen & Winges-Yanez, 2014).

Across this body of literature, two important themes are common. The first is that many countries, my own included, are dedicated to documenting and improving the pedagogy of preservice teacher education on sexuality and sexual diversity. The second point that is often made is that, while there is a degree of enthusiasm for such an undertaking, experience in real-world settings shows that much work is still to be done. These general findings are supported by the feedback given in the large scale, longitudinal study of LGBT youth health and well-being in Australia, *Writing Themselves In* (Hillier et al., 2010, pp. 83–84),[1] in which respondents felt that school-based sexual education, while perhaps well intentioned, was still problematic.

This Australian report finds that while the Internet is now the dominant source of information about sexuality for same-sex attracted and gay-questioning young people, they still look to the school system to improve its sex and sexuality education. The authors write that, out of 1,949 responses to the open-ended question, "My school could better support my sexuality by ...", over 40% of respondents "wanted Sexuality Education to be more inclusive of same sex attraction and gender diversity" (Hillier et al., 2010, p. 88). This report also found that while the queer-supportiveness of Australian school culture in general is improving, there is still more to be done, stressing the "importance of addressing homophobia in ... school culture in order to improve the mental health and wellbeing of SSAGQ [same-sex attracted and gender-questioning] students" (Hillier et al., 2010, p. 87).

The results of this survey reflect the fact that schools, whether in Australia or elsewhere, continue to be spaces in which negotiation, contestation, discovery, and discrimination around sexual identity occurs. As a consequence, teachers are involved—whether they are prepared for it or not—in the lives of young LGBT people. Indeed, they will have significant input into whether or not schools are safe and supportive environments in which all students might come to understand their own sexual identities and those of others. For this reason, how we educate preservice teachers around sexual and gender diversity has a direct correlation with the intellectual as well as health and well-being outcomes of the students they teach.

It is over two decades ago now, but I remember very well the day I was caught reading a collection of Truman Capote short stories during a high school math class. My teacher was furious and brought up this transgression in a parent-teacher interview some days later. To my relief my mother took this in stride, informing the rather pompous and self-important mathematics teacher that at least I had good taste in literature and pointing out that the book was in all likelihood more interesting than his approach to algebra. *Touché!*

Behind this anecdote lies another story that is particularly relevant to this chapter. This book of short stories, among a few significant others, had been given to me to read by another teacher. He was—unsurprisingly perhaps—a teacher of English and English literature, and he had recognized in me a great need for reading material that went beyond what the school library could offer. Moreover, this teacher recognized that I needed reading material that would allow me to connect with my identity as a young gay man, something I had not yet acknowledged to the world but was beginning to realize for myself.

Now, there is very little in Truman Capote's writing that might explicitly be identified as "gay," and it was not as if the Internet was available at that point to provide me with juicy information about Capote and his private life. However, there was something about his writing to which I felt myself responding, almost viscerally. For the first time, and ever so subtly, I felt as if an author might be writing for and to me. When the teacher in question lent to me a collected works of Paul Verlaine, this sensation of being addressed by the writing became even stronger.

In hindsight, this was a very thoughtful gesture by the kind of person we might now describe as a "straight ally": someone who, though they are not LGBT identifying, understands how important it is for young people to connect with representations, stories, and ideas that reflect their emerging identities. By connecting me with those books, this teacher had given me a lifeline; a catalyst for a life-affirming relationship with texts of all kinds.

However, I understand that this "teacher intervention," seen from a contemporary perspective, also illustrates some of the anxieties and fears we have about teachers and the education of LGBT students. In today's litigious environment, many teachers would feel extremely nervous about lending an individual student a book, let alone one that might be, even loosely, associated with homosexuality. So how do we overcome such fears? How might we appropriately and effectively harness the power of literature to help us understand our sexual identities and those of others?

I raise this question and attempt to answer some of them below, as I see a profound and important capacity for teaching and learning with literature that deals with LGBT histories, themes, politics, experiences, and identities. In particular, I argue that it is essential that we teach our teachers to critically examine how literary texts for and about young people shape thinking about sexual identity with the desire that this informs their own classroom practice in relation to sexual diversity. There is now, across the spectrum of young adult novels, online short stories, fan fiction, and children's picture books—that is, the whole gamut of texts that might come under the very broad umbrella of "child and young adult literature"—a recognizable body of literary texts that deal with sexual diversity, and it is to this group of texts that I now turn.

Two picture books in particular really set the cat among the pigeons when it came to representing queerness in children's texts: *Heather Has Two Mommies* (Newman, 1989) and *Daddy's Roommate* (Wilhoite, 1991). The American Library Association website listing the "100 most frequently challenged[2] books 1990–1999" has *Daddy's Roommate* at number two and *Heather Has Two Mommies* at nine (http://www.ala.org/). It is also interesting to note that in the list of most challenged books for the period of 2000–2009, another children's picture book about same-sex parenting came in fourth place: *And Tango Makes Three* (Richardson & Parnell, 2005), a story about same-sex attracted penguin-parents in the New York Zoo.[3]

And Tango Makes Three (Richardson & Parnell, 2005) might best be described as narrative nonfiction[4]; it is based on a true story but is quite clearly using the penguins' story to point toward human relationships. While some may wish to dismiss the humble picture book as somehow devoid of ideology, scholarship in the discipline has long since debunked this myth (John Steven's 1992 book *Language and Ideology in Children's Fiction* is a valuable treatise on this topic). Indeed, the active censorship around such a text tends to prove its ideological power. The negative reaction of some adults to a text such as this one acknowledges, at least subconsciously, that even a child's picture book is a vehicle for values and beliefs around the politics of same-sex attraction, same-sex parenting, and so on. After all, if adults did not believe these books had some power to influence or reflect what young people might think, they would hardly cause a stir.

Both fiction and nonfiction picture books such as those described above often provide an important counterpoint to the preponderance of both fiction and nonfiction books dealing with hetero-normative representations of family and reproduction. Indeed, they are evidence that alternatives to heteronormative texts are increasingly available to young readers. However, it is perhaps in the realm of young adult literature that we see the greatest development in literary representation of young LGBT people. For example, gay, lesbian, and bisexual characters, themes, and communities are now featured in the popular writing of authors such as Julie Anne Peters, Nancy Garden, David Levithan, and Brent Hartinger. While these names may not be immediately recognizable to readers outside of queer youth culture, their names are now synonymous with young adult fiction for and about young LGBT people.

This subgenre of texts is growing in scope and popularity. This is illustrated by the website www.gayya.org, which focuses on all things related to LGBT young adult fiction, including authors, characters, stories, themes, histories, and experiences. The website features book lists, reviews, and links to other literary resources, including publishers, as well as a space where interested users can post their responses to LGBTI texts. Discussions on this site also include reference to fan fiction and to reader responses to nonqueer texts that are interpreted from a queer perspective (the *Twilight* and *The Hunger Games* series being popular examples).

In line with the new popularity of such texts in queer youth culture, some studies have now been made into the inclusion of LGBT-focused children's texts in primary and secondary school curricula, including research by Sanders and Mathis (2013), Blackburn and Clark (2009, 2011), Blackburn and Buckley (2005), and Schall and Kaufman (2003). However, this research is quite limited; as Blackburn and Clark (2011) put it, "Scholarship focused on reading and becoming readers of LGBT-themed children's and young adult texts, whether in the U.S. or international school-settings, is incredibly sparse" (p. 150). Even fewer contemporary studies focus on the use of such literature in the education of preservice teachers, with the exception of Hermann-Wilmarth's "More than Book Talk: Preservice Teacher Dialogue After Reading Gay and Lesbian Children's Literature" (2010) and Steffel and Renzi-Keener's study titled "Breaking Down the Last Taboo: LGBT Young Adult Literature in the Preservice Classroom" (2009).

Hermann-Wilmarth's (2010) research is a case study of her own attempts to do teaching and learning with LGBT-themed children's literature. While a small-scale research project with a limited number of preservice student participants, it is significant insofar as the author rather candidly relays the difficulties some participants had in overcoming prejudice and engaging in productive dialogue. Sanders and Mathis (2013) suggest that the "saturation of LGBT themes" within the resources they discuss "demonstrated that quality texts do exist," and yet the authors do little more than recommend the (perhaps rather obvious) need for "a pedagogy that could be used in classrooms to discuss texts with LGBT characters and themes" (p. 14).

Despite its title, the main focus of Steffel and Renzi-Kaufman's (2009) research is not how the authors choose and use LGBT literature in teaching and learning with education students (this part of their article is all too briefly discussed on pages 31 and 32), but is rather more interested in the social conditions around homophobia that the authors see as influencing student reactions to such texts when they are introduced into the university curriculum. With that said, I cite this article as it pertains to the following in which I more specifically deal with teaching and learning using queer-oriented resources with preservice teachers, and my observations do intersect with some of the general ideas and concerns raised in this article.

Indeed, the articles mentioned above raise a number of general concerns relevant to this chapter, which I have enumerated and described in the following:

- The teaching and learning with LGBT texts covered in these studies often assumed a heterosexual and/or homophobic reader as a starting point.
- This has the unintended consequence of positioning the LGBT subject as always and invariably "Other."
- The use of such texts in schools was most often a one-text or one-class phenomenon: The projects cited showed little evidence of sustained use of such texts or integration into broader curriculum.
- Such texts were in most cases used as a springboard for talking about homosexuality as a kind of "social issue" rather than as part of history, culture, and lived experience in its own right. Moreover, the stories/texts used in some cases reaffirmed the idea that there are negative consequences for people who "come out."
- Indeed, the focus tended to be on reading thematically in terms of the representation of issues/problems/difference—almost always framing sexual diversity in pejorative terms.
- In some of the cases covered in these articles, students were given the option to refuse studying a text with LGBT themes, something that would be unlikely to be tolerated or offered in relation to a text proposing heteronormative values or themes.
- Some of the stories and the discussions they generated did little more than perpetuate stereotypes. On occasion they were used as a window for an assumed heterosexual reader to gain insight into the experience of the Other but rarely were they employed as a mirror-text for LGBT identifying students.

- The available research does not fully investigate whether basic principles of critical literacy are in place before teaching and learning begins; for example, students were not observed participating in a discussion of the connection between narration and values/beliefs before thematic discussion began.
- Moreover, there was little or no evidence of connecting discussion of form and narration with ideology and reader positioning
- The studies tended to focus on the use of texts with fairly obvious gay and lesbian characters or themes, with much less focus on stories relating to other identity positions under the broad umbrella of "queer."
- Queer reading of "straight" texts was similarly absent/extremely rare, missing the opportunity to equip students to interrogate and analyze all kinds of texts from queer perspectives.

After reading this précis of approaches to using LGBT texts in classroom settings, it would be easy enough to despair of the prospects for such activities to contribute in positive ways to the celebration and knowledge of sexual and gender diversity. However, it strikes me that the deficits identified by these studies act as a clarion call for more work to be done to educate teachers on how to use LGBT literary resources more effectively. With this in mind I now want to propose a range of simple but very effective strategies for educating preservice teachers about using child and young literature to do teaching and learning around sexual and gender identity and diversity. In order to explain these ideas I will draw on my own experiences as a teacher educator and as a researcher and writer in the field of child and young adult literature generally.

Before I do so, however, I wish to state openly and plainly that my experience as a queer-identifying male also informs my approach. I do so in order not to overlook the expertise gained from lived experience, as much as from scholarship or professional practice. That is, I know what I know not only and exclusively because of my experience as a teacher of teachers, but also because it intersects with who I am, with an important aspect of my history and identity and how I am in the world. In theorizing this idea of embodied knowledge in education, Johnson (1989) puts it thus: "Knowledge is not some fixed and static thing, but rather an activity (of knowing) by means of which we are able to transform our experience" (p. 363). In effect, I am arguing that we should consider the impact that our embodied knowledge has when we teach; that is, the knowledge that comes from our personal histories and experiences, our lived literacy of a certain realm of ideas, practices, discourses and ways of being.

I mention this as I regret that there have been times when students have raised an idea that would be most effectively discussed if I could speak more openly, at least in general terms, of my life experience. My first recommendation therefore is that we reassess the degree to which teacher educators are able to acknowledge and implement this kind of knowledge in their teaching and learning practices. It is my wish that within the grown-up world of the university setting my sexual identity can be acknowledged as a source of knowledge, and as a resource when planning curriculum. This is because the open acknowledgment of one's subjective position may provide an important model for students to question their own subjective response to texts; if I model the capacity to identify, and even question, "where I'm coming from," it is likely that my students may feel similarly free to do the same.

However, it is also important that teachers and students are encouraged to self-monitor when using anecdotal and personal viewpoints in discussion. Many of my students will have received this piece of feedback from me on their assignments: "To what degree is this subjective viewpoint supported by evidence from the text you are studying?" Getting the balance right between acknowledging that we bring subjective values, beliefs, and experiences to the way we interpret stories and making sure that we are also able to look at things from a range of perspectives, is critical. This balance is, I believe, part of the scene-setting that must go hand in hand with teacher education around sexuality.

By scene-setting, I am referring to the creation of a respectful and yet open forum for the sharing of ideas within the context of the university classroom. This means reinforcing the idea that while different reading/ interpreting positions are possible and encouraged, teaching and learning using LGBT texts does not mean a green card for homophobic statements or discrimination toward other students, regardless of how they identify in terms of sexual orientation or gender. This does not mean placing heavy emphasis on homophobia and discrimination at the outset because, as some of the studies on the use of LGBT literature in education demonstrated, to do so immediately frames any discussion of sexual diversity in terms of fear, hatred, and Otherness (Blackburn & Clark, 2011; Steffel & Renzi-Keener, 2009). In my experience, asking students to collaborate in peer monitoring of language and behavior when studying sexuality tends to be more effective than a strict, top-down, teacher-led approach.

At the same time, we also need classroom spaces for preservice teachers where awkward questions can be asked and answered. For example, some years ago I played a short documentary film about transgender youth for a class studying representations of identity in young adult texts. Afterwards a student tentatively put his hand up to admit that he just "did not get it." He very quietly asked, "I mean, does that girl have a *penis*?" While the question was an uncomfortable one to ask/to be asked, it was an opportunity for us to talk about the various ways, beyond genitalia, that we might be male and female, or indeed, somewhere in between. It was also an opening for us to discuss why such a question might be confronting or offensive to some trans* and intersex people. Over time I have learned that while general rules of engagement can be established to guide discussion and avoid traumatizing each other with reliance on stereotypes, generalizations, and assumptions, this must be balanced with a preparedness to answer difficult questions and to see them as an opportunity to progress, rather than retard, learning.

The second basic point I wish to raise concerns scope, access, and exposure. Little progress can be made unless preservice teachers are given enough time to spend studying the diversity of sexual and gender identity and how it is represented in the literary resources they might use. Therefore, a good starting point would be to ensure that a range of representations in a range of texts are introduced as part of the core curriculum in teacher education, with ample time and resources for fulsome and developed study of sexual diversity. This time, I might add, should amount to days and weeks, not just a few hours.

Before beginning work with texts, it is necessary to involve preservice teachers in discussion and analysis of agenda setting and ideology in curriculum generally. Indeed, it is important to think about who chooses texts set for study and how they are chosen. Along these lines, discussions with preservice teachers around the presence/absence of LGBT-oriented texts in primary and secondary classrooms is an important starting point. For example, with my first-year education students I conduct a tour of the university library's collection of child and young literature, and ask them to identify the range of/absence of identities, histories, and experiences represented within the collection. The students quickly find that, despite my own attempts and that of the library staff to obtain resources that do not always and invariably depict the world as populated exclusively by straight, white, middle-class, Western people, the majority of texts still fall into this category.

Fostering a positive relationship between students and library staff in the tertiary environment is important; it is in liaison with experts in the collection and management of literary resources that students will become adept at locating a wide range of resources that engage with ideas about young people and sexuality. This is particularly important as so many primary and secondary sources, both academic and literary, are now available in online mode, and as such represent a new and exciting opportunity for preservice teachers looking to go beyond the books and journals housed on library shelves.

Teaching and learning that involves digital resources reflects the world of the implied reader, especially when it comes to young adult literature. Thus, ensuring preservice teachers are exposed to a range of text types within the broad genre of child and young adult literature is valuable, as getting kids inspired to read and interact with literature can be half the battle, before connecting this more broadly to a discussion of sexual identity. In light of this I recommend that teacher educators do not simply line up a small selection of gay and lesbian-oriented picture books or novels for study at the undergraduate level, but ask their education students to study short stories, poetry, graphic novels, and online fan fiction as alternatives to traditional text types.

At this point you may be asking, what should teacher educators do with these texts once we find them? To begin with, some groundwork around critical literacy must be in place before tackling the values and beliefs operating in LGBT texts. From my long experience teaching about politics and ideology in texts for young people, it is necessary first to equip students with a basic understanding of representations of identity in the postmodern/poststructuralist context.

Realistically, some first-year university students will require very basic definitional outlines of terms such as *race*, *class*, and *gender*, not to mention terms such as *gay*, *lesbian*, *bisexual*, *transgender*, *intersex*, and *queer*. They may be adept at using some of these terms in everyday life, however, the degree to which they understand how they are mobilized in a range of academic and educational, let alone public and personal, contexts is debatable. While it is important that students feel comfortable and familiar with identity descriptors, at the same time it is important that they understand at least some of the complexities and nuances that go along with their deployment.

In hand with this is the basic requirement that students look beyond common assumptions about children and children's literature (Nodelman & Reimer, 2003, pp. 79–100). That is, students must question their own ideas about what texts for young people do in order to go beyond the idea that this field of literature is merely for play and entertainment. It is critical that students be made aware of the role children's literature plays in setting out values and beliefs and in shaping ideas about what children and childhood are/should be. The ideological nature of children's literature is well documented (Stephens, 1992), and alerting preservice teachers to this area of scholarship introduces them to the idea that whatever books they use in a classroom carry with them certain ways of viewing and understanding the world.

Students must then be taught to identify how texts position their readers in relation to values and beliefs around identity, whether this be in relation to race, class, ethnicity, nationality, gender, or indeed sexuality.

To do this, students must learn how to apply some of the basic elements of narrative theory. Familiarity with narrative strategies such as closure, the use of an implied reader/author, reliable and unreliable narration, point of view, and focalization go a long way to understanding how texts, often subtly and without intention, endorse some ways of being, thinking, and acting and not others (Culler, 2000). Thus, some grasp of form, genre, narration, and representation and the operation of ideology in texts for and about young people is very important as a skillset to apply to texts that represent sexuality.

With a basic grasp of literary theory, it is then possible to identify, understand, and analyze both surface and passive ideology operating within texts. That is, true critical literacy involves a capacity to engage with both the intended and unintended values and beliefs such texts endorse. This is especially important for interrogating heteronormative texts. For example, my own students had quite a bit to say about *The Hunger Games'* Katniss Everdeen along these lines (Collins, 2008). They were interested in the idea that the text positioned them to cheer for Katniss as a representative of "kick-ass" young womanhood. By examining language, closure, narration, and so on, these students were able to see a range of subtle messages about gender identity at play in the text. In particular, they successfully argued, with the evidence they gleaned from applying narrative theory, that young women are encouraged by this story to "play the game" of heterosexual romantic love, even if it is "just for the cameras," with the ultimate prize at the end of the trilogy being the opportunity to "settle down" into marriage and motherhood (with just the occasional afternoon of bloodsport on the side!).

In effect, this sort of reading/interpretation can be described as a queer approach, whereby a seemingly heteronormative text is interrogated for the way it represents values about sexuality and gender. In this sense, discussions around sexual diversity do not always have to extend outward from stories which more obviously and explicitly deal with LGBT themes and characters. As I indicated earlier, testing straight stories for their queer content can be very rewarding indeed.

For some university students who are ardent fans of popular YA fiction, this can be somewhat confronting. And yet it is very important to ask such students to approach their favorite texts from a range of different perspectives that acknowledge, but ultimately challenge them to go beyond, their initial subjective responses. One way of doing this is to ask them to argue against their own interpretations by finding alternative evidence in the textual material in front of them. Another way to encourage reading across subjective positions is to ask students to rewrite parts of the narrative from the point of view of minor/marginal characters. Such exercises are an ideal field in which to consider questions such as Who speaks? Who sees? Who controls the story? Whose perspective is valued? Whose perspective is missing or sidelined?

Indeed, creative practice that asks students to identify and "play" with the values and beliefs of a text can produce interesting results. It is a process of understanding by doing; for example, asking a student to rewrite the ending of a story and change its outcome may reveal how an implied reader is positioned to cheer for one type of character and feel pity or disdain for another. Such an exercise can also lead to valuable discussions about authenticity. What happens when we speak or write on behalf of another person or group? How does this shape their identity for an implied reader?

Any work done with literary texts should acknowledge that not all books that feature queer characters or themes are, *ipso facto*, queer-friendly. As the studies surveyed by Blackburn and Clark (2009, 2011) show, some LGBT picture books and novels can inadvertently perpetuate stereotypes and/or create pathology around sexual diversity. Take for example the much-lauded picture book *10,000 Dresses* (Ewert, 2008). On the surface of things the picture book encourages the reader to accept that Bailey identifies as a girl and should be supported in this aim. However, on closer inspection, the picture book endorses a very particular kind of hyperfemininity for Bailey (and, it might be argued, for her dowdy, poor, depressed mum). Happiness for Bailey cannot be in the middle ground between one gender and another; she must be clearly and unambiguously codified as female, in the most stereotypical of terms. Moreover, to achieve this it is implied that Bailey must draw away from her lower-class family, who fail to recognize her true identity, as if to suggest that discrimination is somehow more likely or even belongs to poor, uneducated people.

Don't get me wrong, *10,000 Dresses* (Ewert, 2008) is in many ways a very valuable book (being one of the few to actually depict a trans kid as a main protagonist) and a great resource for the classroom (it generates discussion very quickly). However, my point is that teacher educators must be at pains to demonstrate to their students that choosing a book for use in the classroom simply because it features a gay theme or a trans character is not enough. When preservice teachers ask, "Well then, what books would you recommend?" I always answer that it very much depends on the context and the aims they had in mind. Sometimes, choosing a really popular text, such as a book from the *Twilight* series (Stefanie Meyers, 2005–2008), the *Hunger Games* series (Suzanne Collins, 2008–2010) or the *Harry Potter* series (J. K. Rowling, 1997–2007) is a good place to start. As I have argued above, there are certainly queer ways of (re)reading texts with which students may already have some degree of familiarity.

However, I also encourage them to look for texts that create a degree of complexity and nuance around queer characters and stories. An example of this kind of reading material is Doug MacLeod's novel for young readers, *Tumble Turn* (2003). The protagonist, Dom, is a primary school kid who seems to be registering high on the "gaydar" of his parents, friends, and schoolmates. And yet, through the use of humor as a narrative strategy, MacLeod reveals that Dom is in many ways the most successful and psychologically "together" character of his immediate circle of friends and family, resisting the idea that we should pathologize difference. Without giving away the ending, the book turns the tables on heteronormative relationships as the ideal, at the same time as it refuses to answer the reader's question, "Is Dom gay?" Rather, it subtly suggests that some people simply do not fit neatly the identity categories we have assigned them. I mention this book in particular as it is an example of a text that is not afraid of nuance and complexity, at the same time as it takes a rather honest, cringe-worthy and oftentimes humorous approach to representing puberty and the development of sexual identity.

To extend upon a point made earlier, to really delve into the complexities of a text such as *Tumble Turn* (MacLeod, 2003) requires time. The studies on the use of literature as a resource for teaching and learning on sexuality mentioned above consistently point out that one of the major limitations in the use of LGBT-oriented texts in education is the lack of time given to reading, analysis, and discussion (Blackburn & Clark, 2011), and this rings true for tertiary spaces as much the primary (elementary) or secondary classroom. Too often so-called minority identities are lumped together as a focal point for teaching and learning in a module or single class without the time or scope to tease out the intersections between such identities or their differences (Carmen et al., 2011).

However, the focus does not always need to be on formal classroom settings, with their inherent time constraints and focus on clear-cut learning outcomes proven via assessment. Positive results can also occur when the process is allowed to wander out of the formal classroom setting into community-based book clubs, where participants are invested in the choice of book for reading and discussion (Blackburn & Clark, 2011). To this end, I suggest that teacher educators consider establishing/becoming involved with extracurricular reading groups for students who wish to specialize in teaching and learning around sexual diversity using child and young adult literature. These may in turn be linked with other community- and/or university-based reading groups organized by queer and allied people. Indeed, queer book clubs abound in major cities in Australia, Europe, and the United States, some of which are also available to participants online. In addition, many universities now include LGBT resource centers that also host these kinds of activities—very pleasingly, they are simply too numerous to list here.

I mention the idea of specialization in the previous paragraph not to suggest that teaching and learning about sexuality and sexual diversity via child and young adult literature should be quarantined for a select group of education students. On the contrary, I think it should be mandatory for undergraduate preservice teachers. However, the carrot is needed more than the stick. If students are given special credit or acknowledgment for furthering their basic skills in this area, they become especially attractive to those schools looking to employ teachers who can successfully do teaching and learning around sexuality and sexual diversity through their knowledge of child and young adult literature. Anecdotally, I would go so far as to say that the alumni who have worked with me to gain critical literacy skills in this area have been highly successful in gaining employment and report back that they employ these skills in a range of different aspects of their teaching practice when education around sexuality and identity occurs in their classrooms. It is for this reason that I recommend to teacher educators that they make special mention of this kind of student expertise if asked to act as a referee for graduates seeking employment.

Thinking about the next generation of teachers excites me. This is because I remain optimistic that, like me, students will encounter teachers who will aid, rather than retard, the natural development of their identities. I feel extremely fortunate that, at an important juncture in the development of my sexual identity, I had a teacher who shared with me the power of literature to transform and enrich existence. For this reason, I feel equally fortunate that the past decade of my life has been spent sharing this revelation with preservice teachers, many of whom will pass this on to the students in their care.

The material above is not meant to be a definitive treatise on sexuality education, but rather is an attempt to isolate one aspect of this process—the use of child and young adult literature—for particular attention. It is neither a proscriptive or exhaustive list of ideas that I offer, but rather a set of pathways that some readers may wish to explore further. In proposing these ideas I do not wish to merely lament the status quo, wallowing in the idea that whatever teachers do in the classroom around sexuality is likely to be flawed. Yes, pitfalls abound. However, it is my hope that some of the practical suggestions around teaching and learning I offer above will be of use to teacher educators and preservice teachers alike. After all, as my friend discovered in the queue of a university café, we must start out somewhere.

NOTES

1. I wish to acknowledge that the inspiration for the title of this chapter came after reading the *Writing Themselves In* (Hillier et al., 2010) report: A remarkable and very valuable piece of public research and scholarship on the lives of young same-sex attracted and gender-questioning young people in the Australian context.
2. The American Library association describes a "challenged" book as one that is subject to "an attempt to remove or restrict materials, based upon the objections of a person or group" (http://www.ala.org/bbooks/about/).
3. Readers may be interested to know that another work of children's literature came in first place on the 2000–2009 list: J. K. Rowling's *Harry Potter* series.
4. Nonfiction informational (as opposed to narrative) picture books on LGBTIQ topics are few and far between. More numerous however are non-fiction prose publications. For a list, refer to the university of Wisconsin's Cooperative Child Resource Center's website: http://ccbc.education.wisc.edu/booksearch/default.asp?TipsDisplay=none/

REFERENCES

Blackburn, M., & Buckley, J. (2005). Teaching queer-inclusive language arts. *Journal of Adolescent & Adult Literacy, 49*(3), 202–212.

Blackburn, M., & Clark, C. T. (2009). Reading LGBT-themed literature with young people: What's possible? *The English Journal, 98*(4), 25–32.

Blackburn, M., & Clark, C. T. (2011). Becoming readers of literature with LGBT themes: In and out of the classroom. In A. S. Wolf, K. Coats, P. Enciso, & C. A. Jenkins (Eds.), *The handbook of research on children's and young adult literature* (pp. 148–163). New York, NY: Routledge.

Carmen, M., Mitchell, A., Schlichthorst, M., & Smith, A. (2011). Teacher training in sexuality education in Australia: How well are teachers prepared for the job? *Sexual Health, 8*(3), 269–271.

Collins, S. (2008). *The hunger games.* Leamington Spa, Ontario, Canada: Scholastic.

Culler, J. (2000). *Literary theory: A very short introduction.* Oxford, England: Oxford University Press.

Ewert, M. (2008). *10,000 dresses.* New York, NY: Seven Stories Press.

Gowen, L. K., & Winges-Yanez, N. (2014). Lesbian, gay, bisexual, transgender, queer and questioning youths: Perspectives of inclusive school-based sexuality education. *Journal of Sex Research, 51*(7), 788–800.

Hermann-Wilmarth, J. (2010). More than book talk: Preservice teacher dialogue after reading gay and lesbian children's literature. *Language Arts, 87*(3), 188–198.

Hillier, L., Jones, T., Monagle, M., Overington, N., Gahan, L., Blackman, J., & Mitchell, A. (2010). *Writing themselves in: The third national study on the sexual health and well-being of same-sex attracted and gender questioning young people*. Melbourne, Victoria: Australian Research Centre in Sex, Health & Society, Latrobe University.

Johnson, M. (1989). Embodied knowledge. *Curriculum Inquiry, 19*(4), 361–377.

MacLeod, D. (2003). *Tumble turn*. Camberwell, Australia: Puffin.

Marshall, D. (2011). The queer archive: Teaching and learning sexualities in Australia. *Transformations: The Journal of Inclusive Scholarship and Pedagogy, 21*(2), 36–46.

Mudrey, R., & Medina-Adams, A. (2006). Attitudes, perceptions, and knowledge of pre-service teachers regarding the educational isolation of sexual minority youth. *Journal of Homosexuality, 51*(4), 63–90.

Newman, L. (2000). *Heather has two mommies*. Los Angeles, CA: Alyson Wonderland.

Nodelman, P., & Reimer, M. (2003). *The pleasures of children's literature* (3rd ed.). Boston, MA: Allyn & Bacon.

Ollis, D., Harrison, L., & Maharaj, C. (2013). *Sexuality education matters: Preparing pre-service teachers to teach sexuality education*. Geelong, Victoria, Australia: Deakin.

Richardson, J., & Parnell, P. (2005). *And Tango makes three*. New York, NY: Simon & Shuster.

Robinson, K. H., & Ferfolja, T. (2001). 'What are we doing this for?': Dealing with lesbian and gay issues in teacher education. *British Journal of Sociology Education, 22*(1), 121–133.

Sanders, A. M., & Mathis, J. B. (2013). Gay and lesbian literature in the classroom: Can gay themes overcome heteronormativity? *Journal of Praxis in Multicultural Education, 7*(1), 1–18.

Schall, J., & Kaufman, G. (2003). Exploring literature with gay and lesbian characters in the elementary school. *Journal of Children's Literature, 9*(1), 36–45.

Simkinson, M. (2009). "Sexuality isn't just about sex": Pre-service teachers' shifting constructs of sexuality education. *Sex Education, 9*(4), 421–436.

Steffel, S., & Renzi-Keener, L. (2009). Breaking down the last taboo: LGBT young adult literature in the preservice classroom. *Language Arts, 24*(2), 29–36.

Stephens, J. (1992). *Language and ideology in children's fiction*. Harlow, England: Longman.

Willhoite, M. (2008). *Daddy's roommate*. Los Angeles, CA: Alyson Wonderland.

CHAPTER 9

"YOU DON'T HAVE TO THINK ABOUT IT IN THAT WAY"

Deconstructing Teacher Assumptions About LGBTIQ Students

Elizabeth Dinkins and Patrick Englert

Educators are working in institutions and, in many cases, creating classroom spaces that promote heteronormativity or centralize heterosexuality as the norm (Nelson, 2009). The 2013 GLSEN (Kosciw, Greytak, Palmer, & Boesen, 2014) survey suggests that 56% of LGBTIQ students experience discrimination at school and that schools are unwelcoming and unsafe for the majority of LGBTIQ students. More alarming is the finding that schools are largely underprepared and lack the necessary resources to support LGBTIQ students. Hostile and underprepared school environments lead to negative impacts on LGBTIQ students' educational success and well-being (Kosciw et al., 2014). When schools become hostile environments, students disengage from the school community. Just under one third of LGBTIQ students report missing one day a month due to feeling unsafe and vulnerable, and over two thirds of these students reported avoiding school functions. Absenteeism can greatly influence students' academic engagement and success by decreas-

Queering Classrooms: Personal Narratives and Educational Practices to Support LGBTQ Youth in Schools, pp. 127–144
Copyright © 2017 by Information Age Publishing

ing instructional time and potentially lowering grade point averages. Avoiding school-based functions and extracurricular activities inhibits students from feeling connected to the school community. Both absenteeism and avoidance, two ways in which LGBITQ students deal with unsafe school environments, are indicative of students who may develop long-term negative associations with education (Kosciw et al., 2014).

Scholarship discusses LGBTIQ students as being invisible (Kosciw & Diaz, 2008; Sears, 2013) in the classroom, meaning that LGBTIQ identities are not recognized or addressed by the teacher. At both the school and classroom levels, students are assumed to be heterosexual, embody traditional gender performances, and have heterosexual parents. This assumption erases the identity of these students and enables policies and procedures to exclude LGBTIQ students and their families. This exclusion spans across academic and social domains. Academic disciplines like biology, history, and English curricula often fail to address LGBTIQ topics and identities while simultaneously employing heteronormative frames (Castro & Sujak, 2014). When social activities like games, school dances, and clubs assume the heterosexuality of students, LGBTIQ students are less likely to form peer relationships where they feel safe to express their identities, connect with their peers, or become involved in the school community (Castro & Sujak, 2014). Invisibility engenders negative impacts upon educational growth and personal development (Bailey, 2005; Sears, 2013). The word "invisibility" connotes something that is unseen or unknown, in this case LGBTIQ students. We argue that LGBTIQ students are not invisible, but ignored by educators. Educators ignore the presence and needs of LGBTIQ students by acknowledging that these students are different but refusing to act in inclusive and anti-oppressive ways. This disregard is grounded in multiple factors; some of these include heterosexism, discomfort, lack of awareness, and fear of retribution by administrators. Fredman, Schultz, and Hoffman (2015) found that teachers associate LGBTIQ topics with layers of controversy reflective of potential backlash from administrators and parents, risks of breaking perceived "rules" (p. 65) about such topics, and uncertainty of their role in these discussions; thus, teachers avoid introducing or addressing LGBTIQ issues. Clark and Blackburn (2009) suggest that preservice teachers are underprepared to teach LGBTIQ-themed texts and struggle with the pressure "to be a value-free enterprise," that is, "neutral and a-political" (p. 25). Despite the perception that schools should be a neutral zone, Kumashiro (2000, 2001, 2002) and others (Asher, 2007; Berg, 2012, 2013; Boyd et al., 2006; Young, 2009) have established the responsibility of schools and teachers to proactively create anti-oppressive learning experiences that embrace the complex identities and empower the role of LGBTIQ students in all classrooms. This responsibility requires teachers and teacher educators to rethink not only the content they teach, but the methods, assumptions, and relationships replicated throughout school culture. Kumashiro (2002) asserts that teaching for social change coexists with a resistance to change because of educators' tendency to repeat practices that affirm who we are and what we believe. For LGBTIQ students, this repetition leads to the perpetuation of heteronormative schools and classrooms. Although these repetitive practices protect educators and learners from the potential emotional crisis of recognizing one's own role in oppressive practices, they limit the possibility of anti-oppressive learning.

LGBTIQ students have historically been classified as victims, but current scholarship reframes them as agents of change with the potential to impact the heteronormative context and environment of schools; Blackburn (2004) suggests that students are victims and agents, emphasizing the importance of acknowledging both roles. Teachers have a responsibility for the difficult task of challenging and supporting (Sanford, 1966) LGBTIQ students to develop resiliency when victimized and to realize the potential of being an empowered agent. It is imperative for LGBTIQ students to not be ignored by teachers, as adolescent sexual and physiological development is occurring, a process through which many students begin to explore and understand their identities for the first time (Bailey, 2005). Teachers serve in the critical role of providing support to LGBTIQ students (Kosciw, Diaz, & Greytak, 2008), challenging norms present within the classroom and school environment (Blackburn & Smith, 2010), and ensuring anti-oppressive learning is occurring through the inclusion of LGBTIQ texts, history, and experiences (Blackburn & Buckley, 2005; Sanders & Mathis, 2013).

PURPOSE

In this chapter we will share vignettes from a qualitative study that investigated how a teacher and students in a middle school classroom negotiated meaning when studying a text with a gay character. Two key factors converged to provide a unique lens for contemplating the ways in which teachers and teacher educators can create anti-oppressive learning communities (Kumashiro, 2001) and meet the needs of LGBTIQ students: the presence of a gay character in the novel and two students who identified as lesbians. Incorporating texts with LGBTIQ representations can provide students and teachers with the raw materials for recognizing multiple perspectives and developing critical frameworks for understanding. Inclusion alone, however, does not create positive change (Blackburn, 2005; Kumashiro, 2001; Schieble, 2012). Educators also need pedagogical methods that facilitate discussions of LGBTIQ topics, embrace moments of discomfort, dismantle knowledge that perpetuates oppressive practices, and create opportunities to explore nuances, themes, and experiences of LGBTIQ identities (Kumashiro, 2001; Lipkin, 1995; Meyer, 2007). Our findings established that, despite good intentions, the teacher missed opportunities for honoring the experiences of lesbian and gay students, empowering them as learners, and creating classrooms that maximize possibilities for positive change. Teacher and students discussed the gay character in relation to thematic understanding of the text, but the teacher's approach tended to limit exploration and perpetuate a heteronormative perspective. Students, on the other hand, engaged the text and each other in both positive and heterosexist ways. These interactions, both teacher and student initiated, demonstrate the opportunities made possible when studying a text with a gay character as well as indicate the need for educator training on LGBTIQ issues and anti-oppressive learning.

Case studies offer preservice and in-service educators the opportunity to contemplate complex, context-rich, real-world challenges from theoretical and applied perspectives. We believe the vignettes presented in this chapter offer teachable moments for preservice and in-service teachers, and teacher educators to analyze the interactions and decisions of the participants, engage in critical self-reflection to establish alternative actions and reactions to enable positive change. Each vignette derives from data collected in the form of observations, interviews with teacher and students, and samples of student writing. Before presenting the vignettes, we describe the context of the original study. We then present each missed opportunity as it happened in the classroom followed by a discussion of what might have been possible had the teacher questioned her assumptions, embraced multiple perspectives, and valued opportunities for unlearning as equally important to learning. We share the vignettes in their natural sequence to demonstrate the cumulative nature of possibilities presented by students and teachers engaged in a study of literature featuring a gay character.

Context

Our study occurred over a nine-week period in an 8th-grade language arts classroom when the curriculum dictated students study a common novel. The teacher originally selected *Tears of a Tiger* by Sharon Draper (2006), but school leadership delivered copies of *After Tupac and D Foster* by Jacqueline Woodson (2008) and mandated she use this text for the unit. The school, located in an urban neighborhood, served a diverse student population where over 75% of the students received free or reduced lunch. The class consisted of 24 students evenly divided between girls and boys, with 11 African American students, 11 Caucasian students, a Hispanic student, an African student, and a Caucasian teacher with eight years of experience. Two of these students (one African American and one Caucasian) identified as lesbian. The curriculum required the study of a whole-class novel and *After Tupac and D Foster* was assigned to 8th-grade classrooms in an attempt to promote the use of culturally relevant texts. The novel tells a coming-of-age story about three friends: a daughter of a single mother, a daughter from a large family, and a foster daughter who wanders in and out of the girls' lives between their 11th and 13th birthdays. The girls bond over their love of double-dutch, Tupac Shakur's music, and their common desire to understand the challenges of growing up. A secondary character in this novel is Tash, the openly gay brother of one of the girls. Described as a "queen" (p. 59), Tash is a talented piano player who serves jail time for a crime he did not commit. The discussions about and around Tash provided us with the opportunity to observe, in rich detail, the stances and interactions of students and teacher as they made meaning of this gay character and their worlds.

VIGNETTES

Each vignette, presented through thick description, focuses on a central theme that emerged from analyzing teacher and student interactions. Because literacy is understood as an inherently social practice involving the ways in which individuals interact with, make meaning from, and produce spoken and written language (Barton & Hamilton, 2005), we paid particular attention to the discourse of students and teacher. The first vignette captures how the teacher introduced Tash, prefaced the chapters in which he plays a significant role, and set expectations for student interactions about the character. The second vignette, derived mostly from teacher interviews, illuminates the teacher's assumptions and decision-making about student attitudes and needs. The third vignette depicts how school culture and classroom-based social interaction illustrate the ways in which teacher and students create a classroom culture that communicated oppressive or anti-oppressive practices. The final vignette captures what Asher (2007) calls "micro-processes" (p. 66) of oppression and resistance as students act as agents to claim a space for understanding Tash's character even when the teacher and other students attempt to minimize it.

Vignette #1: Be Mature

There are just a few minutes left in class. Students are returning to the desks after putting their novels away. The teacher calls everyone's attention to the front of the room.

> Alright. I need to give you a heads-up about the next day's reading before we get to it. I need your attention and I need everybody to be mature. In this book, they just mentioned in Chapter 2, some of you picked up on it—I could tell by your reaction, but most of you did not—they refer to Tash as a queen. In this book, the older brother is gay.

Students giggle. The teacher holds her hand out,

> Hold up. But in 1995, when this book was written, it wasn't as open as it is now. It was not something that people wanted to openly admit to. People necessarily, especially in some neighborhoods, did not take kindly to people being openly gay. So, stop. Stop.

Giggling stops and students look at her.

> In chapter three you are going to learn more about this character and some things that happen to this character strictly because of his sexual orientation. So when we read that, I want you to focus on the fact that—the timeframe, okay. First of all, the fact that they called him a queen. That's not politically correct. That's not how you refer to somebody who would be gay, but in 1995 that is how you would refer to someone who is gay. Just be aware of the timeframe and what is going on. You all know when people say things like hate crimes what that means—that someone is mean towards somebody and has a crime against somebody strictly because they are hating on that person. So be aware of that because you are introduced to that character more in the next chapter. I don't want people getting so caught up in what I'm saying that you don't follow along with the story.

The bell rings and students are dismissed.

Students file into class the next day, grab their books, and make their way to their desks. The teacher directs, "Okay, go to page 32, Chapter three." Most students open books to follow along as the teacher reads aloud. A few students look around the room. Two students turn in their desks to face each other, mouthing words in silent conversation. Tash is introduced. The teacher reads the words "gay" and "homosexual." Students giggle and glance at each other. She stops, looks at the kids and says, "How mature are we going to be here?" Students get quiet again. The teacher begins again and reads, "homos" two more times. Students chuckle more quietly. The teacher looks up from her book and says,

"Stop. Be mature when we are reading about Tash. We already know he's gay. We already know that this is about him, so we don't need to be giggling or anything. Focus and really pay attention." She goes back to reading.

The teacher later explained why she prefaced the chapter the way she did:

> I wanted to make sure that they didn't get so hung up on me saying "homos"—because the word homo is in there and that he was hanging out down in Greenwich Village with his homo friends—that they miss the meaning of that chapter. They are still eighth graders and they are immature. I thought if I read that then they would laugh or go "ahhh" or be so shocked that they would miss the meaning of that chapter. There are some very important things in there.

Setting Expectations and Framing Possibilities

For most educators, LGBTIQ topics are uncharted territory met with hesitation, avoidance, and insecurity (Clark & Blackburn, 2009; Schall & Kauffman, 2003; Young, 2009; Zack, Mannheim, & Alfano, 2010), and this teacher is no different. The limited exploration of these topics may be due to the potential for discomfort and controversy. Literature can act as a conduit for social justice and developing student understanding of LGBTIQ identities (Sims, 1982). Characters, contexts, and problems can function as windows into different perspectives or mirrors, prompting inward reflection about one's beliefs, actions, and reactions (Botelho & Rudman, 2009). Tash provides both teacher and students an opportunity for engaging in the challenges, emotions, and convictions of a gay character, but this learning may not come without difficulties. Discussing LGBTIQ topics opens doors for differing opinions and a range of emotional reactions that teachers are unable to control (Kumashiro, 2001). This teacher is concerned about her students' reactions and their maturity when talking about Tash. She is particularly worried that the language of the text might somehow distract students from the overall meaning of the chapter. She recognizes her eighth graders' tendency to be "immature." Her concern is partially substantiated; her students respond with giggling and side-glances. Her response, however, focuses on managing her students, not building student understanding. In fact, it is possible that she let her concern minimize their interpretation of the character as well as the overall themes of the text. She explains that students focusing on Tash's sexuality may distract them from "very important things" in the chapter. While her intention may have been to insure that students be respectful of the text and the character, her focus on stopping immature behavior precluded the possibility of establishing and expanding student understanding of LGBTIQ topics.

The questions remain: What could be done differently? How does a teacher support student learning about LGBTIQ topics while also ensuring an inclusive classroom climate of safety where students are willing to explore and value multiple perspectives? This teacher believed students should study literature to learn about themselves and the world around them. She regularly used literature to invite students to consider issues of race and class, but she had no experience working with texts incorporating LGBTIQ topics. Further, she admitted she would not have selected this text if the decision had been left up to her. With professional development and support, she may have been able to approach the text and the character of Tash differently. Research investigating how students of all ages engage with LGBTIQ texts and topics highlights the need for student discussion (Berg, 2012, 2013; Blackburn, 2005; Boyd et al., 2006; Greenbaum, 1994; Schall & Kauffman, 2003; Young, 2009); therefore, teacher educators need to prepare in-service and preservice teachers with the skills and dispositions for talking with students about LGBTIQ topics. Kumashiro (2002) argues that these discussions require educators to embrace the unknown, remain open to multiple ways of learning, and question what they and their students already know. This shift from teachers-as-knowledge-providers to teachers-as-questioners-of-knowledge assumes that learning comes with emotional and intellectual dissonance through which teachers must guide students.

Questions are one method teachers can use to shift the responsibility of meaning-making to students. Questions have the potential to slow the pace of learning, disarm students, and create a space for multiple perspectives to be explored. If the teacher in our study had questioned students' knowledge of LGBTIQ identities instead of assuming their lack of maturity, the interactions in our vignette may be fundamentally different. What would have happened if, instead of telling students to stop laughing, the teacher had questioned students about why they were laughing? What if instead of demanding that students "be mature," the teacher asked the students to stop and write their reactions, questions, or concerns about Tash? What if the teacher had asked the students to think like Tash's sister and imagine what she thought, felt, or wondered? Questions may have enabled students to share what they knew about being gay and offered them an opportunity to ask questions, and pushed them to think from a different perspective.

Ashcraft (2012) posits that teachers should approach discussions about sexual identity through code-switching practices that focus on the relationship between language, power, and understanding. Because the teacher was concerned with the novel's use of "homo" and "queen" as distracting and derogatory remarks, engaging students in a discussion about the language of identity may have been beneficial. She could have drawn students' attention to the context surrounding these terms: Who is using them? Where? And with what tone? By asking students to connect language with speakers, contexts, and attitudes, the teacher could have engaged students in a discussion about terms that objectify, empower, and reclaim in relation to the identities of speaker, audience, and context. Finally, because she was concerned with the setting, this teacher could have engaged students to think about how a gay character would be written about today.

The teaching of this text creates possibilities for students to learn about language, representation, power, and visibility of LGBTIQ individuals—a learning experience that combines anti-oppressive education with complex thinking about language, identity, and power. This teacher, however, approaches LGBITQ issues from a stance of controlling student reactions and behaviors. Although her stance may be intended to maintain a tone of respect and tolerance for the LGBITQ individuals, it functions to limit student exploration of LGBTIQ identities and prohibits students from developing critical understanding. By neglecting to seize this opportunity for learning, the teacher implicitly marginalizes the two students who identify as lesbian.

Vignette #2: It's a Normal Thing

Concerned about the difference between today's youth culture and the setting of the book, the teacher explained the importance of students' understanding what she believed is today's more tolerant perspective:

> Things have changed a lot in the last few years and these kids are growing up where it's in the mainstream; they are walking past it, and they see it on TV where there are definitely gay and lesbian couples. We have two in this class who are openly lesbian in the hallway and we are constantly stopping them. That didn't even happen the last time we had 8th grade. That was happening when they got to high school. So because it is so open and even if kids disagree with it they are accepting it. I didn't want them to be so shocked when they heard that people were talking down on it and calling them haters because in 1995 it was not that open and if you were gay or lesbian you were only allowed to be that way in certain sections of town. You were definitely not open and your family members were pretty much disgraced if it came out. They would not see that like it is now. I mean people are very open about it and on TV, they almost glamorize it in certain situations.

When asked how other students reacted to there being out students in the class she explained,

> They just let it go. I mean they may talk about them behind their back, but I don't know if they even do that. So, they just let it be. It's a normal thing. I wanted to make sure that they were aware that that's not the situation and that the book would use politically incorrect terms that we would not use today and that's because it was not a positive thing back then. Even though it was just 15 years ago, it seems like a long time.

Examining Assumptions

Asher (2007) explains how immersion in pop culture images can provide a false sense of progress when working toward social justice. The teacher assumes that, because there are out lesbians on the team and LGBTIQ characters on television, her students are accepting and understanding. Her assumption is problematic. First, it positions inclusion as an acceptable goal for social justice. Multicultural education has evolved beyond including diverse voices to advocating for critical understanding of diverse perspectives in order to empower all students. Second, her assumption prevents all participants from expanding or revising their understanding of LGBTIQ identities and issues. From a teacher perspective, this assumption allows her to shirk the responsibility of initiating discussions that explore and expand student knowledge. From a student perspective, she is potentially ignoring issues of equity, safety, and social justice for the students who identify as lesbians. National survey results indicate that more than half of LGBT students feel unsafe at school with almost two thirds of students hearing homophobic remarks on a regular basis (Kosciw et al., 2014). These national statistics act as a mandate for teachers to guarantee safe and productive learning environments for LGBTIQ students. As we discuss in the final two vignettes, the teacher's belief that being lesbian is something her students consider "a normal thing" does not reflect the reality of student-to-student interactions about LGBTIQ issues.

Although images of LGBTIQ characters and individuals have increased in popular culture, it is false to assume that these images adequately represent the range of LGBTIQ identities (Asher, 2007) or that students develop critical understanding of these characters. Teachers should treat this increase as an invitation to explore complexities and nuances of LGBTIQ representations rather than assume that the representation itself is enough. Literacy is a socially mediated practice in which individuals create meaning through interactions with texts and their sense of identity (Barton & Hamilton, 2005; Berg, 2012). How a student understands a character is shaped by their understanding of self, text, and context; therefore, the messages students derive from LGBTIQ images in popular culture is shaped by a multitude of factors—not the single experience of exposure. Berg's (2012) examination of how students made meaning of gender and sexual orientation through video games, fan fiction, and social networking indicates that students recognized complex queer identities but also developed an awareness of heteronormative expectations. It is possible then, as students develop an awareness of LGBTIQ identities, they also develop an awareness of how these identities are marginalized by heteronormative forces. Teachers must engage students in discussions about visibility, representation, heteronormative expectations, and power of queer identities in order to identify beliefs and actions that counter such forces.

In order to have these conversations, teachers must be willing to examine their own beliefs, which can be a challenging process. Reflection is a core practice in many teacher education programs; educators are taught that reflection leads to refinement of teaching methods, student learning, and assessment results. Asher (2007) and others (Berg, 2013; Boyd et al., 2006; Kumashiro, 2001) argue that teachers must also engage in critical, self-reflexive thinking to unpack the assumptions, biases, and emotions enmeshed in their understanding of LGBTIQ identities and topics. Teachers, like students, carry complex funds of knowledge built from their experiences and beliefs. This knowledge can be as influential as any formal pedagogical training in shaping how teachers interact with LGBTIQ identities and issues (Greytak & Kosciw, 2014). Questions like What do I believe, feel, and know about LGBTIQ people?; What experiences have I had?; How have these experiences shaped me?; What biases do I carry?; and What concerns do I have about talking to students about LGBTIQ topics? can push teachers to look closely at their own beliefs about sexuality and gender. From the beginning of preservice teacher training, teacher educators can lay a foundation for disciplined self-reflexive practice parallel to the reflection of daily lessons. The difficult nature of this work should not be diminished. Kumashiro (2002) explains that when educators question what they know and do, they may discover their own participation or complicity with homophobic or heteronormative practices. Because this new awareness may lead to emotional dissonance, teacher educators and school leaders must guide pre- and in-service teachers through this difficult work.

Vignette #3: Men Wear Pink, Too

The classroom is a flurry of excitement; it is Valentine's Day. An administrator comes to the door, interrupting class to announce that the school is having a Valentine's Day dance complete with food, music, and games.

He states that tickets are cheaper if bought as a couple and a couple "can be just two friends, okay?" Several students are focused on folded pieces of paper at their desks. These papers are the pairings of a personality inventory, titled Matchmaker, a game which pairs students with other students of the opposite sex. This fundraiser, sponsored by the school, has created much conversation among students throughout the school. There was no option provided for same-sex matching.

Amidst the excitement the teacher quiets the classroom down and asks students to, "Face forward. This is a review." She begins by reviewing figurative language and notices two students not paying attention. She stops and looks at the two male students who are distracted. The students are talking and laughing—comparing the cuff bracelets they each wear on their forearm. The teacher moves to stand directly in front of the two students and interjects, "Alright. What are we? This is not bracelet class. I'm trying to teach you about figurative language and you are comparing his pink bracelet to his gold bracelet." The classroom responds in laughter, and one student whispers loud enough for others to hear, "faggots." The teacher continues, "I didn't think that would ever happen—my class would get disturbed over who had the prettiest bracelet. I think the pink one is prettier. Put the bracelet away." Another student in the classroom intervenes, "Some girls say it's brave for a man to wear pink." The teacher responds, "Well yes, but we don't discuss it in class and you are going to get a detention for being disruptive." The other students laugh, again. She closes the interaction and says, "We've got more things to do in this class besides compare that pink bracelet to his pretty little gold bracelet. So we'll get back to figurative language."

Gender Performance and Sexuality

The classroom setting within this vignette was rife with gender bias and heteronormative assumptions common in many schools (Sanders & Mathis, 2013). The administrator who enters the classroom to invite students to purchase tickets to a Valentine's dance only creates normative scenarios for the students. Couples are defined as opposite sex or "just two friends." It also becomes clear through this interaction that school environment and classroom context are enmeshed. It is unlikely that the teacher could have intervened or objected to the solicitation of tickets in her classroom; however, she could have voiced additional examples of types of couples who may purchase tickets.

The Matchmaker game was extremely popular and exciting for students. Although the teacher may not have been able to influence the option for same-sex matching, she could have engaged students in conversations about the game that would challenge norms. In a class period later that week she asks the students whether or not they feel their matches are accurate. A student who identified as a lesbian suggests her matches were not accurate at all. This interaction served as an entry point to delve deeper, however the teacher ignored the opportunity. The teacher could have explored questions such as What does the Matchmaker game assume about you? and How does it limit your options or preferences? Through this questioning the students may be able to recognize and regulate multiple positions of gender and therefore work more proactively against oppressive contexts (Blackburn, 2008).

Numerous opportunities were presented for the teacher to discuss how sexuality and gender are enmeshed. The teacher positioned the students wearing bracelets in a gender binary that shamed and labeled them as breaking the existing norms through her use of words such as *pretty* and *little*; her language positioned students to believe that males and females maintain specific roles. Davies (1993) encourages moving away from gender binaries to focus on each individual's presence of multiple subjects. The interaction modeled for students did not raise awareness of gender norms and marginalized individuals who did not fit within these norms.

The teachers' action is a micro-aggression. Through shaming the two male students for wearing bracelets, the teacher establishes acceptance of behavior that attacks an individual based on nonnormative behaviors and interactions. One student was empowered to step forward as an agent of change; the student challenges the teacher and gender norms in his statement that "wearing pink is brave." This action demonstrates how students are capable of recognizing injustice and pushing the classroom toward anti-oppressive engagement.

Self-reflexive practice would offer the educator the opportunity to revisit the incident and engage the students in what binaries exist and how society generalizes gender roles (Butler, 1999). The text describes Tash as a "queen" (Woodson, 2008, p. 59). Tash, throughout the text, expresses his sexuality in varying ways. In one particular scene, his mother admonishes him for being too flamboyant, and wishes that he would just be himself, which fails to recognize the range of gender performance that exists on a continuum. This scene provides a perfect entry point into exploring how gender and sexuality intersect. It also foregrounds LGBTIQ identities as more than a set of alphabet letters or a concept beyond the four walls of the classroom. Students have the opportunity to explore transgender and intersexed identities, which are often confused as being based on sexuality instead of gender. Dialogue may have been prompted by questions, such as Do we try on different personas than ourselves? Is Tash being himself? How do gender and sexuality connect or disconnect via the character of Tash? These questions could have been approached through journaling or classroom discussion to explore Tash and the adolescent perspectives of developing self.

Lastly, this vignette challenges us to consider what is relevant for class discussion. The teacher ends the bracelet scenario by saying that class is not the appropriate place to discuss whether pink is a brave color for a man to wear. It would be impossible to address every topic, but this particular exchange was a missed opportunity to connect textual content to students' daily lives. If the teacher had approached classroom content from the perspective of what do "we" as a community need to learn versus what are "we" going to learn, anti-oppressive barriers may have been removed.

Vignette #4: Defending a Friend

The use of heterosexist language such as "homo," "gay," and "fag" are commonplace in schools. These terms became more noticeable as the content centered on a gay character. As the teacher introduces several chapters that detail how Tash ends up in prison, a student from another class enters to retrieve a book and leaves. A minute or so later a student, who identifies as a lesbian, tells another student to "shut up." The other student counters, "I didn't say anything." The lesbian student says loudly, "You called him a fag!" The students argue with one another; the lesbian student defends her peer, while the other student continues to deny he said anything. The teacher tells them to stop arguing and explains that she heard the student "defending a friend" and that she "isn't going to stop her from defending someone who is being treated unfairly."

The teacher reminds the class to be mature as she directs them back to focusing on Tash. She reads about the relationship between Tash and a man, Sly, who betrays and assaults him. The teacher frames the discussion as the love between two people. A male student says, "Oh my god" and looks at his friend. The friend shakes his head and the other student nods knowingly. Both boys look back at their books as the teacher continues:

> Now that's the end of that chapter. Before we read on, because it changes topics, we got to stop here and talk about Tash. So we know what happened, but why did it happen? That's the important part. Why did it happen to Tash?

One student says, "Because he was in the wrong place at the wrong time." The same student who shook his head in aversion earlier says almost to himself, "'Cause he's gay." The teacher ignores this statement and another student interjects, "'Cause he loves Sly."

The teacher responds,

Yeah. He loves Sly. He trusted Sly. He thought Sly was there to take care of him. Everyone else sees the bad, but when you love somebody you don't always see the bad. Does that make sense? So people saw the bad in him, but Tash could not see the bad in Sly. That's how Sly was and Tash fell for that because he loved him. I know I heard somebody say "eee" because Tash is loving a man, but think about someone loving anybody. You don't have to think about it in *that* way. Some of you have experienced your first love and loving somebody, but think about grown people you know that love the wrong person. You think, "Why are they spending so much time with that person? Why are they even liking that person?"

Sense of Agency

While microprocesses (Asher, 2007) are present within most classrooms on a daily basis, instances of micro-aggressions were blatant during the exploration of the book. Students used heterosexist language and engaged in actions that marginalized and shamed peers. Numerous missed opportunities occurred as the teacher ignored micro-aggressions of students. In the vignette above, the teacher has the opportunity to discuss the impacts and implications of the word "faggot," but fails to unpack the incident, leaving the oppressive actions of the students unaddressed and further ignoring the LGBTIQ students in the classroom. The character of Tash provided an opportunity for the teacher to draw parallels and allow the students within the classroom to consider how micro-aggressions impact others. Bullying via verbal and physical interactions for LGBTIQ students occurs frequently within middle schools, and teachers are cited as being one of the strongest impacts upon influencing school climate (Chesir-Teran, 2003; Kosciw et al., 2014). Teachers and school administrators must be aware of how ignoring verbal or physical acts further victimizes LGBTIQ students.

The teacher uses the text to advocate and empower LGBTIQ students when she discusses the love that Tash feels for Sly. She uses the context of the book and the depth of the characters to reduce the heteronormative context present within the classroom (Blackburn & Smith, 2010). This highlights that there is more than one reality with regard to what a relationship may look like. This instance is undermined, however, when she states, "You don't have to think about it in *that* way," underscoring the need for educators to be mindful of how their words may be perceived by students in the classroom. Within the context of this statement, the teacher acknowledges her belief that same-sex relationships are abnormal. The presence of students willing to act as agents made small impacts within the classroom and provided space for LGBTIQ students to be present and acknowledged. The lesbian student who stood up for a student who was called names was another instance of student-initiated advocacy. It is unclear how the response of the teacher in each of these situations empowered or disenfranchised the student's willingness to intervene in future scenarios.

CONCLUSION

LGBTIQ students are not invisible, but in many cases their experiences and perspectives are ignored. Most classrooms lack literature with LGBTIQ characters; classroom examples and anecdotes are largely heteronormative, and educators' discomfort to engage in meaningful discourse limits possibilities for students and teachers. Asher (2007) suggests that critical self-reflexivity can help teachers and students recognize their own assumptions and unpack the complex layers of classroom contexts. In order for educators to develop self-reflexive practices and engage students in productive discussions of LGBTIQ topics, teacher educators must model the practices that promote anti-oppressive education. Preservice teachers deserve multiple and ongoing opportunities to think deeply about their knowledge, experiences, assumptions, and comfort levels examining LGBTIQ topics. Teacher education programs can incorporate these opportunities in both foundation courses focused on developing teacher identities and classroom culture as well as discipline-specific methods courses where students have opportunities to consider how LGBTIQ topics and identities can be pulled forward in the content they teach. These vignettes present opportunities for teachers to stop ignoring LGBTIQ identities and topics, co-construct understanding with students, deepen self-awareness, recognize how gender performance intersects with sexuality, and empower LGBTIQ students to act as agents of change.

REFERENCES

Ashcraft, C. (2012). But how do we talk about it?: Critical literacy practices for addressing sexuality with youth. *Curriculum Inquiry, 42*(5), 597–628.

Asher, N. (2007). Made in the (multicultural) U.S.A.: Unpacking tensions of race, culture, and sexuality in education. *Educational Researcher, 36*(2), 65–73.

Bailey, N. J. (2005). Let us not forget to support LGBT youth in the middle school years. *Middle School Journal, 37*(2), 31–35.

Barton, D., & Hamilton, M. (2005). Literacy practices. In D. Barton, M. Hamilton, & R. Ivanic (Eds.), *Situated literacies: Theorizing reading and writing in context* (pp. 7–14). New York, NY: Routledge.

Berg, M. A. (2012). Tolerance to alliance: Deconstructing dichotomies to advocate for all students. *Voices in the Middle, 20*, 32–36.

Berg, M. (2013). Teens' explorations of gender and sexual identities in conversations about/around preferred text. *Journal of Language and Sexuality*, *1*(1), 15–34.

Blackburn, M. (2004). Understanding agency beyond school-sanctioned activities. *Theory into Practice*, *43*(2), 102–110.

Blackburn, M. V. (2005). Teaching queer-inclusive English language arts. *Journal of Adolescent & Adult Literacy*, *49*(3), 202–212.

Blackburn, M. (2008). The experiencing, negotiation, breaking, and remaking of gender rules and regulations by queer youth. *Journal of Gay and Lesbian Issues in Education*, *4*(2), 33–54.

Blackburn, M. V., & Buckley, J. F. (2005). Teaching queer-inclusive English language arts. *Journal of Adolescent & Adult Literacy*, *49*(3), 202–212.

Blackburn, M. V, & Smith, J. M. (2010). Moving beyond the inclusion of LGBT-themed literature in English language arts classrooms: Interrogating heteronormativity and exploring intersectionality. *Journal of Adolescent & Adult Literacy*, *53*(8), 625–634.

Boyd, F. B., Ariail, M., Williams, R., Jocson, K., Sachs, G. T., McNeal, K., & Morrell, E. (2006). Real teaching for real diversity: Preparing English language arts teachers for 21st-century classrooms. *English Education*, *38*(4), 329–350.

Botelho, M. J., & Rudman, M. K. (2009). *Critical multicultural analysis of children's literature: Mirrors, windows, doors*. New York, NY: Routledge.

Butler, J. (1999). *Gender trouble: Feminism and the subversion of identity*. New York, NY: Routledge.

Castro, I. E., & Sujak, M. C. (2014). "Why can't we learn about this?": Sexual minority students navigate the official and hidden curricular spaces of high school. *Education and Urban Society*, *46*(4), 450–473.

Chesir-Teran, D. (2003). Conceptualizing and addressing heterosexism in high schools: A setting-level approach. *American Journal of Community Psychology*, *31*(3/4), 269–279.

Clark, C. T., & Blackburn, M. V. (2009). Reading LGBT-themed literature with young people: What's possible? *English Journal*, *98*(4), 25–32.

Davies, B. (1993). Beyond dualism and towards subjectivities. In L. Christian-Smith (Ed.), *Texts of desire: Essays on fiction, femininity and schooling* (pp.145–173). London, England: Falmer.

Draper, S. M. (2006). *Tears of a tiger* (Vol. 1). New York, NY: Simon and Schuster.

Fredman, A. J., Schultz, N. J., & Hoffman, M. F. (2015). "You're moving a frickin' big ship": The challenges of addressing LGBTQ topics in public schools. *Education and Urban Society*, *47*(1), 56–85.

Greenbaum, V. (1994). Literature out of the closet: Bringing gay and lesbian texts and subtexts out in high school English. *English Journal*, *83*(5), 71–74.

Greytak, E. A., & Kosciw, J. G. (2014). Predictors of US teachers' intervention in anti-lesbian, gay, bisexual, and transgender bullying and harassment. *Teaching Education*, *25*, 410–426.

Kosciw, J. G., & Diaz. E. (2008). *Involved, invisible, ignored: The experiences of lesbian, gay, bisexual and transgender parents and their children in our nation's K–12 schools*. New York, NY: Office of Policy of GLSEN.

Kosciw, J. G., Diaz, E.M., & Greytak, E. A. (2008). *The 2007 National School Climate survey: The experiences of lesbian, gay, bisexual and transgender youth in our nation's schools.* New York, NY: GLSEN.

Kosciw, J. G., Greytak, E. A., Palmer, N. A., & Boesen, M. J. (2014). *The 2013 National School Climate survey: The experiences of lesbian, gay, bisexual and transgender youth in our nation's schools.* New York, NY: GLSEN.

Kumashiro, K. K. (2000). Toward a theory of anti-oppressive education. *Review of Educational Research, 70*(1), 25–53.

Kumashiro, K. K. (2001). "Posts" perspectives on anti-oppressive education in social studies, English, mathematics, and science classrooms. *Educational Researcher, 30*(3), 3–12.

Kumashiro, K. (2002). Against repetition: Addressing resistance to anti-oppressive change in the practices of learning, teaching, supervising, and researching. *Harvard Educational Review, 70*(1), 67–92.

Lipkin, A. (1995). The case for a gay and lesbian curriculum. In G. Unks (Ed.), *The gay teen: Educational practice and theory for lesbian, gay, and bisexual adolescents* (pp. 31–52). New York, NY: Routledge.

Meyer, E. J. (2007). "But I'm not gay": What straight teachers need to know about queer theory. In N. Rodriguez & W. Pina (Eds.), *Queering straight teachers: Discourse and identity in education.* New York, NY: Lang.

Nelson, C. D. (2009). *Sexual identities in English language education.* New York, NY: Routledge.

Sanders, A. M., & Mathis, J. B. (2013). Gay and lesbian literature in the classroom: Can gay themes overcome heteronormativity? *Journal of Praxis in Multicultural Education, 7*(1), 1–18.

Sanford, N. (1966). *Self and society: Social change and individual development.* New York, NY: Atherton.

Schall, J., & Kauffmann, G. (2003). Exploring literature with gay and lesbian characters in the elementary school. *Journal of Children's Literature, 29*(1), 36–45.

Scheible, M. (2012). A critical discourse analysis of teachers' views on LGBT literature. *Discourse: Studies in the Cultural Politics of Education, 33*(2), 207–222.

Sears, J. (2013). *Gay, lesbian, and transgender issues in education: Programs, policies, and practices.* New York, NY: Routledge.

Sims, R. (1982). *Shadow and substance: Afro-American experience in contemporary children's fiction.* Urbana, IL: National Council of Teachers of English.

Woodson, J. (2008). *After Tupac & D Foster.* New York, NY: Putnam's.

Young, S. L. B. (2009). Breaking the silence: Critical literacy and social action. *English Journal, 98*(4), 109–115.

Zack, J., Mannheim, A., & Alfano, M. (2010). "I didn't know what to say?": Four archetypal responses to homophobic rhetoric in the classroom. *The High School Journal, 93*(3), 98–110.

CHAPTER 10

TEACHING TOLERANCE THROUGH LITERATURE

How Including LGBTIQ Titles in Your Library Can Increase Acceptance

Tiffany Renee Droege

BACKGROUND

In 2010, a fellow teacher approached me about sponsoring a Gay-Straight Alliance (GSA). This was the first I had ever heard of a GSA, and I was excited about the challenge. I am a high school English teacher in a diverse St. Louis suburb, and I have observed many of our nearly 2,000 students suffer from homophobic bullying, so I wanted to do whatever I could to improve our school culture. Since its inception, our group has grown to nearly 50 active members. We hold yearly events and fundraisers, and though we don't have any hard evidence, many students and teachers have said that the bullying climate in our school has drastically improved since we founded our GSA.

After co-sponsoring our group for nearly 5 years, I thought it might be valuable to present what I have learned, so I applied to present at the Illinois Reading Council Conference in Springfield. I wanted to do a lesbian,

Queering Classrooms: Personal Narratives and Educational Practices to Support LGBTQ Youth in Schools, pp. 145–154
Copyright © 2017 by Information Age Publishing

145

gay, bisexual, trans, intersex, queer (LGBTIQ) book talk, where I would present young adult and children's titles that address LGBTIQ issues. To my delight, my presentation was accepted.

I worked with my school librarian as well as the librarian at the public library to assemble a list of titles. To my surprise, my school and public libraries had many options for all ages, including titles like *Heather Has Two Mommies* by Leslie Newman and Laura Cornell (2015), *And Tango Makes Three* by Justin Richardson and Peter Parnell (2005), and even *Revolutionary Voices: A Multicultural Queer Youth Anthology* by Amy Sonnie (2000). Through gathering and presenting these resources, I learned that having and promoting LGBTIQ literature, as a librarian and a teacher, is essential to helping LGBTIQ youth feel included in our community. LGBTIQ students and students with LGBTIQ parents are like other minority students; they need to see themselves in the literature covered in their classes, and in the books they read for pleasure. It is the job of teachers and librarians to make these titles available and to promote the use of these titles schoolwide.

RATIONALE FOR LGBTIQ LITERATURE

Although the LGBTIQ movement has made great strides in the last several years, being an LGBTIQ student in a public school still has many challenges, especially for students who come from more conservative communities. In the wake of the US Supreme Court's ruling in favor of gay marriage, it may be even more important to help these students feel included in the classroom when the community is unsupportive. According to the LGBT Foundation's (2009) website, young LGBTIQ people are three to six times more likely to self-harm than heterosexual young people (see http://lgbt.foundation/news/new-report-highlights-self-harm-needs-to-be-taken-more-seriously/). It is also estimated that 40% of all young LGBTIQ people self-harm or attempt suicide at least once (Malley, Posner, & Potter, 2008, p. 39).

Books can be a source of comfort to LGBTIQ students who are struggling with their identity and seeking acceptance from their teachers and peers. According to Oltman (2015), "providing positive resources for LGBT young adults who are in the process of 'coming out' can lessen the confusion and pain often experienced at this time" (p. 26). In addition, LGBTIQ literature can help LGBTIQ students, as well as straight students, establish positive self-identity through positive messages about diversity and self-expression (Mehra & Braquet, 2006, p. 13).

I have found that LGBTIQ texts are not only beneficial to LGBTIQ students, but they can also benefit straight students because they often emphasize universal themes like empathy and acceptance. Once, when I was introducing a list of optional titles for a literature circle[1] project, I gave students the option of reading *Middlesex* by Jeffry Eugenides (2002), a critically acclaimed novel about a young intersex character who undergoes a transformation when they[2] learn they have a genetic mutation that makes their gender identity somewhat ambiguous. One of my straight students approached me after the introduction and asked if she could read the book, but asked if she could keep it in my room because she knew her parents would not approve. I, of course, obliged and she stayed after school every day for at least an hour, devouring the book until the end. When I listened in on her group's discussion of the book, I discovered that she had undergone a transformation of her own. She discussed candidly her family's prejudice against LGBTIQ people, and admitted that she had once shared their bias. But, she said, through reading the book, she understood that some people don't get to choose who they are, and they shouldn't be punished by society. I cannot imagine this student arriving at this profound conclusion through any other vehicle besides literature.

DEFINING LGBTIQ LITERATURE

Usually when we think of LGBTIQ literature, we think of books about queer[3] characters, or books that directly address queer themes like *Boy Meets Boy* by David Levithan (2002), *Giovanni's Room* by James Baldwin (1956), and *Am I Blue?* by Marian Dane Bauer (1995). Though these books are very important works of literature and can be included in any curriculum, the definition of LGBTIQ literature can be much broader to include stories that simply have queer characters, or address queer themes more indirectly. For example, *Cat on a Hot Tin Roof* by Tennessee Williams (1958) does not have any openly gay characters, or characters who are overtly grappling with their sexuality. The issue is much more nuanced in this text (the protagonist is not interested in his wife, so she assumes he is gay). Another example is *The Vampire Chronicles* by Anne Rice, in which the vampires are attracted to both sexes, but it is not an integral part of the story. In addition, many Shakespeare plays, including *The Merchant of Venice, Twelfth Night,* and *As You Like It,* deal with gender identity as well.

SELECTING LGBTIQ LITERATURE

When selecting LGBTIQ literature for the classroom, it is important to choose both obvious and subtle titles. Books like *The Perks of Being a Wall-flower* by Stephen Chbosky (1999), *The Hours* by Michael Cunningham

(2000), and *Fried Green Tomatoes at the Whistle Stop Cafe* by Fannie Flagg (1988), which have queer supporting characters or subplots, can be invaluable to teaching acceptance because they are not only less controversial, but they may even be approved already by the school board. The choices for LGBTIQ titles are as diverse as the community itself. The key is to have plenty of options, both fiction and nonfiction, in many formats, at many levels.

Many schools already have LGBTIQ titles in their libraries, as mine did. But for some small town and rural libraries, there may be fewer options, and it is hard to know where to begin (Oltman, 2015, p. 30). Teachers and librarians can start by going to GSANetwork.org and find an extensive list of titles recommended for youth of all ages, including fiction and nonfiction titles. GoodReads.com also has a list of thousands of LGBTIQ books. Once teachers find some interesting titles, they can search for reviews on the American Library Association's Young Adult Library Services page (http://www.ala.org/yalsa). Then they can decide what is appropriate for their class.

OBTAINING LGBTIQ LITERATURE

If teachers are asking their department chair or administrator to purchase books with department money, they should make sure to emphasize that they are using LGBTIQ literature to meet existing curricular, state, and national standards. If teachers and librarians want to add titles to their school or classroom library but don't have the money to do so, several foundations offer grants. The Ben Cohen StandUp Foundation's mission is "to raise awareness of the long-term, damaging effects of bullying and to raise funds to support those doing real-world work to stop it" (http://www.standupfoundation.com/about/vision/). The Arcus Foundation is based in New York, and their mission is to promote harmony among all people, and they have specific programs for social justice for LGBTIQ people. They offer grants on their website, http://www.arcus-foundation.org/what-we-support/social-justice-lgbt/. The Gill Foundation supports nonprofits, which includes schools that bolster equality for the LGBT community (http://gillfoundation.org/it-takes-money/outgiving/). Teachers who are new to grant writing and are not sure where to start should try Donorschoose.org, an easy, user-friendly way to use crowd-sourcing for funding. Create a profile and a "project" on the website (a class set of books, for example), and Donorschoose will publish your project online. Teachers can share projects with their friends, family, co-workers and community (http://www.donorschoose.org/).

PROMOTING LGBTIQ LITERATURE

Once a library or classroom has developed a collection of LGBTIQ books, it is important to promote the collection. If students and teachers are not aware of the titles, they may go unutilized. The best way to promote these books is simply to advertise them. Create vibrant displays during the month of October, LGBTIQ History Month, or any time of the year. Display them in a New Books section of the library, along with other new titles. Another innovative way to advertise these books is to host an LGBTIQ book "walk" after school. Display the titles on tables, and allow students and teachers to walk around the tables and peruse the collection, allowing time for checkout at the end.

Teachers can also create curricular connections during research units, encouraging students to explore topics and people like the Stonewall Riots, Harvey Milk, and Matthew Shephard. One option is to create a list of LGBTIQ topics and share them with fellow teachers. I teach a unit every year on oppression, for example, where students research various forms of oppression and write an expository essay. Systematic homophobia is one option on my list, along with racial profiling and sexism. I shared this assignment with a US history teacher, and she taught a version of the assignment with her students as well.

Something to keep in mind when promoting LGBTIQ literature is that many LGBTIQ students may not necessarily be ready to, or even want to, read LGBTIQ literature. I would not recommend approaching a queer student and saying, "Hey, Jim, I just got this copy of *Rainbow Boys* by Alex Sanchez (2003), and I thought you might want to read it!" Some students may not fully understand their sexuality or gender identity yet. Or they may be completely comfortable with their identity and ready to explore other topics. Do not assume that just because they are queer they want to read about it. The best strategy is to expose everyone to these titles, present yourself as an open-minded individual, have plenty of titles to choose from on your shelves, and be ready to recommend books if and when students ask.

DEFENDING LGBTIQ LITERATURE

When teachers and librarians decide to include queer literature in the classroom or library, it is almost certain that they will come under fire at some point. It is important to remember that not only is the research on your side, but the law is as well. Students do not shed their First Amendment rights when they walk into school. Several court cases, including *West Virginia State Board of Education v. Barnette*, 319 U.S. 624 (1943) and *Tinker v. Des Moines Community School District* have set precedence for students' rights to freedom from censorship in schools.

When defending titles, it is important to be sensitive to parents who may not agree that teaching queer issues is necessary. I have had dozens of parents call me to complain about books on my shelves. Here are sample "scripts" to follow when parents complain:

> Your son/daughter is in no way obligated to read [insert book title], but many of our students find the messages in [insert book title] relevant to their specific situations, and I have a duty to create an inclusive classroom environment where students from all backgrounds feel represented in the literature available to them.

Another possible response is the following:

> I'm so sorry you feel the way you do about [insert book title]. You have every right as a parent to have a say in what your child is exposed to, and I will respect your wishes when it comes to the books your child reads individually. However, many other parents support the inclusion of [insert book title] in the curriculum, and our curriculum is approved by the school board. If you have a concern regarding the curriculum, I suggest you contact the principal, Mrs. Such-and-such.

To prevent confrontation with parents, inform the department chair and perhaps even the principal of any controversial titles on the shelf. Administrators prefer not to be blindsided if a parent decides to call them directly (which has happened to me many times). In addition, I would highly recommend including a list of books that will be covered by the entire class on the syllabus and ask parents to sign the syllabus at the beginning of the year. That way, if a parent has a complaint, the teacher can say, "I provided you with a list of titles at the beginning of the year, and I see here that you signed your approval."

If parents are complaining about books found in the library, most school libraries have a School Board-approved collection development policy (CDP), a document that explains the goals of the library, what kinds of books it is going to obtain, and how it will address complaints, challenges, and censorship of the collection. Familiarize yourself with your library's CDP, and inform parents of the Board-approved process for challenging a book when they complain. Parents do not have the right to demand a book be removed from the shelf simply because they don't believe their child should read it.

INCORPORATING LGBTIQ LITERATURE

It is not a question of whether or not to address LGBTIQ issues in the classroom (the answer is yes, you should); it is a question of how. Teachers, especially preservice and novice teachers, are inherently idealistic, but LGBTIQ issues can be divisive and are not to be introduced casually without caution. Teachers should ask themselves several questions: Is your community mostly liberal or conservative? Is there a Pride festival in or near your community, and is your community receptive? Are there many openly queer people in your community, and how are they received? Do you have LGBTIQ students in your class? Do you have religious conservatives in your class? Is your administration supportive? Understanding these nuances will guide teachers when they decide what kinds of book titles their community is ready for. Perhaps it would be wiser to discuss gender identity with Shakespeare's *As You Like It*, rather than diving into *Invisible Lives: The Erasure of Transexual and Transgender People* by Viviane Namaste (2002), for example.

An entire unit on LGBTIQ literature may not be appropriate or even necessary. An easy way to justify the use of LGBTIQ literature is to simply fit it into the existing curriculum. Social studies teachers can conduct a unit on civil rights; language arts teachers, a research unit for which LGBTIQ issues is an option; elementary teachers, a unit on empathy or acceptance.

The most important factor to consider is the students in the class. Be aware of and sensitive to students who are LGBTIQ, and also remember that the class may have students who are not "out" yet. Keep in mind the maturity of the class as a whole, as well as individual students, when selecting titles and deciding how to incorporate them. For instance, if the whole class is reading a book with a queer character, and there's a particularly homophobic student in a class with an openly gay student, the teacher may want to avoid whole-class discussions and opt for small group discussions instead.

In order to ward off potential naysayers, I would not recommend making books that focus solely on LGBTIQ issues mandatory. For example, I would not recommend having an entire class read *Stone Butch Blues* by Leslie Feinburg (1993). Though this is a fantastic book that may be appropriate for a young woman grappling with her sexuality, you could lose your job, and then you wouldn't be helping anyone. It is much easier, and more productive, to simply have these books available for independent projects, recommend them to specific students, or have these books as options for a small reading group.

Another way to expose students to LGBTIQ issues is through an Article of the Week assignment. Article of the Week is a project initially designed by Kelley Gallagher (http://www.kelleygallagher.com). Teachers choose a nonfiction piece each week from a newspaper, a journal, magazine, or online publication, and as a class students read the article and annotate it as a close reading activity. Teachers can choose articles dealing with LGBTIQ issues and discuss them in class. Some great sources for LGBTIQ articles are www.lgbtqnation.com, a website that houses news articles related to LGBTIQ people; *The Advocate*, a print magazine for and about queer issues that is also available online at www.advocate.com; www.glaad.com/news is a page for news stories on the GLAAD website. GLAAD is a US media monitoring organization founded by nongovernmental LGBT people in the media. These and other mainstream news sources often have articles suitable for students.

Teacher book studies can also be effective. Every year, many teachers at our school participate in a schoolwide book study where we read a book related to education, and we have a meeting to discuss the book, much like a book club. For our book study, we read texts on myriad topics, from classroom management to Common Core. Discussing books like *Dignity for All: Safeguarding LGBT Students* by Peter M. DeWitt (2012) would give teachers ideas for how to foster a more nurturing environment for all students, as well as give them a safe space to voice their concerns and ask questions.

Each year our library celebrates Banned Books Week, a national event celebrating the freedom to read controversial texts in school and in the public library (http://www.bannedbooksweek.org/). We display titles such as *And Tango Makes Three*, *Heather Has Two Mommies*, and other books that have been banned at other libraries in the past in order to highlight the injustice of censorship. More ideas, information, and supplies are available at www.bannedbooksweek.org.

CONCLUSION

We cannot force students to be accepting, but we can model and immerse them in a culture of acceptance. Literature can open up new worlds for children and adolescents, as well as help them understand the world in which they live. Providing copies of, or recommendations for, literature with LGBTIQ themes and characters can help all students feel more included.

Teacher-education programs can prepare teachers to incorporate LGBTIQ literature in their future classroom by visiting the local LGBTIQ Center or inviting a spokesperson to speak to a class. LGBTIQ centers often have many resources for parents, teachers, social workers, and other people working with the community.

Another way teacher education programs can prepare future teachers is to require them to design a professional development session for a group of teachers on the topic of LGBTIQ issues in the classroom. Students could design a hypothetical professional development session, say for a school or district in-service day, that includes a presentation, literature review, and interactive activities. The future teachers could present their hypothetical inservice to their fellow education students in class.

For students who are unfamiliar with the wide range of children's and young adult LGBTIQ literature, an annotated bibliography of LGBTIQ titles appropriate for their students would be an enriching assignment. Annotations could include a summary of the work, the work's age appropriateness, as well as how it could be used in the classroom. In addition, students could be required to read one of the books and do a full-length book critique.

In my education courses at my university, we were often assigned case studies in order to prepare for discipline issues, as well as ethical quandaries in the classroom. Having students discuss and even create case studies related to LGBTIQ issues in the classroom would certainly prepare them to address these issues in their careers. Here is a sample I created and gave to my fellow teachers at a recent inservice:

> Every week, you allow your students to free write in their journals for 10 minutes about anything they want. You tell them that you usually don't read them word-for-word, you simply skim them to make sure that their journals are school appropriate and that there's nothing alarming, since you are a mandated reporter. Last week, Steven wrote about how he hates another student in your class, Tom, because he's a "fag." Steven doesn't threaten Tom or say that Tom has done anything that has made him uncomfortable, he simply repeats that he hates Tom and he hates fags. Do you report Steven, talk to him one-on-one, have the whole class read an article about homophobia, or ignore it all together?

A final option that would be most beneficial is for the university education department to create an elective survey course on LGBTIQ children's literature. In this course, students could experience all the options I listed above as well as discover myriad texts specifically for LGBTIQ education.

NOTES

1. A literature circle is a small group, in-depth discussion of a text.
2. I am using the personal pronoun *they* as a gender-neutral, singular personal pronoun.

3.   I use the word *queer* here not as a derogatory term, but because it is a word that has been reclaimed by the LGBTIQ community, and it is used as an umbrella term for sexual and gender minorities.

REFERENCES

Baldwin, J. (1956). *Giovanni's room.* New York, NY: Dial Press.

Bauer, M. D. (1995). *Am I blue?: Coming out from the silence.* New York, NY: Harper-Collins.

Chbosky, S. (1999). *The perks of being a wallflower.* New York, NY: Pocket Books.

Cunningham, M. (2000). *The hours.* New York, NY: Farrar, Straus and Giroux.

DeWitt, P. M. (2012). *Dignity for all: Safeguarding LGBT students.* New York, NY: Corin

Eugenides, J. (2002). *Middlesex.* New York, NY: Farrar, Straus and Giroux.

Feinburg, L. (1993). *Stone butch blues.* Ann Arbor, MI: Firebrand Books

Flagg, F. (1988). *Fried green tomatoes at the Whistle Stop Cafe.* New York, NY: Random House.

LGBT Foundation. (2009, February 11). *New report highlights self harm needs to be taken more seriously.* Retrieved from http://lgbt.foundation/news/new-report-highlights-self-harm-needs-to-be-taken-more-seriously/

Levithan, D. (2003). *Boy meets boy.* New York, NY: Knopf Books for Young Readers.

Malley, E., Posner M., & Potter L. (2008). *Suicide risk and prevention for lesbian, gay, bisexual, and transgender youth.* Newton, MA: Education Development Center.

Mehra, B., & Braquet, D. (2006, March). A "queer" manifesto of interventions for libraries to "come out" of the closet!: A study of "queer" youth experiences during the coming out process. *Libres: Library and Information Science Research Electronic Journal, 16*(1). Retrieved from https://www.researchgate.net/publication/238689260_A_Queer_Manifesto_of_Interventions_for_Libraries_to_Come_Out_of_the_Closet_A_Study_of_Queer_Youth_Experiences_during_the_Coming_Out_Process

Namaste, V. (2002). *Invisible lives: The erasure of transexual and transgender people.* Chicago, IL: University of Chicago Press.

Newman, L., & Cornell, L. (2015). *Heather has two mommies.* Somerville, MA: Candlewick. (Original work published 1989)

Oltmann, S. M. (2015). Variables related to school media center LGBT collections. *International Journal of Libraries & Information Services, 65*(1), 25–33.

Rice, A. (2002). *The vampire chronicles.* New York, NY: Ballantine Books.

Richardson, J., & Parnell, P. (2005). *And Tango makes three.* New York, NY: Simon & Schuster.

Sanchez, A. (2003). *Rainbow boys.* New York, NY: Simon & Schuster.

Sonnie, A. (2000). *Revolutionary voices: A multicultural queer youth anthology.* Los Angeles, CA: Alyson Publications.

Williams, T. (1955). *Cat on a hot tin roof.* New York, NY: Signet.

SECTION IV

K–20: CREATING A SAFE AND POSITIVE LEARNING CLIMATE IN ALL EDUCATIONAL SETTINGS

CHAPTER 11

WHAT BEING A GSA SPONSOR HAS DONE FOR ME AND OTHERS

Alexandria Henry

During my time as an undergraduate, I was a very shy individual. I knew that I was part of the LGBTIQ community, but was not very sure I wanted other people to know that, especially when I was not sure where I was on the LGBTIQ spectrum. I have always been one of those types of people who are more comfortable when knowing others are accepting. The first school that I worked for after graduation was at the middle school level. Working in a school was very exciting to me and meant I could start working with today's youth. Throughout my early teaching, I learned about students' needs through programing like Gay-Straight Alliances (GSA) and how that type of programming would have helped me along through my high school to college years as a person on the LGBTIQ spectrum. I learned that programming like GSAs could help more students feel accepted in their school environment. For the past 3 years as a GSA sponsor, I have learned a lot about myself and about what issues today's youth are facing. I had no idea what a positive impact was about to be made by the GSA clubs in my district, which I will talk about soon. During my quest to find a teaching position, I have been able to dedicate my time to after-school programming at the middle school level. I have participated

Queering Classrooms: Personal Narratives and Educational Practices to Support LGBTQ Youth in Schools, pp. 157–167
Copyright © 2017 by Information Age Publishing

157

in after-school programs such as coaching athletics and different types of at-risk youth leadership-building programs. I have been involved longer in programs that address LGBTIQ issues.

THE NEED FOR THE FIRST MIDDLE SCHOOL–LEVEL GSA

The district's middle school GSA at my school started transforming our students and then our school climate. Being part of a Gay-Straight Alliance has not only motivated me to be a better student advocate, but has motivated other staff members to be better educators for all students. Students and staff became more conscious of what type of LGBTIQ-inclusive atmosphere our school was trying to build. I offered to be a co-sponsor of the newly formed GSA with a fellow teacher. The school was the first middle school GSA in the state. Being part of this club was much more than helping students. It also helped me become comfortable with who I am. I originally started sitting in on the GSA meetings at our school to support and check out what students did. At the time the GSA club started, I wasn't really openly out as someone on the LGBTIQ spectrum. This club helped me focus on the type of role model I wanted to be for my students. I couldn't tell them to be more comfortable with themselves unless I was comfortable about myself. Being an "out" member of the LGBTIQ community would help my students to provide them with an LGBTIQ role model within their school. Being a part of this club helped me in amazing ways. It helped me come out of my shell and be more proud of who I was as a member of the LGBTIQ family. Our students need confidence, proud leaders, and role models. That's what I wanted to be for the students as an educator.

ORGANIZATIONS THAT HELPED OUR GSA BE SUCCESSFUL

There are some great organizations out there such as statewide organizations and local PFLAG (formerly known as Parents, Families and Friends of Lesbians and Gays) chapters. Having a resource like PFLAG in our community is a great opportunity since PFLAG helps parents in the area embrace LGBTIQ issues. There was a need for something within the school to be a resource or hub for all the information from these organizations in the area. These area organizations were a great way for people of the LGBTIQ spectrum to seek resources. Having a GSA was important for so many students within our school. GSA is meant to be a student-run club. Some of our middle school students heard what a GSA was and knew immediately that they wanted to have one in their school. These students wanted a place within their school where everyone, no matter what their story was, could be themselves. The fact that a GSA club was started because a couple of middle school students requested it shows there is a need for middle school level GSAs. There is also a statewide organization that helped support our middle school GSA as it was getting started. Our school's assistant principal worked closely with this organization to make establishing a GSA happen for our school district. This organization is the only agency in some counties of the state that is dedicated solely to serving LGBTQ youth. Their mission is to provide wellness education on a variety of topics, leadership development, and social space. A student of ours told us she learned a lot during her time in the GSA, such as "ways to talk to people who don't feel safe and just a lot of ways to make everyone more included." Our GSA members were looking for LGBTIQ information to learn about themselves and to learn how to deal with bullying issues within their school. Thanks to organizations such as these, our students are being educated by surrounding organizations and school sponsors about LGBTIQ and how they can teach others about the importance of being accepting. My colleague and I are always looking for training we can share with our staff so that they can learn content that will make them better educators for all of our students, including LGBTIQ students. For example, some staff within the school district have been able to take free training held at a local university. This ally training has been a great resource for community members to show support for the LGBTIQ community. We have been able to have in-district training by outside organizations to engage our staff that helps them learn how to be better allies and better listeners to our students. The biggest issue we have had in our school is not knowing what to do or say when an LGBTIQ situation occurs. That makes it even more important for school GSAs to educate students and staff. Some of these bullying issues include how to combat the use of the phrase "That's so gay" and other hurtful anti-LGBTIQ language. Our school's GSA would focus on those needs and find appropriate resources for our staff and school personnel to use within school. Other middle school resources came from another statewide organization whose mission is to promote safety, support, and healthy development for LGBTIQ youth. The students in our rural community were looking for a safe place that focused on subject areas that were not talked about anywhere else. The subject of LGBTIQ identity was not commonly talked about in the school setting, and the education needed to be present if our school district was going to start addressing LGBTIQ issues at the middle school level. We were ready as GSA sponsors to lead our students in opening the LGBTIQ doors within our school and community.

THE IMPACT A GSA CAN HAVE ALONG WITH THE STRUGGLES

Regardless of the negative experiences we had in the beginning, we knew that we were meeting the needs of some students right away. Students who requested a GSA had every right to request a club that made them feel like they belong. The beginning struggle we observed in our middle school GSA was not that students didn't want to join, but that students were worried what other people would think if they did join. A common issue for our GSA each year has been that our students feared being labeled LGBTIQ. Students did not want to be labeled or to stand out right away. As our students learned about their sexuality and learned about LGBTIQ identity, they felt more comfortable teaching others and made them more comfortable with themselves. Even though they were more comfortable with themselves, they still often wondered what their middle school classmates thought of them, and what they were calling them behind their back.

Changing the School Climate With Our GSA

Our middle school climate was heading in a positive direction for LGBTIQ students. Our GSA worked hard to change the climate by educating the staff and students on LGBTIQ subject matters and create a school climate worth coming out in. We created an LGBTIQ-inclusive school climate through a variety of different approaches throughout the district. At the beginning of each school year I made an LGBTIQ resource packet for all school personnel. This packet was something that could be hung up in the classroom and used as a guide for topics such as LGBTIQ common language and what to say when someone says, "That's so gay." My school's GSA had many pro-LGBTIQ happenings throughout the school building. For example, the Safe Spot Ally sticker was helpful in changing our LGBTIQ school climate. This sticker was offered to any staff or personnel that wanted to display that their room was a safe space from not only LGBTIQ bullying but bullying of any kind. Our middle school students and staff took kindly to the safe space sticker and it even made an impact on our middle school families. One family, new to town, was touring the building and noticed the safe space symbol on the library door. Our middle school counselor mentioned that this particular family made positive comments with regard to the safe space symbol. He said, "While commenting, she smiled and squeezed her partner's shoulder." This was an amazing occurrence during a school orientation/tour given to a student who just moved into our district. The counselor could tell by the positive reaction of the family that our school was doing the right things to make it a warm and inviting environment.

There was a lot of fundraising to pay for materials that would help educate staff so that they could help their GSA students fight for LGBTIQ rights within their school. I used an amazing fundraising site called DonorsChoose (Donorschoose.org). This website is designed for teachers to list supplies needed; anyone in the United States can choose which school receives the donations. I created educational LGBTIQ binders that were placed in teacher's lounges of each school. I used student feedback to construct an informational binder that would help staff combat anti-LGBTIQ situations. Thanks to DonorsChoose I was able to purchase LGBTIQ-inclusive stories to put in the library for students and LGBTIQ educational books for staff wanting to know more about LGBTIQ education. The LGBTIQ books that were purchased were from a list provided by one of the statewide agencies and include works such as the Russel Middlebrook series. The middle school age-appropriate books from the list we were provided help supply our library with LGBTIQ-inclusive stories for our students to read, which helped make LGBTIQ language more of a common language within our school. We also had books such as "The Trevor Projects: It Gets Better." All of these books provided our students with resources about coming out, as well as stories about others' bullying experiences, to show that they are not alone. The books that were purchased for staff were of various themes, from LGBTIQ rights to how to be a better support for middle school students who are part of the LGBTIQ spectrum. Our students checked out the books from the library often and several staff borrowed books from me to read. We also were able to purchase color printers and button makers and even GSA shirts that helped make it easy for GSA-related dialogue. The visibility and positive support throughout school made it easier for students to join GSA and help out. The staff and students were all given good resources to help with positive LGBTIQ discussions within the school environment. Our school GSA sold almost 100 shirts that said, "Don't Hate, Educate." The staff support was tremendous and has been the number one reason for our GSA's fast success.

Our Middle School Was "Coming Out"

As our school climate changed, we noticed more allies coming out and more students coming out of their shells. Students became more comfortable testing social norms and were not focused on what others thought about them. More and more students participated in GSA events held during lunchtime. For example, each year our school had an event during lunch to hand out GSA buttons and LGBTIQ informational packets in an effort to help stop bullying. We have had a couple cases over the last 2 years wherein students moved out of our school because their parents did not like that we have a GSA. We were hopeful of the positive impact our GSA would have on the many other students who attended the school. The staff was able to see how some of these students went from being the quiet kid in class to the social butterfly with positively developing youth leadership skills.

There are many opportunities for staff and students to learn about LGBTIQ issues in our district. These opportunities range from staff training to the information given out by our school's GSA. There are so many opportunities for not only school personnel to learn, but also for parents. Our school partnered with one of the statewide organizations to host a parent night at the school. This event was to showcase our GSA and provide community members with LGBTIQ basic training. As our GSA became more popular, word about our work reached the community that we were talking about LGBTIQ issues. Some parents and staff had concerns about what was being taught within our school GSA. For example, one parent expressed that we were teaching our GSA students about "gay sex." Education is needed for all, especially those who are hiding their families from LGBTIQ-related topics. We used experiences such as these to focus on getting the word out about who we were as a group and what we stood for.

The attention our school was as a result of our LGBTIQ activism caused our school to "come out" in a way. When I say coming out, I mean first and foremost as an ally. Not only were our students coming out because they were part of the GSA, but our staff supporters were coming out as well. Our GSA members and staff were first and foremost allies— allies for the entire student body, no matter what their sexual or gender identity. A lot more positive LGBTIQ activism happened at the school since the implementation of GSA. There was so much drive for change that our GSA won two Ally of the Year awards during the 2013 school year. These awards were presented to the school by the statewide organization and by our local university. This award is given to a person or organization from the state each year for leadership in making schools safer for those who identify as LGBTIQ. Those same guidelines and expectations are part of the Ally Award presented by the local university.

These awards meant great things for our school environment. This was another reason people could be proud of the district. Many of the staff and I were proud to share this news about our school. The school's GSA was very proud for all the hard work they had done to positively impact their school and community. The school and the school district did however face some negative attention. There were struggles with parents and other community members who thought other ideas being taught during GSA, particularly what content was being presented to middle school students with regard to LGBTIQ issues. Without ever asking the school or students, some parents assumed we were teaching our students about LGBTIQ sex at the middle school level. Proper LGBTIQ education for staff, students, and community members would help create a better ally base so that we can help fight negative rumors about the club. Rumors such as these led to the belief that the GSA was forcing students to be gay and forcing all students to be quiet on events such as the "Day of Silence."

These negative experiences were, despite the misinformation floating around, amazing teaching tools for what school GSAs should be working on with regard to educating others. When we had negative encounters with nonsupporters, it was our administrative staff who were on the front lines, supporting our club and what we stand for. Our principal supported our school's GSA for months during a battle with a group of parents who did not believe our school should be supporting LGBTIQ rights in the middle school. Parents were informed that if they wanted the GSA shut down, all student clubs would need to be discontinued in the school. Our principal did a tremendous job supporting all of our students, including those on the LGBTIQ spectrum. Battling these negative issues was easy due to the amount of support we had within our school environment.

Our GSA Impact on Families and Staff

The impact our middle school GSA has had on the school and community has been a positive and inspirational experience. This was determined by family and staff feedback. We have had numerous positive parental comments while hosting events such as 6th-grade orientation before school starts each year. Our school has set up a small orientation for activities to show what our school has to offer for student involvement. The first year the GSA participated, parents approached staff many times, smiling and letting us know they appreciate what we are doing. Our GSA club table was never lonely. We had parents and students ask what we were about and were seeking more information. Having orientation is great practice for our middle school club members to speak to the community members and get the positive LGBTIQ information out. As the next couple of years progressed, our school staff took a bigger interest in LGBTIQ rights and sought out more information than ever before. I always had staff approach me in the building and ask what our GSA was going to do next and how they could support us. I also had a few parents tell me what an impact our school GSA has made on them, such as help-ing their children become more outspoken and more positive about who they are. These are the reasons we do what we do within our school dis-trict and hope to make an impact like this every year.

TEACHER-EDUCATION PROGRAMS AND LGBTIQ EDUCATION

It would help the LGBTIQ progressive movement if we had teacher preparation programs with inclusion-integrated lessons and train-ing. Current LGBTIQ training would be beneficial for student teachers or those who are about to graduate. I have been to LGBTIQ-inclusive training and I would have benefitted a long time ago knowing the infor-mation from such opportunities. For example, anyone working in the school environment can benefit from knowing gender-neutral pro-nouns. This has benefitted me at the middle school level greatly since there are many students who don't identify as they may appear to me. Diversity training can be beneficial at any level. It helps people get a sense of how different everyone is and how we can accept and affirm each other in a positive learning environment. LGBTIQ training for teachers can help educate these future leaders on how to approach the different types of students they will encounter. I would have also benefited in col-lege knowing more about LGBTIQ terminology. If I knew then what I know now from training sessions, I would have sought out more organiza-tions to be a part of at the college level. Teachers need to be prepared for the issues they will experience in the educational field. These issues go further than just content knowledge in their subject area. Working with students and being seen as someone who promotes a safe space is benefi-cial in creating bonds with students. Issues such as bullying can be more easily addressed when staff is knowledgeable about what is happening in their school.

Despite there being college-level courses available, such as current and critical issues, we need more than a current issues course to cover the importance of gender and sexuality as it relates to K–12 educa-tion. LGBTIQ training and education should be infused throughout the university or college to better educate those who will be working in teacher education programs and in many other programs. I would rec-ommend having safe-zone programs that focus on LGBTIQ terms and how to approach different types of students in the classroom environ-ment. For example, pronoun preference is not anything I ever knew about until joining my school's GSA. Learning there are female, male, and gender-neutral ways to be addressed has opened my eyes to the dif-ferent ways students identity in the educational setting. For example,

many students and staff are unaware that some people prefer the pronoun "Zir" instead of his or her. Asking about someone's pronoun preference is important. Something as simple as pronoun preference can be
easily implemented in the classroom and can make a huge difference in a
student's learning experience. For example, learning how to properly
start the beginning of the school year and make roll call a less anxious
event can be a great start to bonding with students. Teachers can learn to
ask for pronoun preferences on the first day of school. This sets the safe
space tone for the rest of the year. If students aren't comfortable being
labeled in the classroom by others' perceptions, rather than by how they
view themselves, that takes away from their learning focus.

Taking courses or training like the ones set up by LGBTIQ programs
can help provide understanding for why people in targeted or oppressed
groups become bombarded with unfair treatment from society. Training
on the experiences and needs of oppressed groups can help create educated allies to make safe spaces for those experiencing discrimination and
violence. Teacher education programs should be providing material on
how to address current student issues and how to interfere with bullying,
such as what to do when you hear anti-LGBTIQ words being used. There
is also a great deal of useful information out there for educators that can
be easily taught in a safe-space program. There is information readily
available to hand out, such as a list of hotline numbers meeting the different needs of students. For example, an amazing hotline is the Trevor
Project, founded in 1998 for those who need 24/7 counseling. Crisis
intervention and suicide prevention for LGBTIQ youth ages 13–24 can
use the number to seek help (Trevor Project, 2016). These partnerships
can be used to create an amazing portal of resources so that teachers can
provide what their students need.

Training and classes have taught me about the growing statistics when
it comes to bullying in middle school. I have gone through a physical
education program and I can say that I would have benefitted greatly
knowing how to enforce inclusion in the way of gender and sexuality. According to a school climate survey, 35.3% of students in gender segregated spaces felt uncomfortable in their school's locker room (Kosciw,
Greytak, Palmer, & Boesen, 2015). Knowing what areas have more specific bullying would make it easier to plan on how to take action against
it. If I had known 10 years ago what I know now about sexual identity and
gender expression, I would have approached most of my physical education lessons in a different light. If you ask most physical education educators now, they would most likely say games such as dodgeball are not
acceptable to play in physical education anymore because they can cause a
negative atmosphere for many different types of students. This same
negative atmosphere can occur when you divide your class by male and

female lables. Learning about gender expression and learning about how middle school students identify in terms of sexuality and gender expression can shed some light on how splitting students up by gender can be socially unjust. With regard to other classroom subjects, such as a middle school health class, teacher-education programs can teach how to make their lessons LGBTIQ inclusive. For example, a student who is not sure how they identify may sit through a health class that only addresses heterosexual health education. Saying things in health class such as "How many of you girls have a boyfriend?" further excludes students who do not fit within the binaries that drive our assumptions about youth. Furthermore, noninclusive LGBTIQ health education can lead to a negative atmosphere for students. There are other potentially dangerous situations that can occur in the area of physical education and gender separation. We see so many issues with regard to locker rooms and the creating of gender-neutral bathrooms. I have seen many students who are uncomfortable with changing in the locker room, but there has been an increase in gender nonconforming students who are having issues changing in either a female- or male-only locker room. The middle schools I have worked at have done a tremendous job of accommodating students with use of the nurse's office or school bathroom. If educators are not aware of these issues, especially physical education teachers, then it makes it more difficult to connect with a student and makes class tension even worse for the student on many levels.

There are so many great LGBTIQ-inclusive lessons available, such as GLSEN's Changing the Game, which sheds light on inclusive physical education atmospheres. Many lessons are available across disciplines, such as how to include a gay rights activist in a history lesson. In so doing, teachers show to learners that all people, regardless of their sexual identity or gender expression, can and will be successful. Wrapping your head around the fact that times are changing and our students are changing can help educators immensely if they know the right approach to focus on. Our school district has been a great example of using student advocacy skills and has shown what acceptance and affirmation along with education can do for the good of our students and our community.

RECOMMENDATIONS FOR BEGINNING EDUCATORS

Being a better educator takes dedication and motivation to want to continuously learn about today's youth and issues. It would be very beneficial for all school districts, community organizations, and other workplaces to go through LGBTIQ and acceptance training. More universities and schools are offering training that helps teach acceptance and shed some light on diversity. There is great training and education on gender identity and sexuality and that can help teachers adapt their lessons to be more inclusive. For example, a teacher using gender neutral words can make a positive difference to a learner. You, as teachers, can use the Internet to your advantage for seeking out people in your area who are activists in the same areas and network with them. Start a GSA or a youth program in your school that can help create safe spaces for at-risk youth. If you are not sure how, research ways to get training or read literature. One thing that has been growing is the literature on how to be an active GSA sponsor for your school. I encourage everyone to research antibullying training in their area and if there is none, help create it.

The best advice I can give to anyone in the education field is to be open-minded and learn as much as you can about the diversity of the students you will be teaching. We need teachers and school personnel that are willing to help start and sponsor programming to meet the needs of their students. It is important for new and beginning teachers to not only make sure they have age-appropriate content, but that it relates to the current needs and concerns of today's students. As educators, we can never make assumptions about what happens to students when they leave our supervision, and we can never take the job as a student's parent; but we can create a safe place for students to grow socially, emotionally, and academically. A GSA student said at an award ceremony that "We're this little town in this little school and we were doing something for ourselves and we ended up making a bigger change for everyone." As an educator there is nothing more rewarding than seeing your students achieve success. With the right education, support, and allies, the world can help all students succeed in any way they want to. As soon as we learn how to be good allies, we can work in better partnership with others. Students today need their educators to be willing to change with them and advocate for them more than ever before.

REFERENCES

Kosciw, J. G., Greytak, E. A., Palmer, N. A., & Boesen, M. J. (2014). *The 2013 National School Climate Survey: The experiences of lesbian, gay, bisexual and transgender youth in our nation's schools.* New York, NY: GLSEN. Retrieved from http://www.glsen.org/nscs

Trevor Project. (1998). *About the Trevor Project.* West Hollywood, CA: Author. Retrieved from http://www.thetrevorproject.org/section/about

CHAPTER 12

A CALL TO ACTION

The Importance of School Climate, Professional Development, and Teacher-Education Programs in Fostering LGBT Supportive Educators

Melissa Doellman

Professional development for current educators and teacher preparation programs for preservice professionals play a crucial role in providing learning opportunities to foster the appropriate pedagogical and professional skills needed by today's educators. Many school districts require educators to attend a certain amount of professional development activities within the district as well as participate in professional education associations or educational conferences each year. Preservice teacher programs require teacher candidates to document their professional development through coursework, clinical experiences, and student teaching. Both arenas are designed to have the same effect: prepare the educational workforce to properly handle situations that arise and create a well-developed curriculum in the classroom to promote student learning. Topics for teacher training spread across many areas of education including curriculum, content, learning standards, classroom manage-

Queering Classrooms: Personal Narratives and Educational Practices to Support LGBTQ Youth in Schools, pp. 169–186
Copyright © 2017 by Information Age Publishing

ment, technology—the list continues on and on. It is hard to claim that one area is more important than another because each plays a critical role in school climate and in promoting effective student learning. However, as new issues and topics arise in the educational world, it is important to address them. The issues of students in the World War II era are not exactly the same as the issues facing current students. Times have changed and so have the challenges that educators experience on a daily basis. As society pushes forward, it is important for teachers to remain culturally relevant and aware of issues that students endure. One area that is in need of attention by teacher education programs and professional development activities is the issues facing lesbian, gay, bisexual, and transgendered (LGBT) students.

THE IMPORTANCE OF SCHOOL CLIMATE FOR LGBT YOUTH

School climate is a key social development context for LGBT adolescents (Hatzenbuehler, Birkett, Van Wagenen, & Meyer, 2014). Research has shown that intolerance and prejudice make school a hostile and dangerous place. Couple this with an unfortunately elevated nationwide and worldwide occurrence of victimization of LGBT youth at school due to sexual orientation, gender identity, and/or gender expression (Greytak & Kosciw, 2014; Kosciw, Palmer, Kull, & Greytak, 2013), and the importance of school climate for LGBT students is elevated.

The negative experiences of LGBT students at school range from verbal and physical harassment, sexual harassment, social exclusion and isolation, and other problems with peers (Kosciw et al., 2013). The Gay, Lesbian, and Straight Education Network's (GLSEN) 2013 National Student Climate Survey found that 55.5% of LGBT students felt unsafe at school due to their sexual orientation, 37.8% felt unsafe due to their gender expression, and over one third avoided gender segregated spaces because they did not feel comfortable and/or safe. In addition, 71.4% of LGBT students heard "gay" used in a negative way and 64.5% heard other homophobic remarks such as "dyke" or "faggot" frequently or often in school. Some 90.8% of the students also reported that this language caused them distress (Kosciw, Greytak, Palmer, & Boesen, 2014). Furthermore, LGBT students are exposed to an increased level of victimization at school, including harassment and assault. The numbers are staggering: 74.4% of LGBT students were verbally harassed due to sexual orientation (55.2% due to gender expression); 36.2% physically harassed (22.7% due to gender expression); 16.5% physically assaulted (11.4% due to gender expression); and 49.0% harassed via electronic communication in text messages or social media (Kosciw et al., 2014). Not only does victimization occur, much of it goes unreported (56.7% of LGBT students) because students doubt that school staff could effectively intervene or believe that reporting the incident would make things worse (Kosciw et al., 2014).

A study conducted by Kosciw et al. (2013) collected data from 50 random community groups that served LGBT youth and from an online survey posted to LGBT youth-oriented websites and e-mail lists. They utilized data from 5,730 LGBT students who indicated they are in K–12 schools from all 50 states and the District of Columbia. Participants were asked about their experience with verbal and physical harassment and assault due to their sexual orientation or gender expression. They also gathered data on how many school days participants missed due to negative experience at schools, on student grade-point averages, and on available support systems in the school. Results from the study indicate that in-school victimization resulted in decreased self-esteem, more missed days of school, and lower GPAs (Kosciw et al., 2013).

Analysis of focus group interviews by Grossman et al. (2009) revealed common themes for experiences in school. Two themes emerged in their experiences with school violence: lack of community and lack of empowerment with no sense of control over their experience. Students reported feelings of not being a part of the school community; in fact, many reported feeling marginalized and having no control over how other students treated them. Even worse, they felt that nothing could be done to remedy the situation. Furthermore, they felt that they could not act alone to address issues. However, in the rare instances that they were given assistance in school, once they left school property they were again on their own. Some reported that heterosexual students made it clear they perceived themselves to be superior to the sexual and gender minority youth. Frequent name-calling, hate speech, harassment, and violence were common experiences for many participants in the study. According to the participants, the climate of their school, in which harassment was not rare and where support (even when incidents were reported to teachers or school staff) was hard to find, led to their feeling of exclusion from the school community (Grossman et al., 2009).

When school may not often be a safe and affirming environment for these students, there are negative impacts on their well-being and achievement (Kosciw et al., 2013). In the academic realm, the hostile school environment has detrimental impacts on student attendance, academic performance, and "educational attainment" (Greytak & Kosciw, 2014). LGBT students who experience higher levels of victimization due to sexual orientation and/or gender expression were more likely to have missed school in the past month, had lower grade-point averages, were more likely to report that they did not plan to pursue postsecondary education, and had lower levels of self-esteem and a higher incidence of depression (Kosciw et al., 2014). In general, victimization of LGBT students leads to poorer psychological well-being (Greytak & Kosciw, 2014).

Russell, Ryan, Toomey, Diaz, and Sanchez (2011) conducted a study of 245 participants from California-based LGBT young adults (ages 21–25). The study included a retrospective scale assessing their experience with school victimization due to their actual or perceived LGBT identity when they were between the ages of 13 and 19. The analysis of data tested association between LGBT victimization and depression, suicidal ideation, life satisfaction, and self-esteem. They found that LGBT-related school victimization was strongly linked to mental health and risk for sexually transmitted infections and HIV. In particular, they found that there was an elevated level of depression and suicidal ideation among young males that may be explained by high rates of victimization in school (Russell et al., 2011).

CREATING A POSITIVE SCHOOL CLIMATE

Given the importance of school climate on LGBT students' academic outcomes and psychological well-being, it is vital to create a supportive school atmosphere. Hatzenbuehler et al. (2014) provide suggestions to create a more supportive school climate by having a Gay, Straight, Alliance Club (GSA) and safe spaces for LGBT youth, including curriculum related to health matters for LGBT people, prohibiting harassment based on sexual orientation and gender identity, encouraging professional development for teachers to learn to create safe and supportive climates within the school, and facilitating access to off-school property providers for health and special services directly related to LGBT issues. Creating a supportive climate is important because there is a correlation between positive school climate and a reduced risk for suicidal thoughts. The results of this study indicate that youths with a greater school connectedness and who reside in districts with more protective school climates were significantly less likely to report suicidal thoughts and fewer suicide attempts (Hatzenbuehler et al., 2014). Research has shown that each of these has benefits to LGBT students (GLSEN, 2007, 2011; Greytak et al., 2012; Hatzenbuehler et al., 2014; Kosciw et al., 2014; Kosciw et al., 2013; Murphy, 2012; Toomey, Ryan, Diaz, & Russell, 2011).

Gay-Straight Alliance Impact on School Climate

The presence of a GSA is linked to a decrease in victimization, an increase in the feeling of school belonging, and better mental health for

LGBT students (Kosciw et al., 2012). These student-led, school-based clubs are open to all members of the school regardless of sexual identity or gender orientation. They often advocate for improved school climate, educate the community on LGBT issues, and provide a support system for LGBT students and their allies (GLSEN, 2007). Compared to students who did not have a GSA available at their school, students at schools where a GSA is present were less likely to hear "gay" used in a negative way or other homophobic remarks, were more likely to report that school staff intervened when hearing anti-LGBT remarks, were less likely to feel unsafe, experienced lower levels of victimization, and felt more connected to their school (Kosciw et al., 2014). A research brief conducted by GLSEN (2007) found that students in a school with a GSA were less likely to hear homophobic comments (57% compared to 75%), less likely to report feeling unsafe in school because of their sexually orientation (61% vs. 68%) or because of gender expression (38% vs. 43%), less likely to miss school because of feeling unsafe (26% vs. 32%), and students were more likely to report that students, faculty, and administrators were more supportive (52% vs. 37%) (GLSEN, 2007).

In a 2011 study, Toomey, Ryan, Diaz, and Sanchez examine how the presence of a GSA impact young LGBT students' well-being. Utilizing retrospective survey results from 245 LGBT young adults, they analyzed the presence or absence of school GSAs, student participation in their school's GSA, and perception of the effectiveness of the GSA on improving student safety. Only 86 of the 245 participants (~35%) reported that their high school had a GSA. Of those 86 students who reported the presence of a GSA, 55 reported some sort of participation in the organization and the average rating of the effectiveness of the GSAs were low (Toomey et al., 2011). However, the results of analysis showed that there was a significant impact of the presence of a GSA on increased self-esteem and decreased depression in students. The presence of the GSA was also associated with less of a school dropout risk and greater future college attendance. They also found that participation in a GSA appears to buffer the negative association of LGBT school victimization and well-being (Toomey et al., 2011). However, GSAs are not the only facets of K–12 schools that can promote a positive school climate.

Role of Inclusive Curriculum in School Climate

An inclusive curriculum is one that is inclusive of diverse groups and promotes respect and equity. It can directly influence a student's feeling of self-worth (Kosciw et al., 2012). Inclusive curriculum has been shown to contribute to a safer school climate for LGBT youth with connections to a decreased victimization, an increase in feeling safe, and a decrease in the number of days missed due to feeling unsafe (GLSEN, 2011). The inclusive curriculum also helps students feel more connected to the school with and increase in comfort and frequency talking to teachers about LBGT issues that arise in the school. Finally, an inclusive curriculum can reinforce peer acceptance with a decrease in the likelihood of hearing homophobic language and an increase in student intervention when hearing remarks (GLSEN, 2011). In addition to benefits of an inclusive curriculum to LGBT students, benefits to all students include exposure to more accurate and inclusive accounts of historical events, development of a more empathetic understanding of LGBT people and their contributions to society, encouragement of critical questioning of stereotypes about LGBT people, and promotion of acceptance of all people (GLSEN, 2012).

Advocacy for LGBT students can be accomplished through inclusive curriculum. Advocates "promote 'effective learning environments for the social-emotional success of all children'" (Graybill, Varjas, Meyers, & Watson, 2009, p. 570). Schools in which there is an inclusive curriculum where LGBT issues are addressed in courses have a higher percentage of students who feel comfortable talking with a teacher about LGBT issues (73.1% vs. 50.1%) and are more likely to have talked with a teacher about LGBT issues (79.9% vs. 64.1%). However despite the benefits of an inclusive curriculum, one study showed that 86.6% of students reported never having been taught anything about LGBT history, issues, or events in their classes (GLSEN, 2011).

Another study on LGBT inclusive curriculum surveyed 26 students in California (Snapp, Burdge, Licona, Moody, & Russell, 2015) where Senate Bill 48 (the FAIR Education Act) was passed in January 2012. This update to the California Education Code requires "the inclusion of age-appropriate, factual, and relevant information about the roles and contributions of LGBT(Q) people and people with disabilities into history and social studies instruction" (Snapp et al., p. 250). Students in this study reported that LGBT issues were most common in history, government, health, and English classes. In social science classes, current events discussed in class included those relevant to LGBT issues. Health classes commonly addressed issues regarding sexual orientation, gender expression, and related terminology. Speakers were brought to the classes to speak with students about personal stories and health issues facing LGBT people. English courses included LGBT-relevant literature and examined texts from LGBT historical events (e.g., the riots at Stonewall, the Holocaust, etc.) (Snapp et al., 2015).

When attempting to implement an LGBT-inclusive curriculum, educators need to look for places to include LGBT-related content. For example, when teaching the scientific method in science classes, teachers can include information on the scientist who created the method (Francis Bacon) who identified as a gay individual (GLSEN, 2012). In addition to planning when to include LGBT-related content, teachers need to be careful to consider the placement of the curriculum to prevent fragmentation that leads students to believe that these issues are separate from those of other individuals. The Common Core Standards also allow areas for inclusion of LGBT-related content. GLSEN (2012) provides examples of how this can be done for a number of standards. Some of these suggestions include using LGBT-related essays for writing standards in English and history/social studies and using census data on LGBT individuals in data analysis for reaching statistic and probability standards in high school math classes (GLSEN, 2012).

Antibullying and Harassment Policies

Antibullying and harassment policies have also been shown to decrease victimization of LGBT students (Kosciw et al., 2014), and policies that explicitly include sexual orientation yield a lower risk of suicide attempts among LGBT students (Hatzenbuehler et al., 2014). Students where a complete policy that includes sexual orientation and gender identity/expression is in place are less likely to hear "gay" used in a negative way or homophobic remarks frequently and are more likely to report that staff intervenes when hearing homophobic remarks (Kosciw et al., 2014).

Educators have an ethical and legal obligation to ensure that all students have an equal opportunity to learn in a healthy and safe environment (Jacob, 2013). The Tenth Amendment of the U.S. Constitution declares that state governments have the duty to educate children. However, the Fourteenth Amendment, which does not directly address education, has been the basis of lawsuits against schools for cases that involve LGBT discrimination and failure to provide equal protection for LGBT students from harassment. In fact, over $4 million was awarded to LGBT students after filing a lawsuit against their schools for failing to protect them from harassment between 1997 and 2007 (Jacob, 2013).

In order to combat bullying and harassment in schools, a number of states have enacted legislation to protect students, some of which directly address the protection of students on the basis of their sexual orientation, gender identity, gender expression, and specific laws for K–12 education (Russell, Kosciw, Horn, & Saewyc, 2010). For example, Illinois (Senate Bill 3266—Prevent School Violence in Illinois) and New York (Senate Bill 1987B—Dignity for All Students Act) both have laws in place that address discrimination, harassment, and bullying with clear inclusion of sexual orientation, gender identity, and gender expression in order to protect students (Russell et al., 2010). However, there have been attempts from some states to prevent the inclusion of LGBT students in local antibullying policies. The trend seems to be to try to avoid the issue all together. In Tennessee, the "Don't Say Gay" bill(s), would have banned schools from talking about LGBT issues at school even in relation to antigay bullying and harassment (Sanders, 2013).

Currently, there are two federal laws under consideration that address antibullying measures in schools. These would provide explicit protection for LGBT students in public schools. The Safe Schools Improvement Act (SSIA – HR2262) is an antibullying approach that would require schools and districts to implement policies that have prevention and intervention strategies, professional development for teachers and staff, student and parent notification of rights, and responsibility to report incidents to state and local authorities (Russell et al., 2010). The Student Non-Discrimination Act (SNDA – HR4530) is a nondiscrimination law that would provide protection and provisions for legal assistance for students who are victims of violence based on their actual or perceived sexual orientation or gender identity (Russell et al., 2010).

Supportive Staff as a Critical Component of Positive School Climate

While all of the aforementioned measures are important for creating a supportive and positive school climate, supportive staff may have the strongest influence on school climate; previous research has shown that having a supportive adult helps alleviate the negative effects of a hostile climate (Greytak & Kosciw, 2014). It has been reported that LGBT students in the United States believe that having one or more supportive teachers or staff members is critical to surviving in a hostile environment (Greytak & Kosciw, 2014). In a similar manner, Kosciw et al. (2012) found that a supportive staff was the strongest predictor of a less hostile environment and greater student self-esteem. A supportive adult may provide a personal connection to keep students in school and buffer victimization. They can create a safer and more affirming environment by intervening when homophobic remarks are made or victimization occurs (Kosciw et al., 2013). Not only do supportive adults create a safer environment by intervening, they also become more aware of incidents that happen to LGBT students who were victimized, because having more supportive adults in their life leads youth to be more likely to report issues (Kosciw et al., 2013). Having a supportive teacher is associated with fewer school troubles, a greater sense of belonging and/or connectedness at school, and better academic outcomes (Greytak & Kosciw, 2014).

Educators have the potential to act as advocates by intervening in instances of harassment and bullying, thus providing an opportunity to positively impact LGBT youth's school experiences by taking action to ensure students are safe and respected (Greytak et al., 2012). Yet, despite all the positive outcomes of supportive staff members in schools, many studies have found that teachers inconsistently or never intervene when hearing homophobic remarks and negative remarks regarding gender expression, sometimes even remaining silent when witnessing the assault of LGBT students (Greytak et al., 2012; Greytak & Kosciw, 2014). A total of 51.4% of students polled in GLESN's 2013 National School Climate Survey reported hearing homophobic remarks from teachers or other school staff, and 55.5% reported hearing negative remarks regarding gender expression from teachers or staff (Kosciw et al., 2014).

Inaction from teachers and staff can contribute to a negative learning environment directly by allowing anti-LGBT behaviors to continue because the inaction may indirectly signal to students that the behavior is acceptable (Greytak & Kosciw, 2014). Educators also sometimes fail to come to the aid of LGBT students even when their support has been sought out (Greytak & Kosciw, 2014). For example, when students report incidents of harassment, bullying, or discomfort due to language or actions of others, teachers may fail to address the issue with the student, fail to report the incident to administration, or may ignore the student to avoid dealing with the situation. This could include something as simple as not addressing or correcting a student who calls another student a derogatory name such as "faggot" or "dyke" or not correcting a student after saying "That's so gay." GLSEN's study found that of the students who did report an incident of anti-LGBT language, 61.6% reported that the school staff member did nothing in response (Kosciw et al., 2014) and only one third of US LGBT students believe that in instances when school staff did respond, that they responded in an effective manner to their reports of bullying and/or harassment in school (Kosciw et al., 2013).

Factors Influencing Educators' Responses to LGBT Issues

Why is it that teachers are so inconsistent with their response to instances of bullying and harassment? What can be done? It is evident from the data presented that teachers are a vital component of creating a positive and supportive school climate. How then, as professionals, can we address this inconsistency? In order to address the need for increased professional development for preservice teacher candidates and current teachers, it is important to understand the factors that influence the likelihood that a teacher will intervene.

In a 2014 study, Greytak and Kosciw looked at the factors related to educators' responses to anti-LGBT behaviors. They found that homophobic attitudes still persist among some educators that may influence whether they intervene or address anti-LGBT behaviors presented by students. Other studies (Norman, 2004; Schneider & Dimito, 2008) have identified fears of negative reactions from parents and other school staff as a key barrier to intervention and that teachers believed intervention would be facilitated by school policies that explicitly prohibit bullying based on sexual orientation, gender identity, or gender expression (Greytak & Kosciw, 2014).

The three key factors identified by Greytak and Kosciw in educators' responses to anti-LGBT behaviors are awareness, self-efficacy, and a sense of obligation (Howard, Horne, & Joliff, 2001; Nesdale & Pickering, 2006; Newman-Carlson & Horne, 2004; Yoon, 2004). Awareness is critical given the prevalence of anti-LGBT harassment in schools. When teachers view bullying and harassment as a serious or urgent issue, they are more likely to intervene (Greytak & Kosciw, 2014; Yoon, 2004). Therefore, awareness may create a sense of seriousness or urgency, increasing the frequency of teacher response. Regardless of personal beliefs, teachers may feel obligated to intervene in instances of harassment and bullying. Research has shown that this sense of obligation or professional responsibility to students may increase the likelihood that teachers will intervene (Greytak & Kosciw, 2014; McGarry, 2008; Meyer, Astor, & Behre, 2004). Self-efficacy is the individual belief in one's own ability to engage in intervention, and the more confident a teacher is in their ability to intervene, the more likely they are to actually intervene (Greytak & Kosciw, 2014; Howard et al., 2001; Newman-Carlson & Horne, 2004; Yoon, 2004). Another important factor that may also be related to the likelihood of intervention is the teachers' own personal exposure to LGBT people. Research has shown that teachers who have personal contact with members of the LGBT community have more positive attitudes, decreased prejudice, and are less homophobic (Anthanases & Larrabee, 2003; Greytak & Kosciw, 2014; King, Winter, & Webster, 2009; McGarry, 2008). Those who are less homophobic are more likely to intervene in instances of bullying or harassment (Collier, Bos, & Sandfort, 2015). The results of the 2014 study (Greytak & Kosciw) show that knowing an LGBT student is a significant predictor of teachers' intervention in incidents of anti-LGBT behaviors. Other results include a higher intervention rate by teachers at public schools compared to private or religious schools. Furthermore, obligation is neither related to the likelihood to intervene, nor to the increased frequency of intervention when there is a greater general awareness of bullying/harassment and greater self-efficacy to intervene in homophobic remarks (Greytak & Kosciw, 2014).

IMPLICATIONS FOR TEACHER-EDUCATION PROGRAMS AND EDUCATOR PROFESSIONAL DEVELOPMENT

These results have a number of implications for improving teacher education programs and to increase professional development for current teachers. Providing opportunities for preservice and current teachers, K–12 districts, and teacher education programs can contribute to the likelihood for intervention when the time comes (Greytak & Kosciw, 2014). It is important to use the knowledge of the various factors that influence how likely educators are to intervene to create better preparation training for teachers. It is with this knowledge and training that teachers can better create a safe climate for LGBT students. The first measure that can be taken to improve teacher education programs is to increase exposure to LGBT people/organizations, including students, to foster correct practices. One way to increase this exposure is to provide opportunities to become acquainted with LGBT students by inviting youth speakers, service-learning projects for members of the LGBT community in local communities, and encouraging interaction with college LGBT centers and student groups. Secondly, it is important to raise general awareness of anti-LGBT bullying and harassment. Finally, it is important to build future teachers' skills to intervene in anti-LGBT behaviors (Greytak & Kosciw, 2014).

It is important to note that while inclusion of these topics in teacher education is an important step in creating safer school climates, it is not enough to stop there. It is also crucial for teachers to have continued opportunities for professional development throughout their careers. These opportunities need an explicit focus on raising teacher awareness of behaviors that target sexual orientation, gender identity, and/or gender expression and on the experiences of LGBT youth in school (Greytak & Kosciw, 2014).

[It is] crucial to help educators feel comfortable in knowing when and how to appropriately intervene with anti-LGBT bullying and harassment in their schools. Providing teachers with opportunities to become familiar with ways of responding to anti-LGBT bullying and harassment so that they would be more comfortable in intervening should be incorporated into both pre-service training and in-service professional development opportunities. (Greytak & Kosciw, 2014, pp. 421–422)

Despite the evidence from studies that educators with professional development or training on LGBT issues are more likely to take action and that schools with this development are safer and more welcoming, many schools fail to provide professional development for teachers that address LGBT issues (Greytak et al., 2012). Greytak et al. (2012) looked at two studies that explored the impact of professional development on educators' beliefs and behaviors. One study, by Horn and Sullivan (2012), looked at an Illinois training program for middle and high school educators. They administered a pretraining survey and a post-training survey 6 months following to assess their knowledge, beliefs, and attitudes. They found that educators were more aware of school climate, their attitudes were more positive about homosexuality, there was an increase in a sense of obligation to create a safe school, and an increase in their intention to intervene. The second study, Greytak and Kosciw (2010), conducted a 2-day training for teachers in New York City. They surveyed teachers before training, 6 weeks following training, and 6 months following training. The results showed an increase in empathy and increase in communication about LGBT issues, an increase in knowledge of appropriate terminology, and increased engagement in activities to create safe schools, such as the presence of a GSA, inclusive curriculum, and so forth (Greytak & Kosciw, 2010). Both of these studies indicate that there are positive impacts on educators' beliefs and behaviors due to professional development targeted at LGBT issues (Greytak et al., 2012).

In the study by Greytak et al. (2012), training was administered to teachers, administrators, and health professionals in schools to assess their awareness, empathy, feelings on the importance of intervention, and self-efficacy. The goals of their training included (a) increase the participants' knowledge about how bullying, harassment, and name-calling impact LGBT students and staff; (b) increase participants' knowledge of how bullying, harassment, and name-calling impact school climate; and (c) develop skills to create a safer school climate for all. The results of their study indicate a growth of knowledge, awareness, and self-efficacy across each group of participants. Teachers were already aware of the bullying and harassment in school, but developed an understanding of the LGBT experience, feelings of importance of intervention as well as confidence and competence in intervening and promoting an inclusive environment. Administrators, on the other hand, showed an increase in all areas but comfort and competence, because it is already a part of their job to do this on a regular basis (Greytak et al., 2012).

The Long Road to Change

However, this is not to say that the road to increased professional development to better train teachers, administrators, and staff will be an easy one. There are a great number of challenges to addressing LGBT topics in public schools. These topics include not only external challenges from outside of the school but also internal challenges with individual faculty belief systems and local school policy. Two studies describing the resistance to the implementation to LGBT inclusion in schools are discussed below.

Fredman, Schultz, and Hoffman (2015) aptly summarized these challenges to addressing LGBT issues in public schools in the title of their study, "You're Moving a Frickin' Big Ship." Teachers must work within the current student perception in the classroom to try to create an inclusive environment. However, many teachers feel unprepared or unequipped to incorporate LGBT issues and are afraid of backlash from parents, community members, and/or administration. They are also afraid of being labeled as gay themselves, face a lack of support, and are already undertaking a very heavy workload with "normal" classroom duties and obligations (Fredman et al., 2015). Many educators also do not want to impose their own values upon students; therefore they stay silent on LGBT topics, unknowingly reinforcing the stigma of LGBT individuals and issues. To add to the uncertainty that many teachers face when deciding whether to include LGBT topics in the classroom or if they should address bullying of LGBT students directly, educators also face the risk of political decisions that may impact their interactions with LGBT issues in schools. As Fredman and colleagues (2015) point out, when public employees are speaking in a setting that is part of their job duties, they are not protected by the First Amendment. They are then vulnerable to employer repercussions as a result of their speech. Educators are, in fact, public employees and are not protected by the First Amendment with regard to what they say in and surrounding their classrooms. This may deter some educators from addressing sensitive issues, such as LGBT topics, in their classroom for fear of repercussions (Fredman et al., 2015).

In their study, Fredman et al. (2015) interviewed 16 teachers. The interviews revealed three main rules that address LGBT topics in schools: (a) teachers should simply just not talk about LGBT issues; (b) if teachers do address LGBT issues, they need to be preapproved by appropriate administrators and governing bodies; and (c) if LGBT topics are included, they must be managed in a way to prevent or limit negative feedback from parents and the community. Teachers in this study also talked about their personal reasons for hesitating to address LGBT issues. One cited reason was the lack of time and energy to devote to confronting perceived risks for inclusion of issues in classrooms. Another reason was fears of maintaining their job security and their happiness in their jobs. Some indicated that it wasn't just a fear of negative experience or marginalization in their job, but losing their jobs entirely. Suggestions from Fredman and colleagues (2015) to help take small steps toward the inclusion of addressing LGBT topics in school include framing the argument for inclusion around the creation of safe environments for all students, capitalizing on potential leeway in curriculum for inclusion, and requesting training on LGBT topics.

In Thein (2013), the resistance of language arts teachers to teaching LGBT literature and related issues was addressed. Thein analyzed discussion posts from an online master's degree course on multicultural literature. The claims by teachers in the course about their resistance to teaching LGBT literature and issues came from a variety of lines of reasoning. These claims concluded that most of the teachers believed that LGBT issues could not or should not be taught in the classroom even though many of the teachers had a positive or neutral stance toward LGBT issues. Teachers were resistant to teaching LGBT issues in their classroom because of the following: (a) they did not feel it was their job (it was the job of health teachers, bullying programs, or those with more power and influence); (b) they argued that their conservative communities and parents would not approve; (c) they reasoned that the schools would receive widespread resistance based on other people's religious beliefs; (d) students are too immature to handle these topics and will respond in immature ways; (e) teachers felt that it is not possible because it would pose a direct threat to their teaching career because it was prohibited or would be teaching about illegal activities (in some states); (f) they believed it would cause more harm than good; (g) they reasoned that it is unfair, because it would discriminate against students and families that hold antigay beliefs; and (h) they didn't know how to or did not have the ability to teach the topics (Thein, 2013).

Future Steps

So what can be done? What actions can be taken to create a more positive school climate and prepare educators to better address LGBT issues in public schools? Teaching Tolerance, a project of the Southern Poverty Law Center, outlines steps that can be taken to create an LGBT-inclusive school climate (Teaching Tolerance, 2013).

Their first set of guidelines covers how to build an inclusive school climate. These suggestions include empowering GSA members to educate their peers by giving them means of communication (i.e., an informational community board, morning announcements, etc.) and publicly praising staff members who actively promote an inclusive environment to encourage more staff members to do so as well. It also includes measures that directly link to transgender students. This involves the enforcement of dress codes equally among all students and empowers students to express themselves in clothing (i.e., do not forbid males from wearing dresses or skirts to school if other students are allowed to wear them), respecting the wishes of trans* students by ensuring that the correct gender is listed on school paperwork, ensuring school staff address the student using the preferred name and pronouns, designating a gender neutral bathroom, and/or allowing trans* students to use the bathroom that they are most comfortable in, and using gender-inclusive language on all event communications. Finally, these suggestions include allowing students to bring same-sex dates and wear clothing of their choice to dances and school events (Teaching Tolerance, 2013).

The second set of guidelines put forth by Teaching Tolerance (2013) covers how to prevent and address problems. The primary means by which schools can help prevent and address problems is the implementation of an antibullying policy or code of conduct. This code is the most public statement of a school's commitment to safety for all students. These policies should include language specifically prohibiting bullying based on sexual orientation and gender expression/identity. Schools need to take a long look at policies and evaluate the effectiveness of it. It is also important to ensure that reactions to reports of harassment of LGBT students do not further stigmatize the students who are the targets of the harassment (Teaching Tolerance, 2013). In addition to having an inclusive antibullying policy, it is important that both community members and faculty members are trained on their part in creating a safe and welcoming school environment. Students and community education should be age appropriate and address the importance of diversity, behaviors considered bullying, negative impacts of bullying, how students should respond to bullying, how teachers should respond to bullying, consequences for bullying, and the process for reporting bullying. Teacher and administrator training should also include root causes of bullying, steps to foster an inclusive environment, review of the policy with an emphasis on faculty responsibility to bullying, and consequences for staff who engage in or ignore bullying (Teaching Tolerance, 2013).

Evidence also argues that training for teachers and administrators on LGBT youth issues should include an active component (i.e., activities that make participants aware of LGBT experiences and needs), a foundational component (i.e., legal rights of students, science underlying sexuality and gender identity), and pedagogical instructions for specific skills (i.e., best practices in teaching LGBT issues, strategies to prevent and respond to bullying, counseling skills to help students, or how to direct students to get help) (Jacob, 2013). In addition to this training for school personnel, schools are advised by Jacob (2013) to provide opportunities to educate parents on the challenges that face LGBT students and parents of LGBT students, as well as to make the school community aware of the school's policies prohibiting discrimination and harassment of students based on their sexual orientation and/or gender identity/expression (Jacob, 2013).

CONCLUSION

The evidence presented has shown that educators have a large impact on LGBT students' experiences in school and that training in teacher-education programs and professional development can have a positive influence on their ability to intervene on their behalf in instances of anti-LGBT behaviors. Therefore, it is vital and necessary for teachers to receive ongoing professional development to empower them to effectively intervene on the behalf of LGBT students in instances of bullying and harassment. In a world where more and more is asked of school districts and educators on a daily basis, where funding for extra programs and professional development can be scarce, where pressure to meet expectations is constant, it is easy to say "pick your battles" wisely. This is a battle that deserves the fight. Educators are responsible for the well-being of students in their care on a daily basis. *In loco parentis* defines the duty of educators that is owed to their students. Under principles of negligence, educators have a duty to anticipate any foreseeable dangers and take reasonable steps to protect students from that danger (Rumel, 2013). In fact, "courts have recognized that schools, administrators and teachers, based on their in loco parentis status, must supervise and/or protect students from foreseeable harm to both their physical and emotional well-being" (Rumel, 2013, p. 716). Educators owe it to their students to respond to the changing times in society and protect their students. In a world where we are told to "pick our battles," it is necessary that teachers are equipped with the skills and tools needed to adequately protect our students and create a positive school climate to promote learning for all students.

REFERENCES

Anthanses, S. Z., & Larrabee, T. G. (2003). Toward a consistent stance in teaching for equity: Learning to advocate for lesbian- and gay-identified youth. *Teaching and Teacher Education, 19*, 237–261.

Collier, K. L., Bos, H. M. W., & Sandfort, T. G. M. (2015). Understanding teachers' responses to enactments of sexual and gender stigma at school. *Teaching and Teacher Education, 48*, 34–43.

Fredman, A. J., Schultz, N. J., & Hoffman, M. F. (2015). "You're moving a frickin' big ship": The challenges of addressing LGBTQ topics in public schools. *Education and Urban Society, 47*(1), 56–85.

Gay, Lesbian & Straight Education Network (GLSEN). (2007). *Gay-straight alliances: Creating safer schools for LGBT students and their allies* [Research brief]. New York, NY: Author.

Gay, Lesbian & Straight Education Network (GLSEN). (2011). *Teaching respect: LGBT-inclusive curriculum and school climate* [Research brief]. New York, NY: Author.

Gay, Lesbian & Straight Education Network (GLSEN). (2012). *Developing LGBT-inclusive classroom resources*. New York, NY: Author.

Graybill, E. C., Varjas, K., Meyers, J., & Watson, L. B. (2009). Content-specific strategies to advocate for lesbian, gay, bisexual, and transgender youth: An exploratory study. *School Psychology Review, 38*(4), 570–584.

Greytak, E. A., & Kosciw, J. G. (2010). *Year one evaluation of the New York City Department of Education Respect for All training program*. New York, NY: GLSEN.

Greytak, E. A., & Kosciw J. G. (2014). Predictors of US teachers' intervention in anti-lesbian, gay, bisexual, and transgender bullying and harassment. *Teaching Education, 25*(4), 410–426.

Greytak, E. A., Kosciw, J. G., & Boesen, M. J. (2012). Educating the educator: Creating supportive school personnel through professional development. *Journal of School Violence, 12*(1), 80–97.

Grossman, A. H., Haney, A. P., Edwards, P., Alessi, E. J., Ardon, M., & Howell, T. J. (2009). Lesbian, gay, bisexual, and transgender youth talk about experiencing and coping with school violence: A qualitative study. *Journal of LGBT Youth, 6*(1), 24–46.

Hatzenbuehler, M. L., Birkett, M., Van Wagenen, A., & Meyer, I. H. (2014). Protective school climates and reduced risk for suicide ideation in sexual minority youths. *American Journal of Public Health, 104*(2), 279–286.

Horn, S., & Sullivan, S. (2012). *Addressing anti-LGBT bias in schools: Changing educators' knowledge, beliefs, and behaviors through professional development*. Paper presented at the American Educational Research Association Annual Meeting, Vancouver, BC, Canada.

Howard, N. M., Horne, A. M., & Jolliff, D. (2001). Self-efficacy in a new training model for the prevention of bullying in schools. *Journal of Emotional Abuse, 2*, 181–191.

Jacob, S. (2013). Creating safe and welcoming schools for LGBT students: Ethical and legal issues. *Journal of School Violence, 12*(1), 98–115.

King, M. E., Winter, S., & Webster, B. (2009). Contact reduces transpredjudice: A study on attitudes towards transgenderism and transgender civil rights in Hon Kong. *International Journal of Sexual Health, 21*, 17–34.

Kosciw, J. G., Greytak, E. A., Palmer, N. A., & Boesen, M. J. (2014). *The 2013 National School Climate Survey: The experiences of lesbian, gay, bisexual and transgender youth in our nation's schools*. New York, NY: GLSEN. Retrieved from http://www.glsen.org/nscs

Kosciw, J. G., Palmer, N. A., Kull, R. M., & Greytak, E. A. (2013). The effect of negative school climate on academic outcomes for LGBT youth and the role of in-school supporters. *Journal of School Violence, 12*(1), 45–63.

McGarry, R. A. (2008). *Troubling teachable moments: Initiating teacher discourse on classroom homophobic speech* (Unpublished dissertation). University of Pennsylvania, Philadelphia.

Meyer, H. A., Astor, R. A., & Behre, W. J. (2004). Teachers' reasoning about school fights, contexts, and gender: An expanded cognitive developmental domain approach. *Aggression and Violent Behavior, 9*, 45–74.

Murphy, H. E. (2012). Improving the lives of students, gay and straight alike: Gay straight alliances and the role of school psychologists. *Psychology in the Schools, 49*(9), 883–891.

Nesdale, D., & Pickering, K. (2006). Teachers' reactions to children's reactions. *Social Development, 15*, 109–127.

Newman-Carlson, D., & Horne, A. M. (2004). Bully busters: A psychoeducational intervention for reducing bullying behavior in middle school students. *Journal of Counseling and Development, 82*, 259–267.

Norman, J. (2004). *Survey of teachers on homophobic bullying in Irish second-level school.* Dublin, Ireland: Dublin City University.

Rumel, J. E. (2013). Back to the future: The in loco parentis doctrine and its impact on whether K–12 schools and teachers owe a fiduciary duty to students. *Indiana Law Review, 46*, 711–751.

Russell, S. T., Kosciw, J., Horn, S., & Saewyc, E. (2010). Social policy report: Safe schools policy for LGBTQ students. *Sharing Child and Youth Development Knowledge, 24*(4), 1–17.

Russell, S. T., Ryan, C., Toomey, R. B., Diaz, R. M., & Sanchez, J. (2011). Lesbian, gay, bisexual, and transgender adolescent school victimization: Implications for young adult health and adjustment. *Journal of School Health, 81*(5), 223–230.

Sanders, C. (2013). Fighting back in a red state: Tennessee's "Don't Say Gay" and "License to Bully" legislation. *QED: A Journal in GLBTQ Worldmaking*, Inaugural issue, 141–147.

Schneider, M. S., & Dimito, A. (2008). Educators' beliefs about raising lesbian, gay, bisexual, and transgender issues in schools: The experience in Ontario, Canada. *Journal of LGBT Youth, 5*, 49–71.

Snapp, S. D., Burdge, H., Licona, A., Moody, R. L., & Russell, S. T. (2015). Students' perspectives on LGBTQ-inclusive curriculum. *Equity & Excellence in Education 48*(2), 249–265.

Teaching Tolerance. (2013). *Best practices: Creating an LGBT-inclusive school climate—A teaching tolerance guide for school leaders.* Montgomery, AL: Teaching Tolerance.

Thein, A. H. (2013). Language arts teachers' resistance to teaching LGBT literature and issues. *Language Arts, 90*(3), 169–180.

Toomey, R. B., Ryan, C., Diaz, R. M., & Sanchez, S. T. (2011). High school gay-straight alliances (GSAs) and young adult well-being: An examination of GSA presence, participation, and perceived effectiveness. *Applied Developmental Science, 15*(4), 175–185.

Yoon, J. S. (2004). Predicting teacher interventions in bullying situations. *Education and Treatment of Children, 27*, 37–45.

CHAPTER 13

IN OUR OWN VOICE

Campus Climate as a Mediating Factor in the Persistence of LGBT Students, Faculty, and Staff in Higher Education

Warren J. Blumenfeld, Genevieve N. Weber, and Susan Rankin

INTRODUCTION AND REVIEW OF THE LITERATURE

Throughout the United States, in elementary and secondary schools and on college and university campuses, in communities, homes, and in the media, issues of sexual and gender identities are increasingly "coming out of the closet." We see some young people developing positive identities at earlier ages than ever before. Activists are gaining selective electoral and legislative victories. Primarily in academic environments, greater emphasis and discussions are centering on what has come to be called "queer theory" (Sullivan, 2003; Wilchins, 2004), where writers, educators, and students analyze, challenge, and deconstruct current sexuality and gender constructions and categorizations.

In the midst of these progressive advancements, however, conditions related to campus climate often remain difficult at best for lesbian, gay, bisexual, transgender, and questioning (LGBTQ) students. Researchers

Queering Classrooms: Personal Narratives and Educational Practices
to Support LGBTQ Youth in Schools, pp. 187–212
Copyright © 2017 by Information Age Publishing
All rights of reproduction in any form reserved.

have developed a number of theoretical models to conceptualize and describe the campus climate at colleges and universities (Hurtado, Carter, & Kardia, 1998; Milem, Chang, & Antonio, 2005; Smith et al., 1997). Rankin and Reason (2008) have synthesized a definition of "campus climate" from their review of the professional literature as comprising "current attitudes, behaviors, and standards held by faculty, staff, and students concerning the access for, inclusion of, and level of respect for individual and group needs, abilities, and potential" (p. 264). Using the dimensions proposed by Smith et al. (1997), Rankin (2003) developed and later conceptualized (Rankin & Reason, 2008) the Transformational Tapestry Model, which posits that campus climate is influenced by six areas within higher education: access and retention (i.e., access to higher education and provision of the necessary supports for success and retention); research and scholarship (i.e., encouragement of diversity in educational and scholarly activity); inter- and intra-group relations (i.e., a diverse student body with educationally purposeful interventions and interactions); curriculum and pedagogy (i.e., diversity education and proactive educational interventions); university policies and services (i.e., university commitment to diversity and social justice through response to harassment, and written and behavioral policies); and external relationships (i.e., acknowledgment of and response to external influences in society and government).

As colleges and universities continue to more accurately reflect the diverse makeup of society, institutions have focused on the importance of creating campus environments that include, welcome, and support people of different backgrounds and social identities (Rankin & Reason, 2008; Worthington, Navarro, Loewy, & Hart, 2008). Although colleges and universities attempt to foster welcoming and inclusive environments, they are not immune to the negative attitudes and discriminatory behaviors stemming from the larger society. As a microcosm of that larger social environment, college and university campuses reflect the pervasive prejudices and discriminatory actions of society (Eliason, 1996; Nelson & Krieger, 1997; Starobin & Blumenfeld, 2012). Consequently, the campus climate often has been described as "racist" for students and employees of color (Harper & Hurtado, 2007; Rankin & Reason, 2005); "chilly" for women (Hart & Fellabaum, 2008; Hall & Sandler, 1984); and "hostile" for LGBTQ community members (Blumenfeld, 2006; Eliason, 1996; Rankin, 2003, 2009).

Within higher education, an early report by the National Gay and Lesbian Task Force (1990) discovered that fully one-fifth of all reported incidents of harassment and violence directed against LGBTQ people occurred on college and university campuses of our nation. Research indicates that LGBTQ individuals often continue to face chilly or hostile campus climates (Blumenfeld, 2006; Dolan, 1998; Noack, 2004; Rankin, 2001, 2003, 2009). Most of these studies underscore LGBTQ individuals as the least accepted group when compared with other under-served populations and, consequently, more likely to point to deleterious experiences and less than welcoming campus climates based on sexual and gender identity.

Campus environments are "complex social systems defined by the relationships between the people, bureaucratic procedures, structural arrangements, institutional goals and values, traditions, and larger sociohistorical environments" (Hurtado et al., 1998, p. 296). Individual perceptions of discrimination or of a negative campus climate for intergroup relations can affect student educational outcomes. Hurtado and Ponjuan (2005) note that when stereotypes "pervade the learning environment for minority students ... student academic performance can be undermined" (p. 236). On the other hand, students attending colleges and universities with more inclusive campus environments will feel better equipped to participate in an increasingly multicultural society (Gurin, Dey, Hurtado, & Gurin, 2002).

The personal and professional development of employees, including faculty members, administrators, and staff members are also impacted by the complex nature of the campus climate. In a study by Settles, Cortina, Malley, and Stewart (2006), sexual harassment and gender discrimination had a significantly negative impact on the overall attitudes toward employment for women faculty in the academic sciences. Sears (2002) found that LGB faculty members who judge their campus climate more positively are more likely to feel personally supported and perceive their work unit as more supportive of personal decisions (i.e., hiring and promoting LGB faculty members) than those who view their campus climate more negatively.

Research that highlights the relationship between workplace discrimination and negative job and career attitudes, as well as workplace encounters with prejudice and lower health and well-being (i.e., anxiety and depression, lower life satisfaction and physical health) and greater occupation dysfunction (i.e., organizational withdrawal, and lower satisfaction with work, coworkers and supervisors (Silverschanz, Cortina, Konik, & Magley, 2007; Waldo, 1999) further substantiates the influence of campus climate on employee satisfaction and subsequent productivity.

The majority of research conducted on campus climate relates to the experiences of students of color and women students. There has been little emphasis on the experiences of women faculty members and staff members, faculty and staff members of color, and even less for LGBTQ students, faculty, and staff. As LGBTQ people and their allies "come out" in greater numbers than ever before, they have become more visible on college and university campuses. Consequently, researchers, educators, and higher education administrators have expressed increasing interest in learning about and responding to their campus climate experiences.

Two decades of limited research suggests that academe has been unwelcoming of LGBTQ students, faculty, and staff. In a 2001 study that included 30 campuses and more than 17,000 respondents, participants indicated that of all the various constituent groups on campus, the climate was "least accepting" of LGBTQ people (Rankin, 2001). Moreover, 42% of LGB respondents indicated they were the target of harassment based on their sexual orientation, compared to 30% of people of color who reported harassment based on their race, and 28% of women who reported harassment based on their sex assigned at birth.

Though conditions for LGBTQ students, faculty, and staff have improved somewhat over the years, a report by the National Gay and Lesbian Task Force (Rankin, 2003) concluded that they still encounter a hostile climate on college and university campuses, even at campuses with strong support systems and campus centers. Of the 1,600 LGBTQ-identified students, faculty, and administrators surveyed nationwide, 36% of LGBTQ undergraduate students and 29% of respondents overall experienced harassment over the previous year. One in five respondents feared for their personal campus safety related to their sexual and/or gender identities, and half concealed their sexual and/or gender identities to avoid intimidation. Additionally, 41% believed their institutions were not adequately addressing issues related to sexual and gender identity, and 43% felt their college or university curricula did not represent the contributions of LGBT people.

In their two-part study, Anderson and Kanner (2011) found student bias against professors whom they perceived as lesbian or gay. In their first study of 545 ethnically diverse undergraduate students at the University of Houston-Downtown, researchers presented a syllabus for a course titled "Psychology of Human Sexuality." One version indicated a fictional professor who was "gay" or "lesbian." Another version indicated a fictional heterosexual professor. Students were then asked to evaluate the professor based on various factors, including the professor's political bias. Students found that the syllabus alone suggested a political agenda when the professor was perceived as lesbian or gay, but no political agenda when students assumed the professor to be heterosexual.

In the second part of the study with a different cohort of students, 622 ethnically diverse undergraduates, researchers gave one version of the syllabus, which indicated the professor was "lesbian" or "gay," while another syllabus indicated a heterosexual professor. One version of the "Psychology of Human Sexuality" syllabus course focused on a conservative view of sexuality emphasizing sexual restraint and abstinence. A second version indicated a more liberal view of sexuality in accepting and celebrating the variety of human sexual behaviors. Researchers then asked students to evaluate the professor based only on the syllabus review on whether the professor held any biased views. The results indicated that students found the syllabus to suggest biased views when the professor was lesbian and gay on *both* the conservative and on the liberal syllabi. On the other hand, the heterosexual professors, in both the conservative and liberal syllabi, were not found by students to hold biased views.

In their study investigating whether degrees of religiosity could be liked to levels of racial prejudice, Johnson, Rowatt, and LaBouff (2010) found a direct effect (i.e., a "causal" relationship) of religion on racial attitudes. They implemented the research technique known as "priming." Johnson, Rowatt, and LaBouff "primed" Christian U.S.-American research participants with religious concepts (e.g., God, religious attendance) to determine whether this would affect participants' racial attitudes. As the researchers noted, historically, priming for religiosity has resulted in both positive and negative changes in attitudes and behaviors.

Researchers were particularly interested in measuring racial attitudes toward African Americans. Methodologically, they ran two different experiments (one to assess "subtle prejudice" and the second to assess "overt prejudice"). Their results concluded that activation of Christian religious concepts increases subtle and overt prejudice towards the racially disadvantaged group – in this study, specifically African Americans (p. 123). They theorized that the "priming" of Christian religious concepts invoked and advanced in-group pro-social solidarity and out-group antipathy. Researchers discovered similar results when priming Christian religion led to substantial increases in negative attitudes toward gay men, Muslims, and atheists (Rowatt et al., 2006, 2009).

CAMPUS CLIMATE AND STUDENT PERSISTENCE

Academic success is a primary outcome for students in higher education. The literature suggests that the campus climate significantly influences students' learning and their overall development (Pascarella & Terenzini, 2005). College students who perceive and experience positive campus climates usually realize positive learning outcomes (Pascarella & Terenzini, 2005). The majority of this literature focuses on race and gender.

Racial Identity and Student Persistence

Much of the literature concerning racial minority students in higher education paints a fairly negative picture of their experiences. Research suggests that students of color perceive their campus climate toward race, campus diversity initiatives, and available resources for minorities more negatively and is less effective at achieving their goals than White students (Harper & Hurtado, 2007; Rankin & Reason, 2005). In fact, students of color may perceive incongruence between espoused institutional values surrounding diversity and actions toward achieving diversity, further impacting their perception of a negative racial campus climate (Harper & Hurtado, 2007). In addition, research suggests that race can be used to predict student persistence in higher education (Astin, 1993). Although both African American and Latino/Hispanic students lag behind their white peers in college attendance and graduation rates (Museus, 2011), black male undergraduate students in particular are severely underrepresented on college and university campuses and have lower persistence rates than any other racial group of either gender (Harper, 2006). In the next section, we explore literature pertaining to sexuality, campus climate, and persistence.

Gender Identity and Student Persistence

Women college students have reported perceptions of differential treatment based on their gender (Steele, James, & Barnett, 2002). Sex discrimination and stereotype threat (Steele et al., 2002) and harassment (Reason & Rankin, 2006) were reported by women in male dominated academic areas, and "although men are currently a minority in certain academic areas, they have not historically been negatively stereotyped or discriminated against in these domains because of their gender, and accordingly, it is perhaps not surprising that their experience differs from those described by women" (Steele et al., 2002, p. 49).

Academically, women have reported a chilly classroom (Salter & Persaud, 2003). However, "though the evidence supporting the chilly climate thesis is somewhat limited, what does exist suggests that compared with men, many women students' perceive their campus to be less supportive of their academic and social needs and that, as a result, their learning and personal development is adversely affected" (Umbach, Kinzie, Thomas, Palmer, & Kuh, 2003, p. 2). Despite this challenging climate, women, overall, earn higher grades than men (Pascarella & Terenzini, 2005). Women also have larger enrollment and degree attainment rates (Perna, 2005).

Sexuality, Campus Climate, and Persistence

While the body of research concerning racial minority students is extensive, few empirical studies examine the experiences of LGBT students in higher education (Rankin, Weber, Blumenfeld, & Frazer, 2010). Particularly lacking is research exploring fluid, intersecting, or non-binary identities (Renn, 2010). As with research on racial minority students, the limited available literature about LGBT students generally highlights their negative experiences in higher education and emphasizes the hostile climates and discrimination they encounter on college and university campuses (Rankin & Reason, 2005; Rankin et al., 2010). Interestingly, outcomes-based research on LGB students is minimal, and hardly any research examines sexual orientation as a predictive factor in student retention (Reason, 2009; Sanlo, 2004). Such information, however, is crucial to LGB student success: as previously mentioned, a recent study found that LGBT students are 30% more likely than other students to consider leaving their institutions (Rankin et al., 2010).

THE CURRENT STUDY

We conducted our comprehensive current study, *2010 State of Higher Education for Lesbian, Gay, Bisexual, and Transgender People*, which was sponsored by the Q Research Institute in Higher Education of the national organization, Campus Pride. This study begins to fill the gap in the literature on campus climate experiences for LGBTQ individuals using a national sample. In our results, we found that LGBTQ students, staff, faculty, and administrators remain at significantly higher risk for systematic institutional invisibility, marginalization, and harassment at our colleges and universities, compared with their heterosexual and gender normative counterparts.

Study Design and Data Collection

We developed our survey questionnaire to investigate how respondents made meaning of their subjective experiences related to the climate for LGBTQ people at their respective campuses in higher education. We sent an announcement of the study to as many of the LGBTQ campus organizations in higher education we could locate through a number of networks throughout the United States and those identified through our community partners (e.g., Campus Pride, National Gay and Lesbian Task Force, American College Personnel Association, NASPA: Student Affairs Administrators in Higher Education, and others). Within the announcement, we invited potential respondents to pass along the research announcement to those who may have qualified for participation in the study. This sampling strategy is termed "snowball sampling" (Glesne,

2006; Groenwald, 2004), one that is advantageous in reaching additional respondents from "invisible" populations or who may not otherwise be aware of the research announcement (Lichtman, 2006). Our research announcement listed the website for participants to access the survey questionnaire and the Informed Consent form. The criteria for selection required that respondents identify in some way as either "non-heterosexual" or "non-gender conforming." Some participants also identified as "ally" to LGBTQ people.

The national sample included 5149 respondents who identified along what we referred to as a "Queer Spectrum" ("lesbian," "gay," "same-sex loving," "bisexual," "pansexual," "asexual," "questioning," and other terms indicating sexual identity) and a "Trans Spectrum" ("transmasculine," "transfeminine," "gender non-conforming," "cross-dresser," "tranny boi," "gender queer," "pre-op," along with other terms indicating gender identity and expression) who completed the on-line survey. Respondents included students, staff, faculty, and administrators representing all 50 states and who attended all the Carnegie Basic Classifications of institutions of higher education.

Qualitative Research Methodology: Phenomenological Grounded Theory

In addition to the use of quantitative research methodology, which we published elsewhere, we also employed qualitative research methodologies, which we found particularly applicable in the present study because this form of research methodology was well-suited to the type of in-depth exploratory examination and analysis we were interested in unearthing (Marshall & Rossman, 2006; Patton, 2012; Seidman, 1998). Bogdan and Taylor (1998), for example, support the use of qualitative research methodology when the researcher pursues "… settings and the individuals within those settings holistically; that is, the subject of the study, be it an organization or an individual, is not reduced to an isolated variable…" (p. 4). Marshall and Rossman (2006) emphasize that qualitative methods give the researcher a deeper understanding of respondents' lived experiences and how people define and perceive their situations.

We employed the systematic methodological technique of Grounded Theory, which involves generating theory from the data, rather than other research methodologies, which begins with a theoretical framework or hypothesis. Within this framework, we employed the technique of phenomenology, which seeks to describe "the meaning of the lived experiences for several individuals about a concept or the phenomenon" (Creswell, 1998, p. 51). Some forms of phenomenological inquiry direct the researcher to find the "essence of a phenomenon," that is, the de-contextualized meaning that a phenomenon has for all individuals, regardless of individual characteristics, experiences, or settings (e.g., Barritt, Beekman, Bleeker, & Mulderij, 1985).

From the qualitative data, we marked a series of open coding procedures in the text of respondents' comments. We then grouped or categorized the codes into similar concepts in order to effectively manage data collected. From there, we employed the technique of "axial coding" defined by Strauss and Corbin (1998) as "a set of procedures whereby data are put back together in new ways after open coding, by making connections between categories" (p. 96). Through this process, we were able to identify a number of emerging themes from which we developed our theoretical framework. The researchers employed the software package known as NVivo in the coding and sorting procedures of the qualitative data.

RESULTS

The purpose of the study was to determine what meanings respondents made of their college and university campus climates specifically for non-heterosexual and non-gender conforming students, staff, faculty, and administrators and with particular focus on individual perceptions and experiences. Although 71% of all respondents expressed relative comfort with their institutions' overall campus climate, 77% with their department or work unit climate, and 65% with the classroom climate, a substantial number (30%) experienced a difficult or hostile campus climate. Further, 21% experienced some form of harassment connected to their sexual identity or gender identity or expression. Along the Queer Spectrum and the Trans Spectrum, 13% of Queer Spectrum and 43% of Trans Spectrum respondents feared for their physical safety, and 43% of Queer Spectrum and 63% of Trans Spectrum respondents concealed their identities (stayed in "the closet") in an attempt to avoid intimidation. These rates were significantly higher for Queer and Trans Spectrum respondents of color.

Thirty percent of both Queer Spectrum and Trans Spectrum respondents indicated that they had considered seriously leaving their institutions due to the hostile climate (Rankin et al., 2010). Following their response to the question on intent to persist, respondents were asked to share "why" they considered leaving and "why" did they decide to stay? The following sections provide the themes that emerged from these questions.

A Qualitative Look at Intent to Persist: The Impact of Campus Climate

Within the open-ended qualitative questions, respondents shared a variety of reasons why they remained undecided on whether to leave their current campuses, why they considered leaving, why they actually left, or why they decided to stay. While the majority of reasons for respondents' decisions rested on issues centering on sexual or gender identity and expression within their current campus climates, for some other respondents, reasons were more general in scope. For example, explanations included dissatisfaction with a program of study, ending a partnership relation, wishing for a higher salary, desiring to live further away from or closer to family, not feeling intellectually or professionally challenged, not "having a good time," failing academics, transferring from a two- to a four-year institution or to a less expensive college or university, taking retirement, as well as experiencing personal or family issues.

What follows is a discussion focusing on issues pertaining specifically to sexual and gender identity and expression and campus climate as reasons for respondents' consideration of leaving their current college or university campuses.

Respondents assessed the overarching question and examined the concept of "campus climate" on a number of levels: some filtered their experiences of campus climate on issues of personal safety (emotional and/or physical), while others projected their lens of analysis on matters of institutional support, personal assessments of them by others, issues of on-campus or off-campus support, and the topic of academic department climate. Others discussed issues of intersecting identities and concerns of campus oppression around these identities, while others focused specifically on their religious affiliations or on the matter of religious oppression on their campuses. In addition, one participant in particular expressed what comprised a major theme by the vast majority of respondents that "'comfortable' as related to campus climate "is a relative term."

While some respondents answered in dualistic or binary ways by assessing the overall climate on their particular campuses as falling under either the "positive" or "comfortable" range on one hand, or the "negative" or "uncomfortable" range on the other, the majority addressed this question comparatively (changes over time) or contextually (for example, department or work unit in relation to the overall campus). The way in which this question was worded on the survey questionnaire lent itself readily to this latter and more holistic interpretation.

Positive Campus Climate

Respondents assessing the climate on their campuses in positive terms included such thematic categories as overall issues of personal safety, on-campus and off-campus support, comparative department to overall campus climate, and institutional support.

Safety

Representative statements expressing a positive campus climate addressed by students, faculty, and staff centered on issues of emotional safety and physical security: "For the most part, campus is a place in which I can freely be myself and not worry." Issues of personal safely were often connected to personal assessments by others. For students in particular who fall under this thematic category: "At the University..., as an out gay student, I feel I am generally accepted by students and faculty. I've never had an incident in which I wasn't accepted," and another student stated that "Professors routinely refer to LGBT issues. I have never felt any discomfort being out."

While the experiences and campus assessment for most respondents who identified as "transgender" were primarily negative, some respondents contradicted this theme when addressing their individual experiences. For two respondents in particular: "I have been transitioning while working for my university, and all of the staff/faculty have been supportive and understanding. Even those whom I expected to be transphobic have been entirely respectful." And, "Once dressing, as the opposite gender, my professors and students have accepted me, and there has not been any backlash, so I am very pleased."

Faculty and staff members as well discussed issues of campus climate in terms of safety and security: "I teach classes called 'Gay and Lesbian Studies' that I created.... I am completely out at the college and in my department. If there are people who dislike that, they haven't said anything to me. My Chair is completely supportive of my classes, and she encourages me to develop more GLBT-related classes." One participant discussed issues of personal safety on a physical level by stating that "I'm out and I'm trained in 3 martial arts so I'm pretty comfortable wherever I go."

On-Campus and Off-Campus Support

A form of a larger community/societal analysis supplied by respondents included comparing and contrasting the campus and the larger community or region. On rare occasions, respondents rated both as mutually positive. For example: "[My community] is a very gay friendly city considering its location in the southern U.S. and therefore the campus at the University... is a good climate."

Some respondents placed their campuses in context of the larger community and generally rated the quality of climate higher *on* their campus relative to the surrounding area. For example: "[Our state] is generally quite conservative, but [our campus] is quite liberal and generally accepting." Other respondents gave a comparative assessment of their institutions over time. For example, on a positive theme: "My department has come a long way since I came along :) The language used is less heterocentric and more inclusive compared to a few years ago when I first entered the department." In addition, respondents compared campus climate of their current with past institutions: "I am an administrator and feel quite comfortable here. More so than at any other institution in which I have worked. The university and the community are gay/lesbian friendly I think."

Comparative Department to Overall Campus Climate

A significant number of respondents voiced satisfaction and comfort within their individual academic or work departments or programs of study, but discomfort with the overall campus climate. The following respondents expressed this general thematic sentiment: "While the overall climate of my institution is 'chilly,' I am fortunate to work in a very supportive department," and "My department is much more friendly about queer issues than the campus climate as a whole."

In this category, respondents named the following departments most often as providing a welcoming atmosphere, many of which included departments in the liberal arts, humanities, and social sciences[1]: Anthropology, Art, Dance, English, the Library, Journalism, Psychology, Social Work, Sociology, Student Affairs, Theater, and Women's Studies.

When comparing the context of differing departments or programs of study, respondents generally rated one over the other in terms of comfortable campus climate: "In the sociology department, things are great. Elsewhere, I might have problems." And "Women's Studies - better, Political Science—not so much." One student detailed his[2] rating: "I take a lot of gender studies classes [r]un through the sociology and psychology department and I feel safe in those classes. But outside of my gender studies classes the classroom environment is very homophobic and transphobic."

Focusing on the issue of gender identity and expression, a Trans Spectrum student concurred:

> I am a full time M2F [Male-To-Female] grad student in Alabama. None of my professors or fellow students in my field of study (fine Arts) has ever expressed an[y] distaste at my presentation. It's the rest of the campus I worry about.

Students also provided a comparative analysis between their programs of study in positive terms and work environments in more negative terms; for example: "In classes I was an English and Women's Studies major, so my classes and the profs mostly rocked. At work the people there are … less than enlightened. I'm also in the closet there." Moreover, respondents compared and contrasted campus environments between graduate and undergraduate levels: "At the graduate level, gender and sexual orientation tend to be more acceptable topics for discussion and study; our undergrads, however, have voiced the opposite feeling."

Institutional Support

In this thematic category, students, faculty, and staff provided a positive overall and general assessment of their campus' climate. Representative comments included, for example, "[My university] is a very safe and accepting campus," and "Faculty, staff, and students all [are] very supportive." And, "My school goes out of its way to be open to all genders and sexualities, and from the campus community to the classroom, that openness is felt."

In addition, positive assessments of institutional support centered also on issues of relationship status in which same-sex partners of faculty and staff were welcomed and treated with respect. Some respondents referred to supportive heterosexual allies: "[My university] seems very LBGT friendly. We have great straight talks." One student linked the former experiences of the students who attended hir university, with empathy on issues of diversity: "The students at school are 'Nerds' who dealt with bullying in school. Because of this, there is very little of any type of hate on campus."

While very few respondents discussed directly issues of campus climate related to bisexual members of the campus community, the majority who identified as "bisexual" assessed campus climate more generally related to overriding issues of sexuality and gender identity. A small number of respondents, however, rated campus climate as positive for bisexual people. According to one bisexual staff member: "I am very out as a bisexual-queer staff member and campus activist, and have met with tremendous support from my colleagues and supervisors."

In summary, themes emerging in this study under the general category of "Positive Campus Climate" included assessment of campus climate in terms of physical and emotional safety, evaluation of climate regarding the overall institution, consideration of the off-campus community, and judgments in comparative terms between the campus and larger community, one institution over time, and academic or work department climate to the larger or overall institutional climate and support.

Negative Campus Climate

Respondents assessing the climate on their campuses in overall negative terms included the thematic categories of diminished or lack of personal safety, negative judgments coming from others, lack of on-campus and off-campus support, negative department climates, negative religious judgments by others, other forms of oppression intersecting with heterosexism and cissexism on campus, and institutional inaction to improve conditions.

Unsafe: "There is a Climate of Fear"

Students experienced risks to their personal safety: "Our campus has recently been the place of multiple attacks against the GLBTA community, so my safety is a serious concern for me." And "I was concerned about the swastikas and other hate crimes going on on campus." For a couple: "My partner and I were shouted at while walking down the street when I first arrived. I never have felt comfortable on campus or in the general community. The reason I stay is it is only a two year master's program, and the program is one of the best in the country." Respondents also discussed physical attacks:

> I considered leaving my campus because during my first semester at [my campus] I was physically assaulted on campus on my way home. The university's response was less than adequate. Two more physical assaults happened on/near campus in the next three days. News of these assaults hit national news before the university even made a statement of any kind. I decided to stay mostly because I couldn't afford to leave.

Personal Assessments by Others

Negative judgments by professors impacted the campus climate playing a major role in the following student's experience: "Professors have pathologized my experiences as a member of the LGBT community by claiming that participating in activism within the LGBT community is indicative of mental illness." Negative campus climates compelled some LGBT persons to remain in an identity "closet": "I am FTM. I do not feel safe enough to be out as trans, so I live stealth on campus, which honestly makes me sad because it prevents me from doing as much activism as I would like to." In addition, as expressed by this respondent, negative campus climate seriously affected issues of identity development: "I considered leaving because I hated the thought that I was actually digressing in my development as a member of the GLBT community. Homophobia and heterosexism is a bigger issue here than on other college campuses."

By publicly identifying as "lesbian," "gay," "bisexual," "transgender," or "queer," some respondents related incidents where others placed them into stereotypical boxes: "If I choose to come out to a class, it generally means that the rest of my opinions will be considered 'leftist' and 'radical' by the rest of my classmates." In addition, a student named the specific issue of marginalization: "I considered leaving because I felt marginalized. It has been difficult being an openly gay student on our campus and I felt that I wanted to be in a safe and welcoming place. I stayed because I'm on a full academic scholarship and I would be unable to afford the cost of any other institution."

Misunderstanding and bias toward issues around gender and gender expression also emerged as common marginalizing themes. For example: "I am vocal in expressing my opinions on inappropriate commentaries that others express about sexuality/gender/etc., and because my gender expression is not normative for the sex that people perceive me to be, this coupling, along with disregard for my vocal rejection of bigotry, makes me uncomfortable in class settings."

And for a bisexual participant: "I thought that people would not be open minded enough to make friends with a bisexual. [I]n a small town atmosphere, I have noticed that people tend to like asserting their own gender values on other people as 'right' in order to secure themselves some measure of collective confidence in the face of an 'intruder' like myself."

Many faculty and staff had concerns centering on experiences of negative assessments emanating from students and other faculty and staff members. They, therefore, either made a conscious decision not to reveal their sexual and/or gender identities, for example: "In the class I teach, I do not disclose my sexuality because I am not comfortable with the responses I might get from my students," or when disclosing, some have encountered disapproving reactions: "Students in classes are, to a large degree, very conservative, and I have received negative comments on course evaluations when I have been open in my classes about my spouse/orientation."

Respondents expressed concern for the derogatory language coming from individuals, faculty and students on their campuses: "I considered leaving for a number of reasons but the most pertinent was the obvious allowance of derogatory language towards gays by campus faculty." And, "The atmosphere is completely toxic for me. Kids would call people fags on dirty campus vehicles. If you don't fit in, you are completely alone."

When asked to recount campus experiences related to sexual and gender identity and expression, a number of respondents addressed the question from their bisexual identity perspective. For one faculty member: "I have had students also tell me bisexuality doesn't exist. I've also been threatened with my job for hanging out with certain colleagues who were seen as negative on campus." And a student reflected that: "I have felt invisible in my classes in terms of my bisexual identity."

Though issues of oppression on the basis of sexual and gender identity and expression emanate from the larger society, often members of these very communities are not immune from internalizing its harmful effects. A bisexual student discussed her experiences with bisexual oppression from members of hir own community

> I expected much more open-mindedness from an allegedly queer campus. I've experienced a lot of biphobia as a result of others' insecurity. I'm not their punching bag, and I hoped this would be a place where I could be affirmed and where I could grow, not where I would meet closed-mindedness from my own people.

On-Campus and Off-Campus Support

Many respondents rated both their campus as well as the surrounding community climate in negative terms: "[I considered leaving my campus because of the very small GLBT community and the surrounding cities are not very accepting either." A staff member gave as reasons for leaving the negative campus climate as well as the surrounding community: "I am interested in working on a campus that is more connected with best practices in the field of student affairs. I am looking for more support from deans above me. And the geographical location is not particularly desirable; my sexual identity certainly plays a part in my dissatisfaction with my geographical location."

In assessing their current campus climate, a number of respondents provided other forms of comparative appraisal such as: "I would best describe the environment as don't ask don't tell. I have witnessed examples of both great acceptance and great discrimination." This analogy to the notorious United States military policy of exclusion of "out" LGBTQ recruits and active service members was a common frame of reference for respondents in our study.

Negative Department Climates

A number of respondents voiced discomfort with the climate within their individual academic or work departments or programs of study, which impacted their overall campus assessment: "My athletics department is why I can't rate my campus as 'very comfortable' climate," and "I am a part of the College of Agriculture, Food, and Natural Resources..., which houses a conservative bunch of professors (generally). I am not 'out' in my classes for this reason."

Though the vast majority in this thematic category did not explicitly identify the department or program of study that they assessed negatively, those who did included the departments of Agriculture, Athletics, Classics, Law, Law Enforcement, Mathematics, Medicine, Political Science, and Teacher Education.

Religion

While a few respondents in particular discussed issues of religion (specifically Jesuit and other forms of Catholicism) in relationship to an overall positive campus climate (e.g., "Although we are a private Catholic-based university, we are very open and accepting"), the vast majority of respondents who brought the issue of religion into a discussion of campus climate referred to its negative and damaging impact. For example, one participant's statement represents the negative sentiments of religion generally related to overall comfort levels and campus climate: "I feel like going to a state university in the bible belt, most people are not very open minded and look down upon people who are different. Making them feel uncomfortable, shunned, or ashamed of who they are." In addition, respondents related experiences of "religiously inspired" calls to violence:

> A preacher rallied students with the cry "we can either accept homosexuals or BURN THEM AT THE STAKE! ARE YOU WITH ME?!" A large group of people were yelling and saying "burn them!" and there I was in the midst of it all with a rainbow flag on my bag, alone and scared. Tried to get him removed from campus—no one seemed to deem it necessary or possible. Thanks for the concern for my safety!

Respondents who specified religions by name as having a negative, damaging, or destructive impact on campus climate enumerated only Christian denominations with Catholic listed most often and Southern Baptist listed second. Representative statements include "Mine is a Catholic university. Questions of sexuality and gender identity are largely ignored—probably in the hope that they will go away. The administration works actively against GLBTQ groups and activities." And for this student,

> I considered a transfer to another campus my sophomore year because of the inadequate counseling services I received through [this] College—I believe a lot of it had to do with the fact I'm one of the few openly gay students here, and that agency is controlled by an order of Jesuit priests that find me offensive.

According to a gay faculty member, "It's hard to be comfortable at a private Baptist university. There's very little queer visibility on campus in general. There's only one openly gay faculty member in the whole school." A staff member discussed the double standard applied to same-sex couples at hir parochial university: "As live-in staff at a Catholic Jesuit institution I cannot have my partner living with me, but my students can have same-sex visitors 24 hours or live with their significant others as their roommates."

Intersecting Campus Oppressions

While some respondents made clear that their campuses generally welcomed people of all social identities, the majority discussed the overt acts, as well as the subtle microaggressions (often brief and frequent indignities, as one participant termed, the "death by a thousand tiny cuts") creating an uncomfortable and emotionally and physically unsafe institutional environment. Respondents related not merely overarching perceptions of heterosexism, biphobia, and cissexism (sometimes referred to as "transgender oppression" or "binarism") on their respective campuses, but also highlighted many of the other spokes maintaining the wheel of oppression that runs rampant throughout their campuses, especially the spokes of ableism, anti-Semitism, intersex oppression, Islamophobia, racism, sexism, and, in particular, xenophobia toward non-US-born people, especially people from Mexico.

At times without giving specifics that led them to their negative assessments of campus climate, some respondents discussed issues in generalized terms, such as "Much tension exists on the ... campus for students, faculty, and staff. The campus climate, related to diversity issues, spills over into classrooms, as well as individual departments." Some respondents provided more depth when judging the negative climate on their institutions by linking forms of oppression: "The campus climate has always been homophobic (as well as misogynistic, racist, etc.), and I have a deep-seated belief that the administrative 'inclusionism' is a public front that hides a conservative nastiness and hatred of anything 'other.'" And "Most students can be terribly offensive, inappropriate and hateful, this is often definitely geared towards queer issues but also issues of race, gender, class and ability."

Institutional Inaction

Respondents often claimed that overall, their institutions are doing little or nothing to improve conditions: "[Our university] is currently experiencing an anti-gay atmosphere that the institution is ignoring," and for another participant, "The administration largely denies that the climate is 'hostile' towards LGBT individuals, despite the fact that the student body feels that the overall climate is very hostile." Faculty and administrative inaction also appeared in the context of cissexism on campus:

When trans students complain to faculty it goes unreported to the proper authorities. If you have the courage to file a legal complaint the universities [sic] policy is to run the student dry of funds thus obviating the possibility of culpability and transparency on the university's behalf. I am in a Title IX discrimination case against my university now and it has cost me $130K so far and I need another $70K to actually get it to trial.

Some respondents made the decision to leave their college or university campus over concerns for their physical and/or emotional safety and security while not receiving the kind of institutional support they needed: "I actually left my first college due to the abusive climate that involved death threats against me and the ... college administration not caring at all." Others remained on their campuses only because they foresaw no other options. According to a Trans Spectrum participant, "I decided that there was no magic other place where being transgender would be OK, so that I should work to become comfortable here."

Negative campus climate assessments concentrated as well on the subject of unequal benefits for faculty and staff based on relationship status. Though a minority of respondents stated that their campuses provide equitable benefits to same-sex partners and families on par with different-sex-headed families, the majority experienced inequities in benefits and services to varying degrees. While the Fourteenth Amendment of the US Constitution includes the provision of "equal protection of the law" to all citizens of the United States, some campuses offer no benefits and services to same-sex households, and in most instances will not cover specialized medical services to people along the Trans Spectrum. Others, while providing equal access to some campus facilities—for example, athletic facilities and libraries—extend no additional benefits to same-sex couples and headed families.

In many instances, while some campuses act equitably to same-sex couples in terms of benefits, in reality, these couples must jump through additional hoops by completing extra paperwork, and more importantly, they are required to pay additional taxes on these benefits, which are not mandatory for different-sex married couples. In the majority of states, campus policy follows state and federal law. If a state, for example, has not passed comprehensive antidiscrimination legislation protecting equal rights for minoritized sexual and gender identities, or does not officially sanction marriage for same-sex couples, campuses oftentimes refer to these statewide restrictions to justify withholding equitable policies, benefits, and services.[3] "[Our university] does not have domestic partner benefits and that is a major concern for me as a longtime staff member. So the climate will never get better as long as this discrimination exists that creates different 'classes' of employees."

Respondents also addressed unequal and lack of accommodations for Trans Spectrum members of the community on campuses related to gender-inclusive restrooms and health issues:

"My institution does NOT cover transgender health; in fact, issues of transgender health are explicitly EXCLUDED by the definitions of our health plan." And related to living accommodations: "I am the only out trans employee to my knowledge at my institution ... I also am a resident director so I live where I work and I can't relax ever because my climate at work is so horrible. So not only is my work climate horrible, but so is my living space."

In summary, then, within the overarching theme of "Negative Campus Climate," themes included perceptions of an unsafe or hazardous campus climate, negative department climates, unequal benefits for LGBT faculty and staff and their partners, religious intolerance and harassment, negative analysis of both the campus as well as the surrounding community climates, intersecting forms of oppression on campus, and institutional inaction to address concerns and problems.

DISCUSSION

Respondents' comments to open-ended questions reflecting negative campus climate concerns vastly outnumbered remarks assessing campus climate more positively. The majority of responses to these questions perceived a campus climate saturated with an overarching heteronormativity (sometimes referred to as "heterosexism"), which Blumenfeld (2013) defines as "the overarching social system that promotes and institutionalizes a heterosexual norm or standard, which establishes and perpetuates the notion that all people are or should be heterosexual, thereby privileging heterosexuals and heterosexuality" (p. 373) In addition, respondents expressed extreme concern over a campus climate drenched with cissexism, which Blumenfeld defines as "compris[ing] a conceptual structure of oppression directed against those who live and function external to the gender/sex binary, and/or the doctrine that they do not exist at all" (p. 374). These forms of oppression result in the exclusion of the needs, concerns, cultures, and life experiences of lesbians, gay males, bisexuals, asexuals, intersex people, and people who live along the Trans Spectrum. These forms of cultural hegemony are often overt, and at times subtle, and are oppression by purpose or design, and also neglect, omission, erasure, and distortion. Under the force of heterosexism and cissexism, minoritized sexual and gender identities are forced to struggle constantly against their own invisibility and make it difficult for them to integrate a positive sexual and gender identity. Within society at-large, and specifically on college and university campuses, they often find themselves as strangers in their own country.

This study indicated that respondents attending unwelcoming and "hostile" campuses reported lower interest in remaining at their current campuses and the discouraging of future students, staff, faculty, and administrators from attending. Campus community members also experienced lower educational outcomes and more negative identity development issues of self-esteem, and emotional, mental, and physical health.

In other studies (Eliason, 1996; Noack, 2004), LGBTQ employees were less likely to report experiences with or observations of heterosexism or cissexism within institutions that had written nondiscrimination policies that included "sexual identity" and "gender identity and expression" in their diversity statements, and offered same-sex partner benefits. They were also more likely to disclose their sexual identity if they had LGBT co-workers and worked in organizations that had nondiscrimination policies in place.

In the current study, respondents who expressed having the most positive experiences and perceived campuses as welcoming, supportive, and equitable in terms of services, academic programming, and health and other benefits, also discussed leaving or wishing to leave their current campuses least often. This was as opposed to those who expressed a desire to leave or actually left campus due to more negative experiences that impacted their perceptions.

Our study, therefore, clearly indicates that the existence or even the appearance of a negative campus climate seriously compromises campus community members in their ability and willingness to persist academically and professionally. In the same regard, a positive campus climate in the areas of policies, procedures, and opportunities can enhance and, indeed, strengthen one's intent to persist.

In the current study, while a large number of students had thoughts of changing campuses because of unpleasant or traumatic experiences and perceptions of negative campus climate, many remained and some entered into campus activism. Through their work, students felt empowered by serving as change agents to transform their campuses into becoming more welcoming and equitable. Young people have been and continue to be at the heart of progressive social change movements. Corrigall-Brown (2005), in her study of youth participation in social movements, found that youth who enter into work to improve campus climate and the larger society develop higher levels of self-esteem and self-efficacy, and this is also associated with verification and crystallization of their identity development.

The current study confirmed Rowatt et al.'s (2006) finding that Christian religious "priming" increases prejudice toward and resistance of minoritized sexual and gender identity groups with the attendant hostile reactions. As the current study also discovered in respondents perceptions of the intersections in multiple forms of oppression on their campus, ultimately, when the campus climate is unsafe and unwelcoming for any segment of the campus community, this compromises the entire campus climate affecting everyone and every group. This point was emphasized by participants who specifically linked issues of heterosexism and cissexism to multiple forms of oppression and negative campus climates for other minoritized social identities. In the final analysis, they clearly showed that we are all diminished when any one of us is demeaned.

IMPLICATIONS FOR FURTHER RESEARCH

Our study was the most comprehensive investigation addressing issues of campus climate for and attitudes regarding retention of LGBTQ students, faculty, staff, and administrators to date. We intend to continue our investigations in the longer term to understand the longitudinal changes in this area, and we invite other researchers to investigate these issues on individual campuses or within and between geographic regions of the country. In addition, comparative studies can address the similarities and differences between US institutions in higher education with their counterparts both in diverse geographical locations around the United States as well as in countries throughout the world.

Another area for future research can measure the relationship between issues of mental health, self-esteem, and substance use and misuse related to campus climate experiences and perceptions. Moreover, there currently exists a relative lack of research examining the retention of LGBTQ staff, faculty, and students, in particular by discipline or area of student engagement. We also suggest additional research on those LGBTQ students who have been successful within their institutions despite the obstacles. A number of studies in the literature on resiliency focus on other populations, and similar studies can focus specifically on LGBTQ students.

NOTES

1. There were, however, some exceptions, for example, "My department is a conservative social science, though individually there are people which provide a comfortable personal climate."
2. Hir (gender neutral pronoun combining her/his); Ze (gender neutral pronoun combining she/he).

3.   This study was conducted before the Supreme Court of the United States granted same-sex couples the right to marry throughout the country in June 2015 in the momentous *Obergefell v. Hodges* decision.

REFERENCES

Anderson, K. J., & Kanner, J. (2011). Inventing a gay agenda: Students' perceptions of lesbian and gay professors. *The Journal of Applied Social Psychology, 41*(6), 1538–1564.

Astin, A. W. (1993). *What matters in college? Four critical years revisited.* San Francisco, CA: Jossey-Bass.

Barritt, L., Beekman, T., Bleeker, H., & Mulderij, K. (1985). *Researching educational practice.* Grand Forks: North Dakota University.

Blumenfeld, W. J. (2006). Christian privilege and the promotion of "secular" and not-so "secular" mainline Christianity in public schooling and the larger society. *Equity and Excellence in Education, 39*(3), 195–210.

Blumenfeld, W. J. (2013). Heterosexism. In M. Adams, W. J. Blumenfeld, R. Castañeda, H. Hackman, M. Peters, & X. Zúñiga (Eds.), *Readings for diversity and social justice* (3rd ed., pp. 373–379). New York, NY: Routledge.

Bogdan, R., & Taylor, S. J. (1998). *Introduction to qualitative research methods: A guidebook and resource* (3rd edition). Hoboken, NJ: Wiley.

Corrigall-Brown, C. (2005, August). *Social psychological correlates of social movement participation among youth.* Paper presented at the annual meeting of the American Sociological Association, Philadelphia, PA. Retrieved from http://www.allacademic.com/meta/p19043_index.html

Creswell, J. W. (1998). *Qualitative inquiry and research design: Choosing among five traditions.* Thousand Oaks, CA: Sage.

Dolan, J. (1998). Gay and lesbian professors out on campus. *Academe, 84*, 40–45.

Eliason, M. J. (1996). A survey of the campus climate for lesbian, gay, and bisexual university members. *Journal of Psychology and Human Sexuality, 8*(4) 39–58.

Glesne, C. (2006). *Becoming qualitative researchers: An introduction.* Boston, MA: Pearson Education.

Groenewald, T. (2004). A phenomenological research design illustrated. *International Journal of Qualitative Methods, 3*(1), 1–26.

Gurin, P., Dey, E. L., Hurtado, S., & Gurin, G. (2002). Diversity and higher education: Theory and impact on educational outcomes. *Harvard Educational Review, 72*, 330–367.

Hall, R., & Sandler, R. (1984). *Out of the classroom: A chilly campus climate for women?* Washington, DC: Association of American Colleges.

Harper, S. R. (2006). *Black male student success in higher education: A report from the national black male college achievement study center for the study of race and equity in education.* Philadelphia: University of Pennsylvania.

Harper, S. R., & Hurtado, S. (2007, Winter). Nine themes in campus racial climates and implications for institutional transformation. In S. R. Harper & L. D. Patton (Eds.), *Responding to the realities of race on campus: New directions for student services* (No. 120, pp. 7–24). San Francisco, CA: Jossey-Bass.

Hart, J., & Fellabaum, J. (2008). Analyzing campus climate studies: Seeking to define and understand. *Journal of Diversity in Higher Education, 1*, 222–234.

Hurtado, S., Carter, D. F., & Kardia, D. (1998). The climate for diversity: Key issues for institutional self-study. *New Directions for Institutional Research, 98*, 53–63.

Hurtado, S., & Ponjuan, L. (2005). Latino educational outcomes and the campus climate. *Journal of Hispanic Higher Education, 4*, 235–251.

Johnson, M. D., Rowatt, W. C., & LaBouff, J. (2010). Priming Christian religious concepts increases racial prejudice. *Social Psychological and Personality Science, 1*(2), 119–126.

Lichtman, M. (2006). *Qualitative research in education: A user's guide*. Thousand Oaks, CA: Sage.

Marshall, C., & Rossman, G. B. (2006). *Designing qualitative research*. Thousand Oaks, CA: Sage.

Milem, J. F., Chang, M. J., & Antonio, A. L. (2005). *Making diversity work on campus: A research-based perspective*. Washington, DC: Association of American Colleges and Universities.

Museus, S., & Maramba, D. (2011). The impact of culture on Filipino American students' sense of belonging. *The Review of Higher Education, 34*(2), 231–258.

National Gay and Lesbian Task Force. (1990). *National anti-gay/lesbian victimization report*. New York, NY: Author.

Nelson, E., & Krieger, S. (1997). Changes in attitudes toward homosexuality in college students: Implementation of a gay men and lesbian peer panel. *Journal of Homosexuality, 33*, 63–81.

Noack, K. W. (2004). *An assessment of the campus climate for gay, lesbian, bisexual, and transgender persons as perceived by the faculty, staff, and administration of Texas A&M University* (Unpublished doctoral dissertation). Texas A&M University, College Station.

Pascarella, E. T., & Terenzini, P. T. (2005). *How college affects students: A third decade of research* (Vol. 2). San Francisco, CA: Jossey-Bass.

Patton, M. Q. (2012). *Qualitative research & evaluation methods* (3rd ed.). Thousand Oaks, CA: Sage.

Perna, L. W. (2005). The benefits of higher education: Sex, racial/ethnic, and socioeconomic group differences. *The Review of Higher Education, 29*(1), 23–52.

Rankin, S. (2001). *National campus climate for underrepresented people* (Unpublished manuscript). State University of Pennsylvania, University Park.

Rankin, S. R. (2003). *Campus climate for gay, lesbian, bisexual, and transgender people: A national perspective*. New York, NY: National Gay and Lesbian Task Force Policy Institute.

Rankin, S. (2009). Climate assessment reports. *Rankin & Associates Consulting*. Retrieved from http://www.rankin-consulting.com

Rankin, S., & Reason, R. D. (2005). Differing perceptions: How students of color and white students perceive campus climate for underrepresented groups. *Journal of College Student Development, 46*, 43–61.

Rankin, S., & Reason, R. D. (2008). Transformational tapestry model: A comprehensive approach to transforming campus climate. *Journal of Diversity in Higher Education, 1*, 262–274.

Rankin, S., Weber, G., Blumenfeld, W. J., & Frazer, S. (2010). *2010 state of higher education for lesbian, gay, bisexual, and transgender people*. Charlotte, NC: Campus Pride Q Research Institute in Higher Education.

Reason, R. (2009). An examination of persistence research through the lens of a comprehensive conceptual framework. *Journal of College Student Development, 50*(6), 659–682.

Reason, R. D., & Rankin, S. (2006). College students' experiences and perceptions of harassment on campus: An exploration of gender differences. *College Student Affairs Journal, 26*(1), 7–29.

Renn, K. (2010). LGBT and queer research in higher education: The state and status of the field. *Educational Researcher, 39*(2), 132–141.

Rowatt, W. C., LaBouff, J. P., Johnson, M., Froese, P., & Tsang, J. (2009). Associations among religiousness, social attitudes, and prejudice in a national sample of American adults. *Psychology of Religion and Spirituality, 1*, 14–24.

Rowatt, W. C., Tsang, J., Kelly, J., LaMartina, B., McCullers, M., & McKinley, A. (2006). Associations between religious personality dimensions and implicit homosexual prejudice. *Journal for the Scientific Study of Religion, 45*(3), 397–406,

Salter, D. W., & Persaud, A. (2003). Women's views of the factors that encourage and discourage classroom participation. *Journal of College Student Development, 44*, 110–121.

Sanlo, R. L. (2004). Lesbian, gay, and bisexual college students: Risk, resiliency, and retention. *Journal of College Student Retention, 6*(1), 97.

Sears, J. T. (2002). The institutional climate for lesbian, gay, and bisexual education faculty: What is the pivotal frame of reference? *Journal of Homosexuality, 43*(1), 11–37.

Seidman, I. (1998). *Interviewing as qualitative research: A guide for researchers in education and the social sciences*. New York, NY: Teachers College Press.

Settles, I. H., Cortina, L. M., Malley, J., & Stewart, A. J. (2006). The climate for women in academic science: The good, the bad, and the changeable. *Psychology of Women Quarterly, 30*, 47–58.

Silverschanz, P., Cortina, L., Konik, J., & Magley, V. (2007). Slurs, snubs, and queer jokes: Incidence and impact of heterosexist harassment in academia. *Sex Roles, 58*, 179–191.

Smith, D. G., Gerbrick, G., Figueroa, M., Watkins, G., Levitan, T., Moore, L., Merhcant, P., … Figueroa, B. (1997). *Diversity works: The emerging picture of how students benefit*. Washington, DC: Association of American Colleges and Universities.

Starobin, S. S., & Blumenfeld, W. J. (2012). Utilization of social ecology of bullying and social reproduction frameworks to interrogate workplace bullying at community colleges. In J. Lester (Ed.), *Workplace bullying in higher education*. New York, NY: Routledge.

Steele, J., James, J. B., & Barnett, R. (2002). Learning in a man's world: Examining the perceptions of undergraduate women in male-dominated academic areas. *Psychology of Women Quarterly, 26*, 46–50.

Strauss, A., & Corbin, J. (1998). *Basics of qualitative research techniques and procedures for developing grounded theory* (2nd ed.). London, England: Sage.

Sullivan, N. (2003). *A critical introduction to queer theory.* Edinburgh, Scotland: Edinburgh University Press.

Umbach, P. D., Kinzie, J. L., Thomas, A. D., Palmer, M. M., & Kuh, G. D. (2003). *Women students at co-educational and women's colleges: How do their experiences compare?* Paper presented at the 28th Annual Meeting of the Association for the Study of Higher Education, Portland, OR.

Waldo, C. (1999). Out on campus: Sexual orientation and academic climate in a university context. *American Journal of Community Psychology, 26*, 745–774.

Wilchins, R. (2004). *Queer theory, gender theory.* Los Angeles, CA: Alyson Books

Worthington, R. L., Navarro, R. L., Loewy, M., & Hart, J. (2008). Color-blind racial attitudes, social dominance orientation, racial-ethnic group membership and college students' perceptions of campus climate. *Journal of Diversity in Higher Education, 1*(1), 8–19.

CHAPTER 14

TYING IT ALL TOGETHER

Making Meaning and a Call to Action

Paul Chamness Miller and Erin A. Mikulec

There is a lot of work that has focused on the experiences of LGBTQ youth both in and out of school. This research is instrumental in understanding how queer youth navigate the classroom and their lives in the community. An important part of this picture, however, that until now has been largely missing, is the current condition of teacher education programs and preparing future teachers to help change the grim climate of schools and classrooms.

LGBTQ YOUTH AND EDUCATION: HOW FAR HAVE WE COME?

We opened our book with Knaier, who led us through her journey over the past 12 years, first sharing an essay she wrote while in school and then reflecting on the state of affairs regarding the climate of school for LGBTQ youth from the time of her paper to present day. As she noted, although progress in society at-large has been made in securing the rights of LGBTQ people in the United States (e.g., the recent U.S. Supreme Court decision that has legalized same-sex marriage nationwide), the

Queering Classrooms: Personal Narratives and Educational Practices to Support LGBTQ Youth in Schools, pp. 213–222
Copyright © 2017 by Information Age Publishing
All rights of reproduction in any form reserved.

213

same cannot be said of LGBTQ youth in school, who continue to experience significant marginalization by peers, teachers, administrators, and other school personnel (see Kosciw, Greytak, Palmer, & Boesen, 2014 for the most recent data). Knaier argues that there are significant benefits for queer youth if teachers create and an inclusive classroom. However, as she suggests, one of the problems is that teacher educators may assume that preservice teachers will simply know how to make their classrooms and curriculum more inclusive once they are hired, which is not often the case. Knaier calls for teacher education programs to strengthen their curriculum to better equip future teachers with the knowledge and skills to effectively promote inclusiveness, thereby creating a sense of community and belonging for all students.

The inclusiveness that Knaier describes is not just for LGBT teachers and administrators to address, but is important for all teachers to embrace, including Allies. Schey raises several important points that are, perhaps, unique to Allies, but many of these points, however, may also be salient to members of the LGBT faculty and staff. First, he points out that being an effective Ally does not happen by applying a cookie-cutter approach to offering support to queer students. Instead, he urges teachers to approach each instance as unique and to focus on the individual relationship. In so doing, "teachers and teacher educators can work to strategically support the actions and needs of LGBTIQ people on a case-by-case basis." Schey argues additionally that being an Ally is not just about focusing on the individual relationships one might forge with students, but also includes delving into social justice where one can work with others to challenge the systemic "inequality, exclusion, and hate via privileging and othering" of society that perpetuates "homo-/transphobia and hetero-/cisnormativity." This activism of Allies, as Schey maintains, should also extend to teacher education, where teacher educators and in-service teachers can provide opportunities for preservice teachers to become Allies as well in their field experiences and in their teacher education courses. Schey reminds us that the plight of queer youth is not just a "gay problem" that must be solved solely by members of the LGBTQ community; rather, Allies can and should play an instrumental role in bringing about the change that is still needed in order for education to be equitable for all youth.

An argument that is commonly raised by antigay members of society is that given that the number of youth who identify as LGBTQ is so small, why should an entire curriculum change to accommodate them? Wickens addresses this argument in a number of ways. First, many studies in recent years have found that youth are coming out at earlier ages than ever before and in far greater numbers than the in the past. The number of children being raised by same-sex couples is also increasing significantly.

Wickens challenges us to consider how society's ideologies about childhood and children has a significant impact on how LGBTQ issues are (or are not) addressed in K–12 schools and consequently in teacher education. Based on this problematic view of children, she offers several changes that must be made. First, teacher education programs must challenge society's ideologies of children and the language used to express these ideologies. A key point that is made is that such ideologies often view children as incapable of understanding or processing what is often viewed as an "adult topic," despite research suggesting otherwise. Wickens also urges teacher education programs to lead preservice teachers to examine how such ideologies influence the policies and practices in the K–12 setting, again creating a binary of topics that are either "adult" or "child" appropriate, and instead find methods of incorporating LGBTQ-related topics into the curriculum in ways that correspond to their developmental abilities. One of the problems related to the notion of content that is "appropriate" for children is the assumption that anything related to the LGBTQ community is about "sex." One of the consequences of this belief is that antibullying programs are avoided in schools because of the misconceived idea that talking about LGBTQ bullying with children means having to talk about sex. As Wickens argues, teachers and teacher education programs can and should discuss how to talk about antibullying in the context of sexual orientation without talking about sex. The problem associated with a lack of antibullying programs is part of a larger problem with censorship in schools and libraries. In order to address such censorship, Wickens suggests that teacher education programs must prepare future teachers and staff to "unpack underlying assumptions of young people, as well as any other lingering bias, for the ways those assumptions can implicitly impact the selection of curricular materials." In order to achieve this goal, teacher education programs must have frank discussions with preservice personnel about LGBTQ issues with youth and, perhaps more importantly, help their students see the connections between childhood ideologies and these issues of sexuality and gender identity.

REFLECTIONS ON PREPARATION:
VOICES FROM PRESERVICE AND PRACTICING TEACHERS

In order to fully understand the state of affairs in teacher education in terms of preparing educators for meeting the needs of LGBTQ youth, it was important for us to include the voices of preservice and in-service teachers.

In the first chapter of this section, Jaime and Tate offer a very personal account of their experiences—Jaime as a professor and Tate as a student—in a very conservative community. They argue that despite the progress being made and the long road ahead in achieving true equity in education, there is hope that such a lofty goal can be reached. They share their narratives to illustrate the need for greater discussions on social justice in teacher education in order to prepare future teachers to live in our global society and to demonstrate the possibilities of what can happen when a high school teacher and a university professor accept all students and work to make their classrooms inclusive. As they note, when more teachers are affirming and foster an environment of inclusion, then the youth of our society will develop greater compassion and stand up against the injustices that exist in our schools and our society as a whole.

DeWilde supports the points argued by Jaime and Tate with his own personal story during his teacher education program. Some messages he received gave him reason to doubt his choice in a career as an art teacher, while at the same time others encouraged him and fostered the courage that is needed to be a teacher. The negative message that is perhaps most often transmitted, as DeWilde points out, is that LGBTQ teachers must never reveal their true selves at school and they should always conform to the biological sex with which they were born. Many LGBTQ teachers fear that failing to follow these two points puts them at risk of termination, or worse. As he discussed in the chapter, DeWilde reminds us that the teaching profession has historically been and is still is largely very conservative. What is more, many US states do not provide legal protections from wrongful termination based on sexual or gender identity; and even in those states that do have such laws, teacher contracts are written in ways that give school administration other "excuses" for firing an educator. Despite the struggles that remain in the teaching profession for LGBTQ teachers and students, it is vital for teacher educators to foster a safe and welcoming learning environment. As DeWilde reminds us,

> School may be the only safe space a student struggling with these issues can turn to.... By providing students with positive role models and accurate information, educators are given a great opportunity to make a difference in the lives of their students.

The next chapter is a collection of reflections of three preservice teachers who had the opportunity to complete two separate days at a unique school that was created to be a safe space for bullied youth as part of a clinical experience for one of their education classes. About half of the students at this school self-identify as a member of the LGBT community, but learners in the school have been victims of bullying for many different reasons. The school also welcomes bullies, as the central disciplinary system that the school employs is restorative justice, designed to restore broken relationships and teach students how to resolve conflicts in nonviolent ways. What these three stories tell us is that preservice teachers need to spend time in the environments of diverse learners, not just read about them or watch them in videos. Another interesting point to these three stories is that these students chose to return to the school, indicating that preservice teachers are open to working with LGBT youth and simply need the opportunity to do so. The reality is that not every teacher education program has access to schools that can provide future teachers with such experiences. This is echoed by Hansen (2015), who suggests a variety of activities both in and out of class to help preservice teachers work with members of the LGBT community. But as this chapter tells us, the goal shouldn't be to have a few schools like this to be the safe haven for bullied youth. Instead, we should see what is good and what works in this school in every school. In order to achieve this goal, teacher education programs must find ways to help preservice teachers develop an understanding of the needs of all youth and instill a desire and willingness to create a learning community in their future classrooms that challenges the educational system that continues to marginalize so many of our youth. Will one or two days at a school make preservice teachers fully prepared to meet the needs of all learners? Probably not. But as these three narratives illustrate, such experiences can begin to challenge what they have always understood about schools and education.

USING LITERATURE TO ADDRESS
ISSUES OF LGBTQ YOUTH IN SCHOOLS

An area in the larger field of queer studies in education that has garnered a lot of attention is that of literature and critical literacy. Literature has the power to challenge educational systems as well as challenge the ideologies that children bring to the classroom that perpetuate homophobia.

Venzo illustrates the potential that literature and critical literacy have to bring about change by examining how teacher education programs can better prepare preservice teachers for the use of literature to challenge homophobia at school. He suggests that by equipping future teachers with a better understanding of critical literary theory, "it is then possible to identify, understand, and analyze both surface and passive ideology operating within texts," where teacher and student look beyond that which is obvious into the "unintended" messages that are layered deeper than the printed words on the page about sexual and (a)gender identity. In so doing, students are able to queer texts, even those that superficially appear to be heteronormative and gendernormative. This is an important point to be made, because even in schools that have taken to the task of censoring books deemed too queer for their libraries and classrooms, teachers and students can still have discussions about society's values about sexuality and gender and how these values are treated in these texts. If teacher education programs were to prepare future teachers in how to creatively utilize these texts, the results can be outstanding! It is about thinking outside of the box at other ways texts might be treated. And when time is an issue, Venzo suggests that critical literacy can wander out of the classroom into community-based book clubs and other sorts of groups, and he encourages teacher educators to also include such activities in their teacher training. Venzo reminds us that literature is a very powerful tool in promoting the identity development of children and youth (see also Hansen, 2015). Teacher education programs must equally invest the time to prepare future teachers to see the benefits in a strong literature program that challenges society's continued marginalization of underrepresented groups.

In the next chapter in this section, Dinkins and Englert further the points made by Venzo by providing illustrative dialogue in the form of vignettes gathered from their qualitative research study in an actual literature class in a high school. Many of the scenarios that are highlighted in these vignettes could be seen in just about any classroom on any given day. Students engaged in homophobic behavior, creating a hostile environment in the classroom, led to missed opportunities for the teacher to address such behavior and foster a learning community that is open and accepting of each other's differences (see Greytak & Kosciw, 2014). These vignettes illustrate the need for teacher education programs to work more diligently at preparing teachers who are aware of these problems, sensitive to them, and have the knowledge to address them effectively. Not only is it important for teachers to address the behavior as a learning opportunity, but they can use text to empower queer students who are in the classroom while fostering a deeper understanding of sexual and gender diversity with the whole class. As Dinkins and Englert highlight, queer youth are not invisible, but often what happens to them and even their ideas and perspectives on the world are, even in the literature that is available in the classroom and library (see also Jennings, 2015, for the need to address heteronormativity in schools through institutional practices and ways of encouraging preservice teachers to increase their comfort levels with members of the LGBT community). Despite Venzo's argument that even with heteronormative literature teachers can queer the text, Dinkins and Englert suggest that preservice teachers' discomfort, lack of training, and unwillingness to meaningfully queer the literature must be addressed in teacher-education programs. This must begin with teacher educators modeling these practices in their own curriculum and teaching, and in creating a self-reflexive culture where future teachers are given opportunities to "think deeply about their knowledge, experiences, assumptions, and comfort levels examining LGBTIQ topics."

Droege, in the final chapter in this section, shared a combination of her personal stories and advice for teachers and librarians who wish to find ways to include literature that is inclusive and representative of members of the school. She offered practical advice for such topics as addressing parental complaints, and even resources for finding financial support for purchasing books when school budgets are limited. Droege reminds us that it is every teacher's responsibility to promote a culture of acceptance, even when some students are resistant.

K–20: CREATING A SAFE AND POSITIVE LEARNING CLIMATE IN ALL EDUCATIONAL SETTINGS

In this last section, the focus turns to the topic of establishing safe and positive learning environments for all students, including those who have predominantly been marginalized by the educational system. The chapters included in this section reveal what has been accomplished in preparing future teachers for meeting the needs of LGBTIQ youth, and what there is yet to accomplish in making tomorrow's educators effective at ensuring that school is a positive learning environment for all adolescents.

Henry is a current classroom teacher, and the honest reflection of herself as a teacher and her work as an advocate for LGBTIQ youth echoes a lot of what previous chapters argued. In particular, she points out that a lot of what she learned happened as a teacher, not in her teacher education program, and she points out that if she had been afforded such opportunities to understand the needs of LGBTIQ youth as a preservice teacher, she would have been better equipped to meet their needs from the start, rather than learning as she went (see Graybill & Proctor, 2016; Kitchen & Bellini, 2012). However, despite her lack of appropriate training, she also highlights what can happen when a teacher has an open mind and the willingness to understand her students' needs. Rather than playing the ignorance card, she found the resources that she needed and learned from those resources. And rather than keeping that information to herself, she also made note of the needs of her school district and fought for what she knew was needed by the students she and her colleagues served. Henry illustrates the kind of results that can be achieved when teachers fight for what they know in their hearts to be right. She realized that her students need a safe space to be true to who they are, so she worked to help create a GSA not only for her school but for other schools in the district. Not only did she create such an environment, but she also worked to educate her colleagues who may otherwise not have had opportunities to understand what the needs of LGBTIQ youth are. The point of her story is that although it would be ideal to have had such training as part of a teacher education program, where understanding the needs of all youth is integrated throughout the program, not in a single "diversity course," as described by Gorski, Davis, and Reiter (2013). Even in such less-than-ideal circumstances, teachers can take the initiative to educate themselves and find the means to make their classroom, their school, and even their district and space that is safe, nurturing, accepting, and affirming of all youth.

Doellman corroborates much of what Henry recounts of her own education and teaching experiences. Despite the improvements that we may see in schools today, current research shows that most teachers are still not equipped to meet the needs of LGBTIQ youth. As she highlights, LGBTIQ youth are still at significant risk, and teachers and other school staff have the ability to create an environment that is safe and affirming (see also Graybill & Proctor, 2016). She further argues that teacher education programs and in-service professional development are needed to prepare future teachers to know how to address anti-LGBT behaviors. She also reminds us that regardless of the excuses and backlash a school or individual may face, it is the school personnel's responsibility and legal obligation to ensure the safety of every learner. It is, therefore, teacher education programs' obligation to ensure that preservice teachers and other personnel have the necessary skills to make school safe.

The final chapter of this section, a study conducted by Blumenfeld, Weber, and Rankin, gives us reason to pause. In an environment where the assumption is that academic freedom will lead to more open-mindedness, their findings reveal that the college/university climate mirrors awfully closely the climate of the K–12 setting when it comes to safety and well-being of LGBTQ youth. They found that LGBTQ students, faculty, and other staff on college and university campuses have significantly more negative experiences and feelings than those that are positive. As they note, "The majority of responses to these questions perceived a campus climate saturated with an overarching heteronormativity" as well as "a campus climate drenched with cissexism," where "minoritized sexual and gender identities are forced to struggle constantly against their own invisibility and make it difficult for them to integrate a positive sexual and gender identity." This is consistent with Hansen (2015), who points out that although preservice teachers are adults, they may react to the issues and experiences of their peers in a less-than-mature way. The effects of this hostile environment are the same as those that occur to youth in K–12 schools, putting college students at risk of physical, emotional, educational, and career danger. Another surprising finding in this study is that the participants did not find teacher education departments to be safe or affirming of LGBTQ students; some even labeled such departments as specifically hostile. If we are to prepare future teachers and other personnel to have the skills and ability to create safe schools, teacher-preparation programs, as well as the overall campus environment, requires significant work.

THE FUTURE OF EDUCATION

Our goal in assembling this collection of theories, personal narratives, and research is to reveal the truth about the current state of teaching and teacher education when it comes to meeting the needs of LGBTIQ youth and what is needed in order to meet their needs. As many of the chapters throughout this volume have shown, it is no secret that while small strides have been made in improving the climate of schools, the environment for most is still significantly hostile. Such a milieu results in negative, and sometimes tragic, outcomes.

At the same time, while the current classroom picture is painted as fairly grim throughout these chapters, many of the contributions reveal the hope of a better tomorrow for LGBTIQ youth if changes are made. Changes are clearly needed in society as a whole—how we view the world, relationships, identity, among others. In order for this kind of societal change to take place, how we educate future decision-makers of our society must also change. This must start with continued efforts to create a safe environment for LGBTIQ youth, teachers, administrators, and other personnel, where such individuals are free to learn, teach, and work free from bullying and other dangers.

We also need a curriculum that is more representative of all members of society, and we need policies in place that will ensure that this happens, whether it is giving educators the freedom to make an inclusive curriculum without repercussion, reconsidering what we deem to be appropriate for children and youth, or even helping allies understand how they can better support their LGBTIQ friends, peers, students, and colleagues. It is also about improving teacher education programs and in-service faculty development to challenge their assumptions about LGBTIQ youth and to better equip educators and administrators so they can make the kinds of changes that are needed to ensure that all learners have the same opportunities to learn.

What we hope the reader takes from this collection of narratives, thought-provoking ideas, and research is that while we are seeing some improvements in the quality of life for the LGBTIQ community in general, there is still a lot of work to do. The work is not just for the queer community, but for everyone, for everyone can be an ally. As we are reminded throughout this volume, it is our duty as educators and educational personnel, not to mention our moral and legal obligation, to provide a safe learning environment for all learners. If we fail to take this matter seriously, we are doomed to perpetually fail students for generations to come. So, dear educators, the time for making a decision is now. Are you going to be an ally and supporter of LGBTIQ youth to fight for their right to the same education as everyone else in a safe, affirming and supportive environment, or are you going to sit back and watch this perpetual nightmare continue for so many youth who simply want to have the same opportunities and to be themselves? The ball is in your court.

REFERENCES

Graybill, E. C., & Proctor, S. L. (2016). Lesbian, gay, bisexual, and transgender youth: Limited representation in school support personnel journals. *Journal of School Psychology, 54*, 9–14.

Greytak, E. A., & Kosciw, J. G. (2014). Predictors of US teachers' intervention in anti-lesbian, gay, bisexual, and transgender bullying and harassment. *Teaching Education, 25*(4), 410–426.

Gorski, P. C., Davis, S. N., & Reiter, A. (2013). An examination of the (in)visibility of sexual orientation, heterosexism, homophobia, and teacher education coursework. *Journal of LGBTQ Youth, 10*(3), 224–248.

Hansen, L. E. (2015). Encouraging pre-service teachers to address issues of sexual orientation in their classrooms: Walking the walk & talking the talk. *Multicultural Education, 22*(2), 51–55.

Jennings, T. (2015). Teaching transgressive representations of LGBTQ people in educator preparations: Is conformity required for inclusion? *The Educational Forum, 79*(4), 451–458.

Kitchen, J., & Bellini, C. (2012). Making it better for lesbian, gay, bisexual and transgender students through teacher education: A collaborative self-study. *Studying Teacher Education, 8*(3), 209–225.

Kosciw, J. G., Greytak, E. A., Palmer, N. A., & Boesen, M. J. (2014). *The 2013 National School Climate Survey: The experiences of lesbian, gay, bisexual and transgender youth in our nation's schools.* New York, NY: GLSEN. Retrieved from http://www.glsen.org/nscs

ABOUT THE CONTRIBUTORS

ABOUT THE EDITORS

Erin A. Mikulec, PhD and Fulbright Scholar, is associate professor of secondary education at Illinois State University in Normal, Illinois, where she teaches introductory and general methods and assessment courses for undergraduate preservice secondary education majors across all content areas. Dr. Mikulec also teaches graduate courses in issues of diversity in education. She works closely with two school partners for clinical experiences, YouthBuild of McLean County and the Alliance School of Milwaukee, Wisconsin. In the spring 2014, Dr. Mikulec completed a Fulbright at the University of Helsinki in Finland where she studied secondary teacher education. Dr. Mikulec's research interests include secondary teacher education and student learning outcomes of participating in clinical field experiences, study-abroad programs, and international learning opportunities. Dr. Mikulec also serves as Director-at-Large for the International Society for Language Studies, where she also serves as conference co-chair and co-editor for the Readings in Language Studies book series. Dr. Mikulec is currently serving as the Interim Director of the English Language Institute at Illinois State University.

Paul Chamness Miller, PhD, is currently professor of the Faculty of International Liberal Arts at Akita International University in Akita, Japan, where he teaches writing and teacher preparation courses. His research focuses on instructional methods of teaching languages, critical pedagogy, and the issues of underrepresented youth and teachers in the K–12 setting. He has published many books and peer-reviewed articles in such journals as *Teaching and Teacher Education*, *Journal of Thought*, *Multicultural Perspectives*, and *Journal of Second Language Teaching and Research*, and was guest editor for a special LGBT issue of the *International Journal of Critical Pedagogy*. He is currently serving a term as President of the International

Society for Language Studies, and is the Immediate Past Chair of the Second Language Research SIG of the American Educational Research Association. He is also editor of *Critical Inquiry in Language Studies*, an international journal published by Taylor & Francis and co-editor of *Research in Queer Studies*, a book series published by Information Age in the United States.

ABOUT THE AUTHORS

Warren J. Blumenfeld, EdD, is author of *Warren's Words: Smart Commentary on Social Justice* (Purple Press); editor of *Homophobia: How We All Pay the Price* (Beacon Press), co-editor of *Readings for Diversity and Social Justice* (Routledge) and *Investigating Christian Privilege and Religious Oppression in the United States* (Sense), and co-author of *Looking at Gay and Lesbian Life* (Beacon Press). He serves as an editorial blogger for *The Huffington Post*, *The Good Men Project*, and *Tikkun Daily*.

Jordan DeWilde is an elementary art teacher in Oregon, Illinois. He teaches his own curriculum of art, history, and culture to grades 4–6. He tells his students, "Great art has been made by men and women of different races, cultures, and communities throughout history. My mission is to teach you that art is for everyone!" His research interests focus on multicultural art education with the inclusion of LGBT artists and issues. Mr. DeWilde is active on social media with the intent of sharing diverse curriculum with art educators around the world.

Elizabeth Dinkins, PhD, is assistant professor in the School of Education at Bellarmine University in Louisville, Kentucky. She teaches classes in methods of literacy instruction and qualitative research. Her research interests utilize qualitative approaches to investigate how critical literacy can be used to help students read and write their worlds. Her work has focused on LGBTQ issues and identities in classroom instruction, the use of young adult literature to foster disciplinary thinking, critical representations of athletes and sports culture in literature, and approaches to teacher development and schoolwide literacy. Her articles have been published in *Middle Grades Research Journal*, *Sex Education*, *English Journal*, and *Electronic Journal of Science Education*. Dr. Dinkins strives to produce scholarship that humanizes and empowers the youth and communities she represents and apprentice her doctoral students to do the same. Previously she taught English language arts and coordinated schoolwide literacy instruction in an urban middle school.

Melissa Doellman is a high school science teacher from Illinois. She primarily teaches life science and also teaches chemistry. In addition to teaching, she is the faculty sponsor for the Gay-Straight Alliance at her school.

Tiffany Droege is an English teacher at Collinsville High School, in Collinsville, Illinois. She primarily teaches American literature, and she also works in her school's writing center, where she works one-on-one with students on personal and academic writing projects. She is an active straight ally (or what she calls a "straight accomplice"), and she is a co-sponsor of her school's Gay/Straight Alliance chapter.

Nora Dunne is an Illinois State University graduate and a Social Studies teacher in the Chicago area. She has taught world history, psychology, and geography. She was the 2014 winner of Illinois State University's Gleynafa T. Ray Scholarship Award, and her paper "Fighting for Their Reproductive Rights" was selected for publication in Illinois State University's student journal, *Recounting the Past*. In her spare time, she enjoys reading and traveling.

Patrick Englert is the interim assistant vice president for student affairs and multicultural affairs at Bellarmine University where he oversees the areas of career development, student activities, multicultural affairs, and student engagement. He completed his master's in education from the University of Louisville, and bachelor's from Western Kentucky University in English literature. He is currently working to complete his doctorate in education and social change from Bellarmine University. He has completed all of his coursework and is working toward defending his dissertation entitled, *Experiences Explored Through the Prism: Out Gay and Lesbian Pathways to Presidency*. During his doctoral program he became enamored with qualitative research and the impact it can have upon impacting communities. His research interests focus on LGBTQ topics surrounding leadership and organizational constructs, community engagement within higher education, and critical inquiry of sexuality and gender. He has had articles published in the *AHEPPP Journal* and *Sex Education*. He has worked as a university administrator for nearly 15 years in roles such as Director of Residence Life and Assistant Dean of Students/Director of Student Engagement, which have contributed to his belief in holistic development of students and life-long learning. Additionally he has taught for the past 5 years in the Interdisciplinary Core (IDC), a key program in the liberal arts tradition, which enables him to incorporate the co-construction of meaning within the classroom. He has taken his passion for working with college students in the diverse setting of higher education and focused on infusing a critical approach in his work with students and the community. Running provides an outlet for mindfulness and reflexive thinking, which he uses to find balance as well as motivation.

Kevin Goffard is a current preservice student teacher and a recent graduate of Illinois State University. Kevin will graduate with degrees in theatre education and theatre design/production with minors in history and political science as well as being endorsed to teach social studies. Kevin's interests include urban education; working with at-risk, underrepresented and LGBTQ youth; nontraditional and alternative schooling; social change/justice; and incorporating the arts back into communities and education.

Alexandria Henry is a certified teacher for DeKalb (Illinois) School District #428. She is an advocate for and is part of the LGBTQ community. She spends a majority of her teaching time with the Special Education population. In 2010, she obtained her Physical Education degree and teacher certification from Northern Illinois University. In addition to teaching, she spends a lot of time in after-school programs such as coaching, at-risk youth programing, and middle school gay-straight alliances. She enjoys getting involved and engaging in community events and projects.

Angela M. Jaime, PhD, joined the College of Education at the University of Wyoming in the fall 2004 semester. She is a member of the Department of Educational Studies and an adjunct and advisory member of the American Indian & Gender and Women's Studies Programs. Her expertise is in multicultural and diversity education, social justice, and curriculum studies. Angela specializes in American Indigenous education and the study of native women and their experiences in higher education. She also served as the Chair of the Shepard Symposium on Social Justice for 5 years. But most importantly, she is a mother of two amazing boys (9 & 14).

Michelle L. Knaier uses queer theory to advocate for LGBTQ-inclusive teacher education and K–12 curriculum. She is a doctoral student at Purdue University, enrolled in the Curriculum and Instruction Department's Curriculum Studies Program. Her research focuses on multicultural education. Michelle also is a graduate of SUNY Cortland, holding a Master of Education in Childhood Education, with an emphasis in Educational Technology; and a Bachelor of Science in Education in Elementary and Early Secondary Education, with an emphasis in biology. She often reflects on her experience as a former middle and high school science teacher while incorporating critical theories into her research on queer(ing) curriculum.

Susan (Sue) Rankin, PhD, retired from the Pennsylvania State University in 2013 where she most recently served as Associate Professor of Education and Associate in the Center for the Study of Higher Education. Dr. Rankin has presented and published widely on the intersections of identities and the impact of sexism, genderism, racism and heterosexism in the academy and in intercollegiate athletics. Dr. Rankin's most recent publications include the *2010 State of Higher Education for LGBT People, The Lives of Transgender People*, the *2011 NCAA Student-Athlete Climate Study, and the 2016 United States Transgender Survey.* Dr. Rankin has collaborated with over 170 institutions/organizations in implementing climate assessments and developing strategic initiatives. Dr. Rankin is the recipient of the ACPA 2008 Voice of Inclusion Medallion and 2015 Diamond Honoree recognizing her outstanding and sustained contributions to higher education and student affairs.

Ryan Schey is currently a doctoral student in education, seeking a degree in adolescent, postsecondary, and community literacies at the Ohio State University in Columbus, Ohio. Prior to returning to graduate school, he taught high school English language arts in central Ohio. Throughout this time, he has been a member of a teacher inquiry group focused on interrupting homophobia, transphobia, and heterosexism. His research interests include literacy, sexuality and gender, and educational activism.

Jacqueline Svetich is a science teacher at Mahomet Seymour High School. She primarily teaches biology and earth science. She graduated from Illinois State University and visited the Alliance School in her clinical experience. Her time and involvement at the Alliance School helped better prepare her for first year of teaching.

Brody C. Tate has an MEd in higher education from Loyola University Chicago and a BA in communications from the University of Wyoming. His work focuses on higher education curriculum, social justice inclusion initiatives, and academic affairs. He also serves as a member of the steering committee for the Shepard Symposium on Social Justice at the University of Wyoming.

Paul Venzo, PhD, is a lecturer in the field of child and young adult literature with Deakin University, in southwest Victoria, Australia. In this role he has worked for over a decade in the education of preservice elementary (primary) school teachers. He has published widely in academic publications and books, including research into representations of queer identities in media and literature. In the early 2000s he was involved in the establishment of support services for GLBTI youth in his local community: a program that continues to flourish. As a creative writer, he is known particularly for his work in poetry in translation across English and Italian, exploring themes of subjectivity and in-between-ness.

Genevieve Weber, PhD, LMHC, is associate professor in the Department of Counseling and Mental Health Professions, School of Health and Human Services at Hofstra University. She is also a Licensed Mental Health Counselor in the State of New York with a specialization in substance abuse counseling. Dr. Weber teaches a variety of courses related to the training of professional counselors including group counseling, multicultural counseling, psychopathology, and counseling the LGBT client. She has over 10 years experience working in community agencies where she provides counseling to diverse clients with both substance abuse and mental health concerns. Dr. Weber also conducts campus climate assessments at institutions across the country as a Senior Research Associate with Rankin & Associates Consulting.

Corrine M. Wickens, PhD, is associate professor in the department of Literacy and Elementary Education at Northern Illinois University. She teaches undergraduate and graduate courses in elementary and secondary literacy instruction. Her research interests focus on disciplinary literacy, LGBTQ young adult literature, and gender and schooling. She has published in such journals as *Sex Roles*, *Adult Education Quarterly*, and *Qualitative Studies in Education*.

Made in the USA
Middletown, DE
28 July 2019